THE QUEEN AND DI

THE QUEEN AND DI

Ingrid Seward

Thorndike Press
Thorndike, Maine USA

This Large Print edition is published by Thorndike Press, USA.

Published in 2001 in the U.S. by arrangement with Arcade Publishing, Inc.

U.S. Softcover ISBN 0–7862–3206–4 (General Series Edition)

The text of this Large Print edition is unabridged.
Other aspects of the book may vary from the original edition.

Set in 16 pt. New Times Roman.

Printed in Great Britain on acid-free paper.

Library of Congress Cataloging-in-Publication Data

Seward, Ingrid.
    The Queen and Di / Ingrid Seward.
       p. cm.
    ISBN 0–7862–3206–4 (lg. print : sc : alk. paper)
    1. Diana, Princess of Wales, 1961– 2. Elizabeth II, Queen of
    Great Britain, 1926—Family. 3. Daughters-in-law—Great
    Britain—Biography. 4. Mothers-in-law—Great Britain—
    Biography. 5. Princesses—Great Britain—Biography.
    6. Queens—Great Britain—Biography. 7. Large type books.
    I. Title.
DA591.A45 D53627 2001
941.085'0922—dc21   00–066673

CONTENTS

ACKNOWLEDGEMENTS

Over the course of seventeen years as editor of *Majesty* magazine and almost as many writing books and articles, I have interviewed many members of the royal family and spoken to their friends, courtiers and members of the staff and household. I was privileged to be invited to Kensington Palace by the late Diana, Princess of Wales shortly before her tragic death, and without her views and opinions my task in writing this book would have been impossible. I would like to thank all those who have helped me and I am grateful for their continued friendship and assistance.

In particular, my thanks go to my husband Ross Benson, my picture researcher Christine Cornick, with whom I worked for many years on *Majesty* magazine, Mike Shaw of Curtis Brown, and Richard Johnson and Marian Reid of HarperCollins.

I have listed separately in the bibliography those books which I have found most useful in my research for *The Queen and Di.*

Ingrid Seward
London, May 2000

PRELUDE

KENSINGTON

Diana told me that 1996, the year of her divorce, was 'the worst in my life'.

She knew that she had finally lost the support of the Queen, the one member of the royal family who had consistently sympathized with, excused and defended her. She believed she was being followed, that her telephone was being tapped, and that her 'enemies' were out to get her. She also felt she was being watched and this scared her so much that there were times when she was afraid for her life.

'I didn't even feel safe in my car,' she said. She was convinced at the time that someone had been tampering with the brakes. A few weeks after our conversation, the Queen would wonder if someone had.

Diana's fears were in recession, however, that summer morning when we met. There was no guard at the heavy, black front door at Numbers 8 and 9, Kensington Palace. It stood half-ajar. All I had to do was push it open and walk straight into her private apartments. I called out, 'Is anyone there?' No one answered. I walked down the beige carpeted corridor and on into the sparsely furnished staff sitting room on the right. Still no one.

1

But enter Buckingham Palace—where, if things had worked out as they were supposed to have, Diana would one day have reigned as Queen—and you have to pass through a cordon of soldiers, policemen, footmen and pages before you get anywhere near 'the Presence', as the staff call the Sovereign. Diana was not going to be Queen. She had turned her back on that lustrous destiny. She was divorced and had shed much of royalty's cosseting paraphernalia.

There were no flunkeys, no liveried pages, no army of maids to attend her, no princely husband, no disapproving courtiers, only her butler and confidant, Paul Burrell, whom I found arranging flowers in his pantry across the passageway. This, she would tell me, was how she wanted it. 'I feel free,' she declared.

Burrell, apologizing for not meeting me at the door, showed me to the downstairs bathroom and loo, which had a cartoon on the wall showing a large turd on a pavement and bearing the caption, 'Has anyone seen James Hewitt?' He then escorted me up the wide wooden staircase to the drawing room.

A few moments later, at precisely 11 o'clock, the Princess strode in on a waft of perfume, her hand outstretched in greeting. She sat down on the sofa and asked me to sit beside her. A catalogue from her sale of dresses in New York still lay open on the coffee table. Dozens of her frocks and gowns had come under the hammer at Christie's but the Princess, despite echoing the complaint of rich women the world over that she had nothing to wear, was not exactly down to her last pair of jeans. She was wearing a bright-blue Versace cocktail dress—'dear Versace, he's so wonderful'—which came to just above her bare knees and was worn tight but without a trace of a panty line. Her shoes were beige and by Chanel. She wore a gold Cartier watch on one wrist and a slim diamond bracelet on the other, and her earrings were sapphires with a small diamond drop. Her skin was honey-coloured, without a blemish or even a hint of a freckle, and she had kept her make-up to a minimum; just a small amount of blue-black mascara around her eyes, and a touch of gloss on the lips of a mouth which was unexpectedly small and stingy. Her hair was immaculate, and looked as though she had just blow-dried the fringe. She was groomed for an evening reception. Did the Princess always dress this way for morning coffee? I wondered. But of course Diana had discovered the power of imagery long ago.

As we sat down Burrell tiptoed in with the coffee and then quietly slipped away as soon as he had put the tray down on the table with a small flourish of his hand. There were no biscuits, and certainly none of the oatcakes her ex-husband makes and sells under his Duchy of Cornwall brand label, which he had served me when I visited him at Highgrove.

'They keep offering them to me on airlines but I always refuse them—they taste like sawdust,' Diana said.

She described Highgrove as 'very small', and giggled at the memory of Prince Charles bobbing out of sight below the window ledges so he would not be spotted by the troops of worthy ladies in stout shoes who visited his garden.

The Prince had served freshly brewed Earl Grey tea poured out of a silver teapot by a frock-coated butler. Diana apologized for her instant coffee. 'Sorry, it's only Gold Blend.' I poured some coffee for myself, realized I hadn't given her any, and poured one for her too. I asked her if she wanted a spoon with her cup, meaning did she take sugar, and she laughed again and said that she had never heard that expression before, but the answer was no, she didn't.

The first thing she wanted to talk about was the concerns she had once harboured for her safety. 'The divorce was hell,' she said. 'I was in pieces. I didn't feel safe anywhere.' She had been consumed, she admitted, with paranoia. 'I know it sounds silly now, but I really did worry about the brakes on my car . . .' and her voice trailed off into another giggle.

I laughed too. It was high summer and Diana, Princess of Wales had less than two months to live, but how could we have guessed that on a morning like this? She always said she would die young. She had said so to me, as she had said it to many others. But death was the last thing on her mind as we sat chatting over a cup of instant coffee. It wasn't even a distant shadow. A vase of the flowers Burrell had arranged earlier stood on the sill of the open window overlooking the front courtyard and, beyond it, her walled garden. The sunshine was streaming in and her disposition reflected the hot summer weather. She was full of life, vivacious, positive, at ease with herself, and certainly more relaxed than I had seen her for some time.

'I'm happy now,' she told me. It was a simple thing to say, but it had taken Diana a long time to get round to saying it. The best part of two decades, in fact. And if she was still afflicted by that inherent sense of insecurity which was an element of her charm but also one of her greatest problems—she would never outgrow the habit of dropping her eyes when she spoke—her prospects had started to look a whole lot better than they had in the fraught aftermath of the divorce. She had her money, all £17 million of it. 'I can't sell a stick of furniture or a piece of jewellery,' she told me. But her home was still a palace.

'I'm not lonely, not any more,' she said, in answer to a question I hadn't asked. 'The only time I do feel on my own is sometimes in the morning after I've read the newspapers, and if they are critical of what I've done it destroys all my confidence. I feel really insecure about going out as I am, meeting people who have never met me and will probably never meet me again, and I have to give them 110 per cent. It makes it very difficult and I find it hard to find the confidence to do it. It really spoils my day.'

But that happened only occasionally, she insisted. She had started to enjoy herself. She was no longer being harangued to quite the same extent as before by the officials at Buckingham Palace. Her campaign to ban landmines was gaining international momentum. She had stopped worrying about the brakes on her car. A summer romance was already in the offing. And she had the holiday with her sons to look forward to.

Any conversation with the Princess eventually, and sooner rather than later, swung round to William and Harry. Their pictures cluttered the top of the grand piano. 'I love them to death,' she said.

She always had, and there had been times when it had almost smothered them. She was still possessive about them. She continued to resent the presence of Tiggy Legge-Bourke, the daughter of one of Princess Anne's ladies-in-waiting, who had been employed by Charles to help look after William and Harry when they were with him. In one unseemly scene, she had approached her sons' minder at a party and said how sorry she was to hear that

Tiggy had lost her baby, falsely implying that the unmarried Tiggy had had an abortion. Tiggy threatened legal action, but the matter blew over and she continued looking after the boys in her jolly-hockey-sticks way.

The antagonism between the two women continued to smoulder, however, and Tiggy declined Diana's invitation to a 'make-up' lunch at Kensington Palace. In her turn, Diana had been deeply upset when William, embarrassed by the attention his mother inevitably attracted, had asked Tiggy, and not her, to join him at Eton's Founders Day. She burst into tears when he told her of his decision. 'He kept asking me, "Mummy, why are you crying?"' she recalled. 'But I couldn't help myself. I hardly see the boys—you can understand why I didn't like it, can't you?' she asked. I said I did.

A few years earlier, the merest mention of it would have brought her to the verge of tears. No longer. Both boys were away at boarding school and distance had given her a better perspective on their destiny and the responsibilities that went with it. She no longer ordered William not to smile at the cameras, as she had done on his first day at Wetherby. She said that William hated the publicity he attracted, 'but I told him he will have to learn to live with it, that he was still young but that he will learn to adjust.'

She had fewer worries about Harry. 'He

doesn't mind anything,' she said. 'He takes everything in his stride. He loves castles and soldiers, and he's always teasing William, "If you don't want to be King, it doesn't matter—I will be."'

It is William who was born to wear the Crown, however—and to head the family she had divorced herself from. 'I would never do anything to hurt the Monarchy,' she said. 'I have no wish to upset what is essentially part of William's inheritance, whether he likes it or not.' But she had, as she very well knew, and the bitterness built up over the previous sixteen years lingered on.

The Princess was once again not talking to the Duchess of York and had gone to the length of changing her number so that the Duchess could no longer telephone her. Their volatile relationship had taken yet another downturn when Sarah had talked about Diana on American television and, worse, mentioned in her biography that she caught a verruca from Diana when she wore a pair of the Princess's shoes. But a photograph taken on the day of Sarah's wedding to Andrew and signed, 'To Darling Diana', still stood on the piano. And Diana did find a few words of pity for her erstwhile sister-in-law. 'She was treated very badly by the Palace and should have been given a lot more money. After all, she is the mother of the Queen's grandchildren.' At one point Sarah's overdraft had stood at £4 million.

'I just can't imagine having that amount of money to pay off,' Diana declared.

Another royal lady whose inability to live within her means had also put her several million pounds in debt, was the Queen Mother. The sympathy which Diana felt for the Duchess of York clearly did not extend to the previous holder of that title. A photograph of the Queen Mother had once had pride of place on the piano. It had been removed.

'Everyone said that she was going to teach me everything—but she didn't teach me a thing!' Diana declared, and the ice-blue diamonds on her wrist would have spoken with more warmth. Despite the antipathy the two had more in common than she cared to admit. Princess Anne pinpointed the similarity when she called them both 'manipulative'—the very word, as it happens, that Diana used in describing the Queen Mother to me.

It was Prince Philip's name, though, that drew the angriest response. 'I don't like the way he shouts at his staff and I always tell William he must never shout at people who can't answer back,' she told me, adding, 'the Windsor men have notoriously bad tempers.'

She knew. She had been married to one for fifteen years. She had given herself a cue but she did not pick it up. Instead of the tirade I was half-expecting, she talked with wistful affiection about the man who had been her husband. 'Charles absolutely loved me,' she said in a silvery voice which sounded as if it belonged to a little girl. 'It's very hurtful to our children when people say we didn't love each other.'

She paused, shaking her head and giving me a sidelong glance to see how I was reacting. She continued: 'It was the people around us. They didn't give us a chance. The trouble with Charles is that he listens to the last person he spoke to.' The words then poured out in a torrent. 'He's surrounded by the wrong people giving the wrong advice and he's very unfulfilled and he really doesn't do enough.' Then, in contradiction of what she had just said, she continued, 'If he becomes King, he will be so restricted and will not be able to do all the things he likes. I worry about him.'

If the thoughts were jumbled, the underlying meaning was not. Diana knew the workings of the Palace and she was astute enough to see its flaws and weaknesses. The system was not hers to change, however. It belonged to the Queen. She had tried to accommodate Diana within it—bending its rules, excusing her indiscretions, making allowances for her illness, overlooking her outbursts, taking note of her grievances, ignoring the way she tried to claim centre stage, and ordering her staff to treat her with respect and courtesy at all times. 'She was reserved—the first and only time I ever saw her cry was at the burial of the Duchess of

Windsor at Frogmore,' Diana said. 'We were at the graveside, Charles and me and the Queen, and when she started crying I said to myself, "I can't believe this is really happening." She had been incredibly kind to the Duchess and paid all her bills in the last years of her life. She was also incredibly kind to me.'

What the Queen would not do, what she was incapable of doing, however, was to restructure the Monarchy to suit her daughter-in-law. Had she become Queen herself, Diana might have made the changes she wanted, just as the Queen Mother had when she was Queen. But that opportunity had slipped away before it ever arose. Diana was now outside the royal orbit and looking to her own future.

'I do want to get married again and I do want more children,' she told me. 'Harry is always asking me to have another baby because he doesn't want to be the youngest any more, and I'd love a little girl. But he seems to have forgotten that I have to be married first.'

And that, she admitted, posed a problem. Her beauty had won her many admirers, more than she would publicly admit to. But her celebrity was an awesome obstacle for any suitor to contend with. 'I am looking for a man who can rise to the challenge of me. A man whose wife was dead—I don't want to be accused of being a husband stealer. And a man who has no children.'

11

Whether Dodi Fayed could have fulfilled her criteria is a question which cannot be answered with certainty, but I somehow doubt it. Having shed one lot of baggage, she was understandably reluctant to pick up another, and Dodi came with a heavy load, even if it was all Louis Vuitton.

Diana was intrigued by Mohamed al Fayed, the owner of the Ritz in Paris, Harrods in London and the house in the Bois de Boulogne where the Duke and Duchess of Windsor had lived and died. 'He invited me to the Windsor House with the boys but I didn't dare do that—I didn't want to put my head over the parapet on that one,' she told me. 'But I like him. His language is so naughty, and so is he—he probably even bugs the soap!'

His behaviour was sometimes worse. Fayed is one of the most contentious figures in British politics, and whose bribery of members of the British parliament contributed to the downfall of John Major's Conservative government. He would have made a highly dubious father-in-law for a princess, just as his son would have made a controversial stepfather for a future king.

Dodi's mother was the sister of Saudi arms dealer Adrian Khashoggi, which did not sit well with Diana's campaign to ban landmines. As a young man in London Dodi had dabbled in drugs and hung out at the Playboy Club. In Hollywood, he had worked his way through a succession of actresses, few of them famous.

Dodi was keen to marry her. His father was anxious that he should: shunned by the Establishment, Diana represented the ultimate social revenge. The package the Fayeds offered was an enticing one, as good as the one Aristotle Onassis had given Jackie Kennedy. Three yachts, a chalet in Gstaad, Switzerland, a castle in Scotland, apartments in New York and London, a house in Los Angeles and a private jet to ferry her from one to the other. But Diana knew her own worth and, with money of her own, she could afford to be choosy.

She also had to consider her son's feelings. William did not want his mother to remarry. Nor did he like the jet-set lifestyle the Fayeds were brandishing before her. 'He's quite happy to have me to himself,' she told me. She added: 'I always tell my boys what I am doing—and I always ask their advice.' Perhaps that explains why, at the end of August, she was telling friends like Lady Annabel Goldsmith: 'I need another marriage at this stage like I need a spot on my face.'

The matter was resolved with brutal finality just a few days later. When I left the Princess, we had agreed to meet again in the autumn. We did not keep our appointment. On the night of Saturday, 31 August 1997, her life ended in the crushed wreckage of a Mercedes in a Parisian underpass, Dodi at her side.

CHAPTER ONE

CALLING DEESIDE

The death of Diana plunged the royal family into chaos, almost drove the Queen to drink, and reduced the Prince of Wales to tears.

It drew millions on to the streets, cutting right across the divisions within British society, and unleashed an outpouring of public anger against the Crown not seen this century.

In life, Diana had been troublesome and difficult. In death, she proved a force beyond control which threatened the stability of the Monarchy. Indeed, such was the rage directed at the ruling house that at one point they looked unlikely to survive.

The royal family, holidaying in their Highland fastness at Balmoral, had no inkling of the crisis about to overwhelm them when they received the news that Diana had been killed in a car crash. The confirmation came from the British embassy in Paris at 3.30 a.m. on the Sunday morning of 31 August 1997. Their first reaction was simply one of dazed bewilderment.

The Prince of Wales was overcome with grief: his shoulders shook, his face crumpled and in the days to come his eyes were often red-rimmed from crying. Sometimes he would

14

maunder dolefully across the surrounding hills. Other times he was to be observed sitting silently in a chair, staring vacantly into space, lost and alone, thinking of what might have been, what should have been, what could never be.

The Queen was equally stunned, and in the trauma of the following week was seen to drink far more Martinis than was advisable. She had grown increasingly exasperated by Diana's behaviour, but she was the only one who had recognized the potential in her daughter-in-law, and she saw her loss for the terrible waste it was. Now she was about to find out just how potent a symbol Diana had become, and she was shocked by the discovery.

She had been woken by her page at 2 a.m. and was the first to be told that the Princess had been involved in a crash. Pulling on her old-fashioned dressing gown, she had gone out into the first-floor corridor where she met Charles coming out of his own bedroom three doors away.

The first information coming in from Paris was that Dodi Fayed was dead but that Diana had miraculously survived. The Queen asked of her son. 'What *is* she up to now?'

The Queen (who normally only shows affection for horses and dogs) and Prince Charles (brought up to keep his emotions under a tight rein) hugged each other; mother and son seeking rare solace in each other's affection.

By now the whole castle had been stirred from its slumbers. Sir Robin Janvrin, the Queen's deputy private secretary who was in attendance that weekend, had taken up his position in the equerries' room on the ground floor, and was liaising with the Paris embassy. Footmen and staff had been roused and the Balmoral switchboard, through which all calls are made, was fully manned.

Charles went into his sitting room, next to the Queen's dressing room, to take the calls now coming in, some through the switchboard, others on his mobile telephone. The Queen ordered tea, which was brought up from the kitchen downstairs in a silver teapot, and then ignored it as mother and son, now joined by Prince Philip, paced up and down the lavender-scented, tartan-carpeted corridor anxiously asking each other what was to be done.

It was a question which the royal family, confused and racked with indecision, found themselves incapable of answering in the week to come.

Their first concern, however, was to discover just how badly injured Diana was. Not too badly, they were told—first reports were that she had walked away from the twisted wreckage of the Mercedes, virtually unscathed.

Their next worry was her sons, asleep in their nursery suite at the end of the corridor.

16

Should Prince William and Prince Harry, each asleep in their own rooms next door to Prince Charles's suite, be woken up and told of their mother's accident? Their father ruled against it. Charles telephoned his deputy private secretary, Mark Rolland, in London, and asked him what had caused the crash, who had been driving, and 'what the dickens' Diana had been doing in Paris in the first place. After the umpteenth telephone consultation with Rolland, Charles resolved to travel immediately to France to be at her side. It was as a flight was being arranged that Janvrin took the call informing him that the Princess was dead. Instantly he called the Prince and said, 'Sir, I am very sorry to have to tell you that I've just had the Ambassador on the phone. The Princess died a short time ago.'

Charles's composure collapsed and the tears which the public never saw started to flow. There had been times when Diana's behaviour had driven him to such distraction that he had declared her to be 'utterly mad'. Confronted with the finality of her demise, however, the residue of bitterness was torn away, exposing the sensitivity which Diana had once found so attractive. The barriers of his self-containment had been breached and even his Eastern sense of fatalism, acquired by listening to such aged gurus as Sir Laurens van der Post, provided no spiritual consolation.

When his close friend Major Hugh Lindsay was killed in a skiing accident in Klosters in 1988, Charles had put his own survival down to what he described in a letter to a friend as the 'wonders of our existence'. He displayed no such stoicism at Balmoral, and in a reversion to the philosophical traditions of his Christian upbringing, was to spend the next few days plaintively pondering what wrongs had been committed that could possibly warrant such savage retribution. He kept asking, over and over again, 'What have we done to deserve this?'

Diana's supporters were to have their own answer to the question. In their view it was the royal family, the Prince in particular, rather than a drunken hotel chauffeur in the employ of the Ritz, who had driven her to her death. As disbelief later gave way to anger, the royal family found itself caught in the startling rip of public rancour. The Queen was bewildered and frightened by the virulence of the reaction, but even she was to be caught up by the mood of suspicion which had given rise to it. Her first comment, on being told of Diana's death, had not been to ask, as has been suggested, if she was wearing the royal jewels. What actually she said was: 'Someone must have greased the brakes.'

It was a remark which echoed the fears

Diana herself had once held, albeit for different reasons. The Princess was convinced that the Establishment—'my enemies', as she called them—which she both disliked and feared, wanted her out of the way. The Queen's thoughts were more rational. It occurred to her, as it would to others, that one of Harrods owner Mohamed al Fayed's many sworn enemies—and they were dangerously real—had contrived the killing of his eldest son and the princess he was bullying him to marry. Her own security advisers would look into the circumstances of her death and rule that the cause of the crash was misadventure. But in the shadows cast over Balmoral's wooded hills on that first sad dawn the sinister seemed distinctly possible and the Queen's reaction was an indication of just how shaken she was by the news coming in from France.

*   *   *

The Queen was not the only one to be shaken. The whole royal apparatus was thrown into disorder. The initial call from the embassy had been taken by Sir Robin Janvrin, who was staying ten minutes' walk away at Craigowan, the house where, ironically, the Prince and Princess of Wales had spent part of their honeymoon and where the fault lines in their relationship had first been exposed. He had immediately phoned through to the Queen and Charles, asleep in the castle. He had then informed the Prince's assistant private secretary Nick Archer, who was staying in another house on the estate. Calls were subsequently put through to both Mark Bollard and the Prince's private secretary Stephen Lamport, who were in London. The rows started almost at once.

Viewed through the opaque window of deference which protects the royal family from the scrutiny of outsiders, the Royal Household appears a dull but smoothly run business which compensates for its lack of imagination with the security of routine. Schedules are prepared months, sometimes years, in advance, and there is not a day when the senior members of the family do not know where they should be or what they are supposed to be doing—right up to and including the moment of death. The courtiers who keep these gilded wheels turning reflect the system they serve. They form the only branch of government service in Britain whose members are appointed not by competitive selection, but on personal whim, and who tend to be of a singular type—stolid, reliable, upper-class, and brought up in the public school ethos of team spirit, namely 'playing the game' and letting convention do the thinking for them. It is an antiquated, undemocratic organization based on patronage—and on the whole it works reasonably well. But it is heavily reliant on precedents which make no allowance for the unforeseen and the unexpected. This flaw—and it soon proved to be a disastrous one—was ruthlessly exposed by Diana's death. Before first light on that fateful Sunday morning, the wheels of royal state were starting to rattle loose.

The first disagreements came when Prince Charles announced his intention of flying to Paris. While the Queen and her heir paced up and down a corridor decorated in off-white wallpaper and embossed with Queen Victoria's cypher, discussing what was to be done, their respective staff were on the telephone elsewhere in the castle arguing about the protocols.

From the mid-1980s onwards, the royal family has been divided into two separate, sometimes antagonistic, bureaucratic camps. While the Queen continues to rely on courtiers of the old school, Prince Charles has surrounded himself with younger, less hidebound, but also less experienced, advisers drawn from beyond the traditional pale. Many of these are state-educated, a number are homosexuals. Given the divergence of views on what the style and role of the Monarchy should be, and with each side working to its own set of priorities, frequent clashes would occur. In the turmoil of that night, they were inevitable.

When Mark Bolland asked for a plane to

take the Prince to France, Janvrin replied that only the Queen could authorize an aeroplane of the Queen's Flight and that in the circumstances such permission was unlikely to be forthcoming. Bolland irritably replied that the Prince would therefore travel by scheduled flight.

The argument was abruptly ended by the announcement that the Princess had died. There was now no question but that a plane of the Queen's Flight would be made available to the Prince.

Charles expressed the wish to bring Diana's body back on the same plane. The Queen's private secretary Sir Robert Fellowes, on the telephone from his home in Norfolk, was vehemently against the notion. He pointed out in his clipped, plummy drawl that Diana was no longer a member of the royal family, that she was a private citizen, and that therefore it would be wrong—and, that increasingly ominous word, 'unprecedented'—to afford her the royal privileges she had specifically renounced. The Queen initially sided with Fellowes.

It was an unseenly quarrel, demeaning to the memory of the Princess, and taking absolutely no account of the enormous affection in which she was held. It proved to be a harbinger of much worse to come, but on this occasion the issue was resolved in Diana's favour. It was Janvrin who settled it when he

22

asked the Queen: 'What would you rather, Ma'am—that she came back in a Harrods van?'

By now the Queen was in a state of some agitation. 'What are we to do?' she kept asking. One of her staff, with an independence of speech that came with many years of service, drily suggested: 'Go to Buckingham Palace in sackcloth and ashes, Ma'am.'

The comment seemed to jerk the Sovereign out of her indecision. It had to be business as usual, she decreed, and she asked that everyone go to church at nearby Crathie that morning. The only people excepted from the royal command were Princes William and Harry. Given the enormity of what had happened, the Queen felt that it was up to them whether or not they attended morning service and faced the inevitable battalions of press photographers converging on Balmoral. After a brief discussion between themselves, both boys decided to go.

The princes had been allowed to sleep through the drama of the night and were not told of their mother's death until the morning. It was their father who broke the news, put a loving arm around them, and offered what words of encouragement he could. They in turn comforted their tearful father. They spent much of the days to come walking on the estate, sometimes together, often with their cousin and peer model, Princess Anne's son

Peter Phillips, who flew straight up to be with them. Peter Phillips, everyone who was there that weekend agreed, was 'an absolute brick'.

* * *

It was a sorrow-torn period for Diana's sons. Yet the staff noted that both William and Harry showed remarkable resilience in the face of the tragedy. Both boys behaved very much as Diana might have predicted. Harry, always matter of fact, appeared to take the loss in his young stride, while William, on the verge of manhood and very much aware of his royal destiny, made the demanding effort of keeping his emotions to himself.

It would be unwise and terribly unfair to read too much into their apparent detachment. There is no doubt that both were deeply affected by the death of a mother who had poured so much of her emotional energy into their welfare and made herself so central to their young lives. They were now of an age, however, when they were able to see their mother's weaknesses as well as her strengths, and fifteen-year-old William in particular had become increasingly concerned at the direction her life appeared to be heading in. The boys had spent several days that summer with her in the south of France as guests of the Fayeds, and William had hated almost every minute. Mohamed al Fayed had pulled out all the stops, laying on helicopters, yachts and speedboats, and even opening a discotheque especially for them in the effort to impress. But it was certainly not the way to impress the princes: it was all too lavish, too embarrassing, too over-the-top, too 'foreign' (their word, not mine) for young men brought up to believe in the virtue of discreet understatement. Diana was lured by the meretricious glamour. Her sons, more royal than she realized, were not.

In her determination to ensure that they should enjoy as normal an upbringing as possible, Diana sometimes inadvertently led them in directions which went against their natural inclinations. William, for instance, much preferred the hills of Scotland to the beaches of the Riviera, shooting to water-skiing, the companionship of his schoolfriends to the company of international playboys like Dodi Fayed, and he was starting to find the programme of entertainments his mother insisted on organizing for him increasingly irksome. The prospect of spending the next few years in Mohamed's jet stream did not appeal in the least.

There was no chance of that happening now that the disruptive contradictions in their lives had been removed so abruptly. And while that had been achieved by the most tragic of events, it nonetheless enabled the princes to see their royal futures with a clarity which hitherto had been denied them.

That is not to insinuate that William and Harry were anything other than distraught. (Indeed, it would have been unnatural if they had not been.) What it may in part explain, though, is why they were able to deal with the tragedy with a maturity which drew such respectful comment from the castle staff. In the chaotic aftermath of Diana's death, it was William and Harry who managed to maintain their emotional equilibrium while so many others around them were losing theirs.

*　　　*　　　*

On Sunday morning after church, Charles flew to Paris aboard a BAe 146 of the Queen's Flight accompanied by Diana's sisters, Lady Sarah McCorquodale and Lady Jane Fellowes, Sir Robert's wife, together with Sir Robert's press secretary, Sandy Henney. Charles had ruled that it would be better if the princes did not accompany him on this mournful mission, and they remained at Balmoral in the care of the Queen and under the watchful eye of Peter Phillips, who arrived later that day, and their father's old nanny, Mabel Anderson. It was just as well they did.

Once in Paris the royal party was driven to the hospital where Diana had died, and taken to the first-floor room where her body now lay. Her butler Paul Burrell had flown out earlier in the day and dressed his royal mistress in one of her favourite Catherine Walker frocks and carefully combed her hair. 'I considered it my duty, and it was right and fitting that I should do that,' he told me.

The Princess had been embalmed, but no amount of cosmetic dressing could hide the damage her body had suffered. The Prince and Diana's sisters were profoundly upset by what they saw. How right it was, Charles said, that the final sight her sons had of their mother should not be this one.

On the flight back from Paris yet another row had erupted when Charles learnt that arrangements had been made, most probably by Sir Robert Fellowes, for Diana's body to be taken to the public mortuary in Fulham, West London. The Prince, furious and again close to tears, immediately countermanded the instruction and ordered Sandy Henney to arrange for his ex-wife's remains be taken straight to the Chapel Royal at St James's Palace.

It was a travel-worn and distraught prince who arrived back at Balmoral that evening. He slept fitfully that night, only to find his mother in sour mood when he awoke.

In her forty-seven years on the throne the Queen had dealt with ten prime ministers, starting with Sir Winston Churchill. She had got on well with some, less well with others and the current occupant of Number 10 Downing Street fell firmly into the latter catagory. 'Too much too quickly', was her unguarded summary of her new prime minister's policies.

Tony Blair had been at Northolt military airfield in West London to meet the plane bearing Diana's coffin draped in the Royal Standard. On the Sunday he had issued a statement which sounded more American than British in its wording. It read in part: 'We are a nation in a state of shock, in mourning, in grief . . . She was a wonderful and warm human being.'

It was the sound bite in the last sentence which caught the nation's attention. Diana, the Prime Minister declared, was 'the People's Princess'.

This was the headline carried by most of the newspapers delivered to the castle on Monday morning and the phrase struck a resounding chord in the hearts of millions who had never met her, knew little about her other than what they read in the newspapers they professed to disbelieve, and yet had come to see her as one of their own.

The Queen was not amused, to put it mildly. She disliked the title 'People's Princess' and the implicit challenge it posed to her position as the Queen of all her people. A traditionalist to the core, she quickly came to the conclusion that New Labour was no friend of the Monarchy or the values she believes it embodies. She distrusted New Labour's plans for the reform of the House of Lords and its decision to accommodate homeless people in Admiralty Arch at the opposite end of the Mall to Buckingham Palace (she called it 'a publicity stunt'). After her regular Tuesday meetings at the Palace with Blair, she would often emerge stony faced. On this morning and in the days to come her irritation became more sharply focused by her belief that the government was trying to expropriate Diana for its own political ends.

It soon became abundantly clear, however, that it was the government, and not the family Diana had once been a member of, which knew best how to deal with the Princess of Wales in death. The Blair administration in London, having been borne to power by the biggest electoral victory in history, could sense and see what the royal family, out of touch in Scotland, could not, namely the mass hysteria Diana's demise was causing. Flowers were left at the gates of Buckingham Palace and on the lawns in front of Kensington Palace where she had lived. They grew into fields, then into vast savannahs. Trees and lamp-posts were ringed with candles. Notes, teddy bears, gifts, photographs and handwritten verses of poetry were pinned to railings. Churches which had stood all but empty for years were filled with people on their knees praying for her soul. It was a spectacle artless in its intensity and decidedly un-British. In its spontaneous desire to honour a woman who had died at the side of her playboy lover, a nation which had always prided itself on its self-control and its reserve threw off its restraints and allowed itself to be swept up in a frenzy of lamentation.

The royal family demanded the right to be left to grieve for one of their own in privacy. They could not have it both ways. In the mind of the public at large it was the royal family who had rejected Diana, isolated her and stripped her of Her Royal Highness, leaving her the title of princess, not in her own right but under sufferance, for as long as she remained unmarried. But the harder they had tried to push her into the shadows, the more potent her appeal became. The royal family were dealing with a real person. The public was captivated by an emotional icon, and it was the illusion which won. In death Diana was posthumously crowned.

The family gathered in the ivory tower of Balmoral simply did not understand what was taking place six hundred miles to the south. More damagingly, nor did their senior advisers, certainly not at first. The politics of the street was something they regarded with well-bred disdain: they ignored the ever-more frantic messages they were receiving from London and instead sought refuge in the battered redoubt of precedent.

The Funeral, the Queen decided, should be a small, family affair at Windsor, followed by a burial in the graveyard at Frogmore where successive generations of the royal family, with the exception of reigning monarchs and their consorts, are laid to rest (since Queen Victoria's time kings and queens have been buried at St George's Chapel, Windsor). Sir Robert Fellowes agreed.

The situation was being wrenched from their control, however. In London the crowds of mourners were perilously close to turning into a mob. Their growing wrath was palpable. They wanted to know why no flag was flying at half mast over Buckingham Palace, why no royal tributes to the Princess had been forthcoming and, above all else, why the royal family had chosen to remain in Scotland instead of returning to the capital to join in the nation's mourning.

In fact, there was nothing unusual or pernicious in their decision to remain where they were. The royal family traditionally does its grieving in private and in a more devout age their wish to keep their sorrow to themselves would have been respected. There had been no complaints when the family had gone into retreat at Balmoral following the deaths of the Duke of Kent in 1942, of the Queen's glamorous cousin Prince William of Gloucester in 1972, or of Prince Charles's beloved great-uncle Earl Mountbatten of Burma in 1979. By ironic coincidence all had died violently, Kent and Gloucester in plane crashes, Mountbatten at the hands of the IRA.

*   *   *

Diana was different. Her death had changed the rules, to such an extent that even the royal family's attendance at Crathie church on the morning of her death was criticized. How was it, the swelling army of critics demanded, that they could go to morning service, taking the bereaved Princes William and Harry with them, and show not a glimmer of remorse? It was a cruel judgement which either missed or ignored the point that the Windsors are a religious family who find quiet solace in their faith, not in an *Oprah Winfrey Show*-style exhibition of public soul-wringing.

A public display of royal grief, however, was exactly what the millions converging on the capital were demanding, and the naked flag staff over Buckingham Palace became the symbol of what was being perceived as the royal family's cold-hearted indifference. By tradition, the only flag that flew over the Palace was the Royal Standard, and then only when the Sovereign was in residence. It never flew at half mast even on the death of the Sovereign, never mind a semi-detached princess, because the Royal Standard is the symbol of the state and the state is ongoing. As the heralds proclaim: 'The King is dead. Long live the King.'

Such arcane niceties were of no interest and little relevance to the multitude outside the Palace gates whose cries soon became a cacophony of abuse aimed at the royal family. To venture among the crowds in the days that followed and hear the insults was to be caught in a swell of raw passion which threatened to sweep all before it. Most had been drawn to Kensington Gardens and St James's Park by the simple wish to share in the communal sense of sorrow but as the numbers grew, so the ambience changed and darkened. Young and old, the well off as well as the dispossessed who had formed Diana's natural constituency, were asking how the royal family could be so uncaring, so out of touch, and so heartless. Her death had proved to be a catalyst, and resentments which had lain dormant for years came spewing to the surface. A moral audit was being conducted, and the royal family was revealed to be deeply in the red. A country which had prided itself on its steadfastness and its stability appeared to be teetering on the brink of razing an institution it had been taught to venerate.

By now the calls to Balmoral had acquired a terrible urgency. Sandy Henney and Stephen Lamport had remained in London and their daily bulletins were becoming increasingly bleak. At Prince Charles's request Sandy Henney flew up to Balmoral to talk to William and Harry. She told them of the millions of flowers left outside the gates of the palaces and warned them the emotion of the people might shock them. She also reported on a growing mood of 'real hatred' directed towards the royal family, while Lamport urged the Prince of Wales to try and persuade his parents to order an immediate return to Buckingham Palace. Maureen, Marchioness of Dufferin and Ava, had felt compelled to ignore etiquette and telephone her friend the Queen Mother, who was staying at Balmoral, to beseech her to come to London as soon as possible.

The turreted battlements of the Gothic keep are remarkably resistant to the onslaught of unpleasant reality, however. Queen Victoria hid behind them following the death of Prince Albert, detached from the world beyond, secure in a realm of her own creation which remains, right down to the furnishings and the wallpaper, very much as she left it. Now her descendants were doing much the same thing following the death of the Princess. After the uproar of the first night, Balmoral had settled back into its old routine, and if the atmosphere was muted, everyone still dressed for dinner.

Charles, apprehensive, depressed, tormented with self-doubt, was all for submitting to public pressure. Others had yet to be convinced. If that was due in part to the royal family's firmly held conviction that in times of trouble, sticking to the rules of protocol offers the best form of defence, it also reflected the antipathy some of them felt towards Diana.

Prince Philip had never bothered to keep his feelings to himself. Nor, even in this most doleful of weeks, did Princess Margaret. The Queen's sister, forced to cut short her holiday in Tuscany to return to Scotland for the Court mourning, complained bitterly about 'the fuss the unfortunate girl who married my nephew has caused'.

Even the Queen, usually so politically attuned, was unpersuaded. While her sister, her mother and her husband had long since given up on Diana, she had retained some of her affection for her daughter-in-law. Alone of all her family, she still found it in herself to sympathize with Diana's problems. Changing the rites of a century for a woman who by the letter of the law was no longer royal was quite another matter.

She had objected to Tony Blair being represented on the Funeral Committee which had been set up under the chairmanship of her Lord Chamberlain, the Earl of Airlie, and it had required another argument to induce her to give way. It was only when Prince Charles insisted that his ex-wife, as the mother of two princes of the blood, was entitled to a state funeral, that she had given up on her desire for a small, private ceremony.

What she said she was not prepared to do at

this stage, however, was defer to the demands of the mob and go scurrying back to London. Such an action ran counter to the dignity she had been brought up to hold dear.

But events were rapidly sliding out of royal governance, and even the Queen's resolve was eventually broken. On the Thursday after Diana's death the Union Flag was hoisted over Buckingham Palace and flew there at half mast for the first time in British history. That same day the family came out of their self-imposed seclusion to look at the flowers and letters of condolence which had been lain against the stone walls of the Balmoral estate.

Of greatest significance was the Queen's decision to return to London a day ahead of schedule. It was tantamount to a surrender.

The final battle between tradition and modern political necessity was fought out in the Queen's tartan-carpeted first-floor sitting room, which has changed little since it was decorated by Queen Victoria. Ever since the crisis erupted the Queen's advisers, including Janvrin and her lady-in-waiting, Lady Susan Hussey, had been monitoring what was happening in London. They had gone by the book but that had not worked, and by midweek it had become clear to everyone but the Sovereign that the royal family was going to have to give way if it was to weather the emotional storm, and this led to yet more strained discussions.

Matters were brought to a head by the appearance of the bumptious Prince Andrew who was staying at the castle. Politically naïve but a pedant for protocol, he walked into the sitting room, heard the arguments flowing backwards and forwards and furiously declared: 'The Queen is the Queen. You can't speak to her like that!' The Queen's word, he said, was their command and it was their duty to carry out any instruction she chose to give.

A week before this might have been true. It clearly wasn't any more and the sitting room was struck into stony silence. It was broken by a courtier who said that if the Queen did not want their advice, they would leave.

Faced with what amounted to an ultimatum from her own staff, the Queen chose to ignore her favourite son and accept the counsel of her advisers. She had no choice. The discussion was no longer about what was appropriate for Diana. It had come down to the future of the Monarchy itself. In the judgement of the men and women whose job it is to guide the Monarchy through the storms of controversy, the situation was critical and their advice was blunt and to the point: like it or not, the crowds had to be appeased if a major constitutional crisis was to be averted.

The Queen at last agreed. The original plan had been for her to travel south overnight by train and go straight from the station to Westminster Abbey. Instead she flew to

London on the Friday, accompanied by Prince Philip, Princess Margaret and the Queen Mother who, royal trooper that she is, had categorically rejected her daughter's pleas to spare her health and stay behind in Scotland.

Back in the capital, she drove straight to Buckingham Palace and, with Prince Philip at her side, left the safety of her own forecourt and went out to mingle with the heaving throng gathered beyond the flower-covered railings.

It proved to be a disconcerting experience for the 71-year-old sovereign. A chasm had opened between the governed and their governors and instead of the respect and polite applause which had been her customary reception all her life, she was surrounded by people whose animosity was blatant. 'About bloody time, too,' someone shouted. 'That gave the Queen quite a turn,' one of her staff remarked later.

With the composure which comes with a lifetime's training, the Queen managed her walkabout with grace and dignity, stopping to chat, asking the right questions, giving the appropriate answers. It was a sterling performance and to look at her—and the people who came within touching distance looked at her very closely indeed—it was hard to see any chink in her self-possession. It was quite clear to those who knew her, however, that she had been very alarmed by the rumpus that had broken out. She could not comprehend why people had been so hostile. 'What do they want me to do?' she asked. No one could remember ever seeing the Queen so agitated, so unsure of herself.

*　　　*　　　*

The Queen was more her usual self by the time she went on television that evening to deliver her valedictory to her dead daughter-in-law. Sitting against an open window of the Palace with the crowds on the street below providing the backdrop, she spoke simply and movingly in a voice whose accent was stripped of its upper-class resonance and was an octave lower than the cut-glass tinkle of her youth. It was a speech loaded with subtly coded messages.

It offered an excuse for what to many had seemed the royal family's indifference to the death of a young woman who was being elevated to secular sainthood. 'We have all been trying in our different ways to cope,' the Queen said, adding, by way of apology: 'It is not easy to express a sense of loss, since the initial shock is often succeeded by a mixture of other feelings: disbelief, incomprehension, anger and concern for all who remain. We have all felt those emotions in these last few days. So what I have to say to you now, as your Queen and as a grandmother, I say from my

39

heart.'

She acknowledged, as she had to, the qualities which had touched the hearts of so many of the people who could be seen in the background. 'First, I want to pay tribute to Diana myself. She was an exceptional and gifted human being. In good times and bad, she never lost her capacity to smile and laugh, nor to inspire others with her warmth and kindness. I admired and respected her—for her energy and commitment to others and especially for her devotion to her boys.'

She explained the royal family's decision to stay in Scotland. 'This week at Balmoral we have all been trying to help William and Harry come to terms with the devastating loss that they and the rest of us have suffered.'

She promised a new beginning. 'I for one,' the Queen said, 'believe that there are lessons to be drawn from her life and from the extraordinary and moving reaction to her death.'

The address was intended to appease a country which, in the space of a few short days, had become thoroughly disenchanted with its ruling family. It was written by Sir Robert Fellowes and checked by Tony Blair's press spokesman Alastair Campbell, who had added the sentimental but apposite 'grandmother' reference. It was not quite the wholehearted apologia many took it to be, however.

The Queen had been drawn to breaking

point and she was flustered, perplexed—and angry. Her authority had been challenged, her good intentions called into question, the character of her family cast into the gravest doubt. The Queen was spared most of the vitriol: even in this moment of crisis the British people's peculiar, almost mystical attachment to their monarch still held. It was the other members of the royal clan—the amorphous 'they'—who were being blamed for what had happened. But that was hardly any reassurance. The atmosphere in the Mall was charged with hostility and the Queen had just seen and heard at first-hand how incensed so many of her subjects were and how thoroughly disillusioned they had become with the family she is head of. It was without doubt the worst juncture of her reign.

But if the situation was grave, she was still the Queen—'your Queen' as she reminded the millions who watched her speech—and this elderly lady who had sat on the throne for half a century was not going to bow too deeply to the hordes at the Palace gates.

As she walked off the makeshift set she asked, 'Was that contrite enough?' It was not a question. It was a joke, but one delivered without a trace of humour, and there was steely resolve in her voice.

*　　　*　　　*

41

It wasn't just the millions of mourners who had to be placated, however. There was also the more intimate problem of the Spencers to deal with. Lady Sarah and Lady Jane were willing to fall in with whatever plans were formulated by the royal family and Jane's husband, Sir Robert Fellowes. Their brother was not.

Charles, who had succeeded their father as the 9th Earl in 1991, had what might best be called an ambivalent relationship with his famous sister and the two had seen little of each other in recent years. As the head of the Spencer family, however, he claimed the right to have a say, and a decisive one at that, in the funeral arrangements.

They were already causing difficulties enough. The royal family is swaddled in ceremonial rituals. In the Victorian era pageantry had become an imperial art form. But the ability to invent a rite to fit the occasion had withered along with the Empire which spawned it. Precedent had superseded improvisation and the House of Windsor and the bureaucrats who serve it had become trapped in the barbed-wire entanglements of their own rules. Without an example to turn to, they had no clear idea of how to honour a princess they had expelled from their fold.

The only model available was the Queen Mother's, and it was in desperation that the Funeral Committee was reduced to plundering the plans she had so carefully laid for what will be her last great imperial occasion. She was the last person alive with any experience of organizing such an event and had spent several years checking over every detail of her own funeral, down to where the soldiers will stand. Without an alternative, this became the template for Diana's funeral.

Britain's last Queen-Empress was piqued at having her own meticulous preparations purloined for a woman who had never been a queen. Along with the rest of her family, she was also nonplussed by Lord Spencer's interference in what, like it or not, was now clearly a royal event.

The Spencers' connections with royalty stretched back to the sixteenth century and the reign of Charles I, who had awarded them their first title. Using their money and the prestige it bought them, they had assiduously moved ever-closer to the Crown until they were firmly entrenched in the inner circle of courtiers. But now even this family of royal acolytes had grown disaffected enough to defy the wishes of their Sovereign and her family. Even their traditional supporters, it seemed, were turning against them.

Despite the Queen's objections, Lord Spencer insisted that Diana be buried, not at Frogmore, but at the family home of Althorp in Northamptonshire. He also said he should be the only one to walk behind the Princess's cortège.

Given that they had effectively banished her, the royal family were in no position to deny Spencer his wishes as to her final resting place. The cortège was quite another matter. In a mark of respect to an ex-wife and a departed mother to his boys, Prince Charles wanted to walk behind the cortège with William and Harry at his side. Another of the by now interminable telephone rows ensued which the Earl terminated by hanging up on the Prince.

This was one point the royal family were not prepared to give way, on, however. It was made clear to Spencer that regardless of whatever private feelings he might harbour, the Prince and his sons would walk behind the gun carriage bearing the Princess's coffin.

The next hurdle was persuading William to join his father, uncle and younger brother in the slow walk from St James's Palace to Westminster Abbey. At first William flatly refused. Charles pleaded with him and said that it would be utterly wrong of him not to accompany them. The Prince, never comfortable in the eye of a crowd and certainly not one so charged with emotion, replied that he simply didn't want to. Prince Philip weighed into the argument and eventually William agreed to take part—but only on condition that his grandfather walk beside him.

Diana had grown to dislike Prince Philip intensely—and he her—but Prince William was devoted to the old man. Philip, in turn, was immensely fond of his grandson. He had taught him to shoot and William liked nothing better than spending his days with his grandfather out in the shooting fields of Sandringham or wildfowling on the foreshore of the Wash. Revered as football or cricket are in other families, field sports provided the common interest which crossed the royal generations and bound them together. Now William wanted his grandfather at his side in what was certain to prove the most harrowing public engagement the young man had ever taken part in. Philip readily agreed and as the cortège trundled under Admiralty Arch it was Philip who put a comforting arm around William's shoulder.

As it turned out, it wasn't William, but his father, who was in urgent need of reassurance. Ever since blank shots were fired at the Queen at the Trooping the Colour ceremony in 1981, the worry at the back of Charles's mind was that some day someone would take a pot-shot at him—and that the bullets would be real ones. As a teenager at Gordonstoun, the Prince was often bullied, and it had left him with a victim's anxieties. They came rushing to the fore as he walked down the Mall and turned into Whitehall.

In the wake of Diana's death Buckingham Palace had received a number of threatening letters. Most were directed at the Prince of

Wales. Charles took them so seriously that he sat down and wrote farewell letters to his mother and two sons, to be opened in the event of his death. As he walked along he could hear the bitter comments of the crowds which lined the route eight-deep and he was convinced that a lunatic was hiding among them, waiting to strike. He told his detectives afterwards that he considered himself fortunate to make it to the Abbey in one piece.

If getting there had been fraught, there was still more upheaval awaiting them in Westminster Abbey. Built by Edward the Confessor in 1065, it is the spiritual font of the British monarchy. Kings and queens had been crowned and buried there for a thousand years. It can therefore only be construed as an act of calculated revenge for the unhappiness he believed they had caused his sister that Lord Spencer chose it as the setting in which to deliver a swingeing attack on the family of the Sovereign to whom, as a peer, he had sworn 'to bear true allegiance'.

The press came in for a fierce lashing in his address. 'She talked endlessly about getting away from England, mainly because of the treatment that she had received at the hands of the newspapers,' he said. 'I don't think she ever understood why her genuinely good intentions were sneered at by the media, why there appeared to be a permanent quest on their behalf to bring her down. It is baffling.

My own and only explanation is that genuine goodness is threatening to those at the opposite end of the moral spectrum. It is a point to remember that of all the ironies about Diana, perhaps the greatest was this—a girl given the name of the ancient goddess of hunting was, in the end, the most hunted person of the modern age.'

Spencer himself had once been a part of the media he so savagely lambasted. Indeed, he had been employed by the giant NBC television network in America specifically because he was Diana's brother. The problems in his own marriage had quickly brought him into conflict with the press, however, and, given his anguish and the paroxysm of recriminations it had induced, his remarks were perhaps understandable.

What was more striking and less expected was his condemnation of the royal family.

When he said 'She needed no royal title to continue to generate her particular brand of magic', he was referring to the Queen's decision to strip her daughter-in-law of the designation Her Royal Highness.

His closing remarks were even more barbed. 'She would want us today to pledge ourselves to protecting her beloved boys, William and Harry, from a similar fate and I do this here, Diana, on your behalf. We will not allow them to suffer the anguish that used regularly to drive you to tearful despair.

'And beyond that, on behalf of your mother and sisters I pledge that we, your blood family, will do all we can to continue the imaginative way in which you were steering these two exceptional young men so that their souls are not simply immersed by duty and tradition but can sing openly as you planned.'

What Spencer was saying in no uncertain terms was that he considered the royal family unfit to bring up his nephews. It was a stinging rebuke of their father and the values of duty and tradition which are the bedrock of royal life. The Anglican funeral service allows no place for allegation, accusation or the settling of scores. Quite the opposite: it is a ceremony of remembrance which is designed to bury the woes of this life alongside the body of the deceased. By going against time-honoured form, Spencer was guilty of gross bad manners. Hypocrisy, too, got an airing because it wasn't Victoria, his wife and the mother of his four children, whom the Earl had brought to the Abbey that day, but his latest mistress, Josie Borain. Spencer was not the person best qualified to deliver a lecture on good parenting to the Prince of Wales from the pulpit of an abbey in front of a worldwide television audience of several hundred million people.

Curiously, though, the Prince's initial reaction was not one of outrage but of relief. Spencer had refused to allow him to see a draft of his address and after the telephone altercations he had had with his erstwhile brother-in-law in the hours leading up to the funeral, Charles had been expecting a lot worse than the admonition which was finally delivered.

The Queen and Prince Philip, on the other hand, were appalled, and their indignation was writ large in their stony glares.

As far as the public were concerned, however, Lord Spencer had hit precisely the right note. He had articulated what so many were feeling. His address was relayed by loudspeakers to the multitude packing the square outside the Abbey and as he finished they gave a great roar of approval. It was borne through into the ancient building where the congregation, echoing the sentiments of those outside, burst into applause.

The Queen Mother and Princess Margaret looked straight ahead. So did Princess Anne, who had viewed the events of the week with all the down-to-earth disdain one had come to expect of that pragmatic, no-nonsense woman.

In truth, there was nowhere else to look. The people had taken matters into their own hands. Instead of being told what to do, they had told the royal family how to behave. The Monarchy had responded—but only after it had been battered into submission.

But now the week was at its end and the beast of public opinion began to settle, its anger vented, its grief expressed. As Diana's coffin made its way up the M1 motorway to her lonely grave on an island in the middle of a lake in Northamptonshire, the crowds began to melt away. A few hardy souls continued to keep vigil in the gardens outside Kensington Palace but for most, the roller coaster had run its course. There was much talk of a new Britain, in touch with its feelings, cut loose from the restraint of its past, but slowly the country returned to normal—exhausted and exhilarated by the experience it had come through, but embarrassed, too, by such a wanton exhibition of emotion.

There was no retreat to the sanctuary of the pedestal for the royal family, however. The door to the past had been slammed shut. As the Queen had said, there were 'lessons to be drawn' from Diana's life and, first and foremost, from the reaction to her death. The regal system had been put to the test—and found to be woefully wanting. Change was vital if the Monarchy was going to survive the next new century, never mind the next millennium.

Bringing this archaic ship into line was never going to be easy, however, and the Queen was left to wonder how it was that the institution she had devoted her life to could have been brought to such a low ebb.

CHAPTER TWO

FIRST IMPRESSIONS

The Queen took Lady Diana Spencer for granted. She had known the youngest daughter of the 8th Earl Spencer all her young life. Diana's father had served as equerry to the Queen between 1952 and 1954 and to the Queen's father, George VI, for the two years before that. She knew her well enough to greet her warmly when she encountered Diana walking, unexpected but by no means unwelcome, in the grounds of Balmoral in the autumn of 1979. Enough to invite her back to the castle the following year. And when it came to it, quite enough to encourage her son and heir in his desire, nurtured in her Highland home, to make her his wife.

The Scottish fastness bought and built by her great-great-grandmother Victoria is the Queen's favourite retreat. It is where she is free to dress down and roam where the mood takes her over its 50,000 acres of hill and moor. There are torrenting waterfalls and great crags, and the views from the peaks, weather permitting, are splendid and stark and uncluttered by the petty protocols of man and her own majesty. There she can 'commune with her Maker' and, on those nights when the

51

sky is wonderfully clear, she will go outside to gaze at the stars, most of whose names she knows. There her time is her own and for a woman whose life is governed by routine and ritual it is a respite to be relished.

She does not have to speak to anyone she does not know. This is the Queen's private reserve and there are no strangers at Balmoral. It was therefore with a surprised but cheerful, 'Oh, Diana, isn't it? How nice to see you, how are you, what are you doing here?' that she greeted the eighteen-year-old striding out across her land.

Diana was staying with her sister Jane and her husband, Robert Fellowes, at their house on the estate, three miles up a dirt road from the castle itself near the Falls of Garawort which is where the Queen takes one of her favourite walks. Fellowes was there in his capacity as the Queen's assistant private secretary, helping her with the dispatch boxes before she went for her early morning ride, staying behind when she set off for her rambles, checking on the workings of the machinery of state which must be kept running even when the Sovereign is on holiday. One of his tasks was to anticipate problems before they developed and take appropriate evasive action.

While he worked, Jane stayed at home. For company, and with her husband's approval, she had her youngest sister up to stay. It was

Fellowes, therefore, who invited what would prove to be his greatest and most intractable problem—one that would consume and eventually overwhelm him. But how could that austere, staunch, colourless and most loyal of royal servants have foreseen that he would be instrumental in introducing the speck which almost ground to ruin the antiquated apparatus he was dedicated to maintaining?

There was no hint of the troubles to come when Diana arrived at their grace and favour home. Diana was delighted to be there. Without a boyfriend or a career (her last job had been as a daily cleaner working for her elder sister, Sarah, and her friends) she had no reason to stay behind in London, where she had just bought herself a flat with money left her by her American great-grandmother, Frances Work. It was summer, the very few friends she had were away, and a holiday in Scotland offered an agreeable break. She was dressed casually and in tune with her setting in corduroy knickerbockers and woolly sweater when she met the Queen who was wearing sturdy shoes, a tartan skirt and a tweed jacket, her hair shielded by a head scarf; two women apart in age but dressed according to the upper-class fashions of the country which, like a secret handshake, are taken at first glance to signify a unity of taste and ideals.

Diana told the older woman how much she loved Scotland, called it a 'magical place' and said she loved it 'beyond imagination'. It was the right thing to say and it made a very favourable impression on the Queen.

It was not just the lure of the Highlands which had brought her north, however. Since she was sixteen years old, Diana had carried an adolescent torch for the Prince of Wales. Her elder sister Sarah had once dated him but Diana had convinced herself that it was she who had really taken his fancy.

This was not just wishful thinking. The Prince had warmed to the vivacious, 'jolly', seemingly untroubled teenager who had fluttered irreverently in the background while he was courting Sarah. He enjoyed her company, admired her figure and her looks, and found her amusing. His opinion was confirmed in their subsequent meetings and, to the irritation of Sarah, he had insisted on inviting Diana to the dance held at Buckingham Palace in celebration of his thirtieth birthday.

*　　　*　　　*

The Prince saw nothing unusual or untoward in drawing Diana into his circle. She was attractive and outgoing and, no small consideration, she came from one of the rich and well-connected families who traditionally make up the royal circle.

Diana, however, was 'amazed' that the

Prince should pay her such attention and read into Charles's early interest more than he wished or intended. It would have been surprising, though, if she hadn't. To be noticed by a prince is flattery indeed and it went to her young head. She started looking out for him and going to places where she thought he might be and it was partly in the hope of catching a glimpse of him that she went for those long walks across the wild heathland of Balmoral.

She didn't encounter the Prince on that trip. Instead she met his mother. It was a fortuitous meeting, for when Prince Charles asked the Queen the following year if it would be all right if Diana came and spent a few days at the castle, she recalled their conversation and said how nice it would be to see her again and have her to stay.

By then Charles's relationship with Diana had moved on apace. In July 1980 they had both been guests at a house party in Sussex. Diana was seated next to him on a hay bale at the barbecue on the first night, and told him how sad and lonely she thought he had looked when she watched him on television at the funeral of his great-uncle, Earl Mountbatten of Burma, who had been assassinated by the IRA the previous summer. She said: 'You should have someone to look after you.'

They kissed—'snogged', as Diana called it—for the first time that night.

On the first weekend of August she was invited aboard the royal yacht *Britannia* for the annual yachting regatta at Cowes. Charles was at the end of his romance with Anna Wallace, known to her friends as Whiplash, the fiery, high-spirited daughter of a Midlands landowner.

It had not been the easiest of relationships. Anna was a wilful woman of his own age with experience of the good life who was not overly impressed by her suitor's unworldly ways. On a visit to Windsor she had asked for a glass of champagne only to be offered a bottle of brown ale Charles had appropriated from a guardsman, explaining: 'Mummy's got the keys to the drinks cabinet.' She had objected to being left on her own at parties while Charles did his dutiful round of the guests, and at the Queen Mother's eightieth birthday she had hissed at him, 'Don't ever ignore me like that again!'

Charles, however, was besotted, and at one point invited her to Balmoral to meet the Queen. It was almost certainly the prelude to a formal proposal of marriage. Anna refused to go. 'Too tedious for words,' she later explained.

After the stormy Anna, Diana seemed to offer the prospect of tranquil waters and at Cowes she endeared herself to his staff and friends alike with her open, friendly manner.

The Queen had been monitoring her son's

romantic manoeuvres. She was not the kind of mother who interfered directly in the lives of her children, but she liked to know what was going on. 'A good gossip is a wonderful tonic,' she once remarked and her staff, rather in the manner of medieval courtiers, saw it as their duty to keep her quietly informed about what the members of her family were up to and who they were seeing. *Britannia* was her yacht and she noted Diana's name on the guest list, knew of her eldest son's interest in her and was not in the least surprised when, a few days later, he asked if he could invite her up to Balmoral. The Queen readily agreed and a formal invitation, including dress instructions, was duly dispatched.

Diana would later say that she was 'terrified, shitting bricks' at the prospect of staying at Balmoral but the only person who noticed was the Queen's footman, Paul Burrell, who later became Diana's butler. He encountered her shortly after she arrived, 'wandering down a corridor looking lost. I took her to her room and she said, "Come in and talk to me because it's awfully lonely in here."'

It soon got a lot better. Diana had again been staying with the Felloweses, helping Jane look after her newborn daughter, Laura Jane. She arrived at the castle in mid-afternoon when everyone was out shooting and the staff were stood down, which was why there was no one there to greet her and show her to her room on the ground floor. It was decorated with a green tartan carpet, cream walls, pine furniture and freshly cut flowers and, Diana noted with surprise, 'a normal single bed!' (The clandestine late-night assignations which are such an integral part of so many aristocratic house parties do not take place under the Queen's many roofs where bourgeois propriety resides.)

By evening, however, the castle had come alive again. It was the beginning of the season when only family and close friends are there and the other guests included Princess Anne's children, Zara and Peter Phillips, and Princess Margaret's son, Viscount Linley, and her daughter, Lady Sarah Armstrong-Jones, whom Diana had befriended and who had been a guest on the royal yacht at Cowes a few weeks before.

Even on holiday, the Queen sticks to an ordered routine. She has breakfast in her room before meeting her private secretary or his deputy to go through the dispatch boxes containing the state papers of the day. At 10.30 a.m. she goes riding and then changes into her kilt and brogues for a walk, sometimes alone, at other times in the company of the other ladies. At 12.30 p.m. she loads up her Land Rover with picnic hampers and drives the women at breakneck speed up the rugged pony paths to join the men for an informal picnic on the hill. Afterwards she will either accompany the men on the shoot or walk her dogs back to the castle, leaving her vehicle for one of the guns to drive back at the day's end.

The ladies always 'freshen up' for afternoon tea, royal speak for a change of clothing. Served at the regular hour of 5 o'clock, it includes sandwiches, freshly baked cakes and scones and constitutes a meal in itself. After that the Queen again takes her dogs for a stroll, comes back for a stiff dry Martini and then goes upstairs for a bath and yet another change.

The candlelit dinner, which is preceded by drinks in the drawing room, is at 8.15 p.m. unless the house party happens to include the Queen Mother, who, much to the chagrin of Prince Philip, always runs at least half an hour late. The Queen does the seating plan herself and, as is her custom, arranged for Diana to sit next to the Princes Philip, Andrew and Edward in turn over the next few days. There is a page, a footman, an under butler and a wine waiter assigned to every eight diners and at dinner's end a piper in full kilted regalia marches round the table playing his bagpipes.

After dinner there is sometimes a film show followed by a few more drinks before everyone retires early in readiness for another day out on the hill shooting or stalking. Manners demand that no one goes to bed before the Queen. When Princess Alexandra's daughter Marina Ogilvy became bored with the evening and set off towards her room, the Queen stopped her and asked: 'And where are you going?' Marina took the hint and sat down again.

Marina described a weekend at Balmoral thus: 'There was so much going on that there was never a quiet time. We had to change clothes constantly. First there was breakfast, then shooting, then you'd come back and change for tea and drinks and then change for dinner. That's a normal day.'

*　　　*　　　*

Diana fitted easily into this grand programme. The royal family live on a lavish scale but so did the Spencers of Althorp, and Diana was not overawed by her surroundings. Nor was she unduly overawed by the Queen. There was no reason why she should have been. In her own home the Queen is relaxed and accommodating and if her conversation is of a pattern—dogs, horses, old sermons forgotten by everyone but herself; and anecdotes about her grandmother, Queen Mary, are her favourite topics—she spices it with humour and dry wit. And besides, as Diana often pointed out, she had known the Queen since she was a little girl. Diana's early life had been spent at Park House, the ten-bedroomed Victorian mansion 200 yards from Sandringham's back entrance which her father had leased from the Queen. Andrew and Edward had played in the nursery there and she in turn had visited 'the big house' for the occasional tea and parties.

In other words, she appeared to know the form. She also seemed to be genuinely enthusiastic about the life that would soon be on offer. While the other women guests preferred to spend their mornings leisurely, Diana was always up at 6 o'clock, three hours before the piper made his 9 a.m. march round the castle. By 8 o'clock she was out to see the guns off. The bags at Balmoral are large, with thousands of brace of grouse and up to three hundred stags killed every year, but the young Diana was untroubled by the slaughter. She was happy to muck in and wasn't in the least worried about getting dirty.

Patti Palmer-Tomkinson, one of Prince Charles's oldest friends, who was a guest that weekend, recalled her going stalking and falling into a bog. 'She got covered in mud, laughed her head off, got puce in the face, hair glued to her forehead because it was pouring with rain . . . a sort of wonderful English schoolgirl who was game for anything.'

At night, dressed in a long Laura Ashley dress with a pie-crust collar, she enchanted Prince Philip with her unaffected manner and lively humour.

She also ingratiated herself with the Queen. Afraid of horses (she had fallen off her pony aged six and, unusually for a girl of her background, had not had the courage or determination to become a proficient horsewoman), she even made the effort to accompany the Queen on at least one ride. She joined her on walks and played a keen part in setting up the lunchtime picnics.

In amongst all this activity, she also found the time to be with Charles who, after all, was the reason she was there. He took her walking and showed her how to fish on the River Dee. 'I thought it was all wonderful,' Diana later recalled.

So did the Queen. Her son was now in his thirties and she had come to share her subjects' concern at his failure to find a wife. He had had his share of romantic adventures and the Queen, according to members of the household, had given clear approval to at least two of his girlfriends.

She had been very taken with Lady Jane Wellesley, the beautiful daughter of her friend the Duke of Wellington, and saw her as an ideal consort. This descendant of the victor of Waterloo was not willing to sacrifice herself on the battlefield of a royal marriage, however. 'I couldn't, just couldn't give up everything to become his wife,' she said.

On another occasion she asked of an inquisitive reporter: 'Do you honestly believe I want to be Queen?' She then dismissed the whole affair with a grand remark of the kind the first Duke would have approved of. 'I don't want another title. I already have one, thank you.'

Amanda Knatchbull was the other girl who the Queen believed fitted the royal bill. She had known the Prince since childhood and had always called him Charles, unlike his other girlfriends, Diana included, who had to start off calling him 'Sir'. And as her dynastically ambitious grandfather, Earl Mountbatten, kept pointing out, as a member of the family she had been brought up to know what the job of being a royal wife involved.

To help chivvy the romance along, Lord Mountbatten provided Amanda with the then considerable sum of £3,000 for a suitable wardrobe and made sure that the young couple were together as often as this meticulous matchmaker could arrange. 'Good,' Prince Philip remarked upon being appraised of his uncle's scheme. 'It beats having strangers come into the family.'

The Queen was at first more circumspect. Like the Queen Mother, whose opinion she respected, she viewed Mountbatten's dynastic machinations with well-founded suspicion. It was Mountbatten who had tried to get the family name of the ruling House of Windsor changed to his own, and had only been prevented from doing so by the intervention of Sir Winston Churchill and Queen Mary. Now he was trying another route to secure his bloodline by seeing his granddaughter married to the heir to the throne, just as he had his nephew, Prince Philip, a generation earlier. On this occasion, however, the Queen saw the logic in his arguments and went so far as to give Charles the use of Wood Farm on the Sandringham estate where he was able to entertain Amanda in seclusion.

By the summer of 1979 matters had progressed to the point where members of the household believed that an engagement was imminent. It had even been agreed that Amanda should accompany the Prince on his forthcoming tour of India where Mountbatten had served as Britain's last Viceroy and first Governor-General.

All came to nought. On 27 August 1979 Lord Mountbatten was blown to smithereens by the IRA while on a fishing expedition in Ireland. Charles, on a fishing holiday of his own in Iceland with Lord Tryon and his wife Kanga, with whom he had once enjoyed an intimate relationship, broke down in tears at the news. His romance with Amanda eventually ended. Without the grand old matchmaker to urge them along, they discovered that they had little in common and the couple went their own ways, amicably and without rancour, more like brother and sister than the lovers Mountbatten had tried to make them.

The field was now clear and by late 1980

Lady Diana Spencer was the only serious runner in these marital stakes. In November she was invited to Wood Farm to celebrate Charles's thirty-second birthday. Back in London Charles took her to the ballet and paid her the rare honour of inviting her to Buckingham Palace.

The Queen did her part and in January, at Charles's behest, invited Diana to Sandringham. The visit was deemed a great success. Diana behaved as she had at Balmoral and declared Sandringham to be 'wonderful'. She made a well-received point of going up to the nursery to visit Charles's old nanny Mabel Anderson, a central figure in his emotional life who was then looking after Princess Anne's son, Peter Phillips. And when the guns set out in the morning, Diana was there to wave them off, just as she had done at Balmoral.

The bags at Sandringham are even more prodigious than those in Scotland, with over 10,000 pheasant shot out of the skies every year. Diana appeared to revel in the activities. 'She was everywhere, picking up the birds, being terribly gracious, full of charm,' one of the household recalls. Basking in the glow of the Prince's attention and with a full social life of a kind she had failed to carve for herself in London, Diana was starting to blossom.

At the same time, she had also won the wholehearted support of the press which declared her, in headlines ever-more strident, to be the ideal bride-to-be for the future king. They went digging into her past and found a blank sheet and an empty bed. 'She, I can assure you, has never had a lover,' her uncle, Lord Fermoy, announced. That made it official. She was a girl without a past—a vital attribute, so the press sanctimoniously declared, in any future Queen.

*   *   *

By now the romance had acquired a momentum of its own. In her youthful eagerness, Diana was happy at the way she was being pushed along. 'She very much wanted him,' observed Patti Palmer-Tomkinson. Charles was less certain. In his determination to do only what is right he frequently ends up doing nothing at all. Faced with the most important decision of his life, he found himself incapacitated by irresolution. He sought the advice of friends and advisers, listened to their opinions and then retreated back into indecision. Almost everyone, including his paramour and confidant Camilla Parker Bowles and the Queen Mother, was in favour of the union. The Prince, however, as he later admitted, was in a 'confused and anxious state of mind . . . I do very much want to do the right thing for this country and for my family—but I'm terrified sometimes of making a promise and then perhaps living to regret it.'

It was not the most kingly of displays and it was causing the Queen some considerable concern. 'The Queen was fed up,' Diana recalled.

The Prince at this stage was closer to his mother than at any other time in his life. He called her 'Mummy', considered her 'very wise', and always made a point of going to say goodnight to her before he went out for the evening. They dined together every evening they were together at Buckingham Palace. The subject of Diana frequently entered their conversation and while the question of his marriage was not addressed directly, by nod and nuance the Queen made it clear that she approved of the young woman she felt she had come to know at Balmoral.

The one person the Queen did discuss the matter with was Prince Philip. Despite their sometimes cold and disconnected public image, the Queen and her consort enjoy a close relationship. They live as man and wife and always have, and in the privacy of their own rooms they talk over their problems and those facing their family. Points are made and argued over and a mutual decision is eventually arrived at. At this conjuncture Prince Philip took over. The Queen is too restrained for the undignified burly-burly of confrontation. 'She confines herself to questions like, "Would you like a chocolate mousse for dinner?" and leaves the tricky stuff to Philip,' said a member of the household. The Prince, as is his wont, communicates himself forcefully. In matters pertaining to the running of the family, however, the opinions he expresses are also those of the Queen.

It was with his wife's agreement, therefore, that Philip wrote to their eldest son urging him, for the sake of propriety, to either end his relationship with Diana forthwith or marry her. Her visit to Balmoral, he pointed out, had caused salacious speculation. Further procrastination, he argued, would compromise Diana's reputation and damage the good name of the royal family.

It was a choice stark in its simplicity. Most modern men of thirty-two would have taken umbrage at being dictated to in such a manner but in the royal family where the practical is afforded precedence over the vagaries of passion, matrimony is as much a matter of state as of personal choice. Charles had been brought up to believe that. 'Marriage is more important than just falling in love,' he once observed, echoing the thoughts of his parents. 'Creating a secure family unit in which to bring up children, to give them a happy, secure upbringing—that is what marriage is all about.'

It was an old-fashioned view and while it does not seem to have occurred to Charles that Diana might have seen herself as more than an obliging brood mare, there were others who questioned her suitability for the role.

Princess Anne did not like her. She saw her as foolish and shallow and called her a 'silly girl'. Penny Romsey was another who harboured misgivings. As the wife of Lord Mountbatten's grandson, Amanda's brother Norton, she had had the opportunity to get to know the young woman well over the previous five months and concluded that she was enraptured, not with Charles but with the idea of becoming a princess. The two, she felt, had little in common.

One of Charles's closest friends, the pompous but astute MP and grandson of Sir Winston Churchill, Nicholas Soames, also saw the union as a grotesque mismatch and went so far as to blame Prince Philip for pushing his son into an ill-conceived marriage.

Even Diana's grandmother, Lady Fermoy, was against it but unlike Lady Romsey, who had given the Prince the benefit of her opinion, she chose to keep hers to herself. 'If I'd said to him, "You're making a very great mistake," he probably wouldn't have paid the slightest attention because he was being driven,' Lady Fermoy later explained.

It was the urgings of his parents, however, rather than the doubts of a few friends which most impressed themselves on the Prince. Dismissing the reservations of Soames and Lady Romsey, he decided to take what he called in cod French, *'La grande plunge'*. In

February, while on his annual skiing holiday, he telephoned Diana from Klosters, invited her to dinner at Windsor on his return and said: 'I have something to ask you.' Diana knew what that was—'instinct in a female,' as she remarked.

In times of emotional tension, Charles retreats into the security of his childhood and it was in his old nursery sitting room at Windsor Castle that he asked Diana to marry him. It was not the most romantic of settings. The room was sparsely furnished and painted a pale shade of green with an old, worn, pale-green carpet. A photograph of the Queen and Prince Philip taken a quarter of a century earlier stood on the mantelpiece and pictures of Queen Victoria's grandchildren hung on the walls.

There were no candles on the white tablecloth, which was the same one Nanny Anderson had served his nursery suppers on. The food was cold poached salmon and salad followed by fresh fruit. There was not even any champagne; instead the couple drank 'lemon refreshers', the concoction of lemon squash and Epsom salts invented by Earl Mountbatten and which the Prince had been served as a boy 'to keep him regular'.

The question, when it came, was a question in itself. 'If I were to ask, what do you think you might say?' Charles enquired.

Diana replied, 'Yeah, OK,' and started

giggling. Charles then ran out of the room to telephone his mother with the news.

The Queen's own proposal of marriage had been made and accepted in a more romantic setting. As the Queen recalled, Philip had asked her to marry him in 1946 at Balmoral 'beside some well-loved loch, the white clouds overhead and curlew crying'. But no matter. The fact that her son and heir had finally got round to asking the question at all pleased her well enough.

Shortly afterwards Diana flew to Australia for a holiday with her mother and stepfather, Peter Shand Kydd. The break, Charles said, would give her 'plenty of time to think about it, to decide if it was all going to be too awful'. There was never a chance of that. 'It was what I wanted,' she said.

*　　　*　　　*

The engagement was formally announced at 11 a.m. on Tuesday, 24 February 1981. The photocall was held on the lawn of Buckingham Palace. The Queen watched from an upper-floor window unnoticed by the cameras, which were entranced by the young woman whose marriage was supposed to make her a queen. The new was in the spotlight. The old was in the shadows, but nonetheless the Queen was delighted. She wrote: 'I am very fond of all three of the Spencer girls.' She had got to know Sarah when she was going out with Charles, Jane through her marriage to Fellowes, and she had grown very fond of the gambolling young woman she had come to know at Balmoral. In the Queen's eyes Diana appeared to have the same qualities she had admired in Lady Jane Wellesley and Amanda Knatchbull. Like them, she had poise and pedigree and as the daughter of one of her own courtiers, Diana, the Queen believed, had absorbed enough over the years to know what to expect. It was not one of the 'strangers' Prince Philip was so wary of, who was marrying into the family. As the Queen observed: 'She is one of us.'

Many years later when I asked Diana whether the marriage was arranged, she told me with some irritation: 'It was Charles and I who decided on the marriage. Not the Queen. Not my grandmother. Us. No one else.'

That was true, to the extent that no one actually ordered Charles to propose or Diana to accept. But without the Queen's explicit approval, no proposal would have been made. In law the Prince of Wales needs his Sovereign's permission to marry but regardless of that requirement, Charles would not have gone against his mother's wishes. He looked to her for approval, and Sabrina Guinness was one who had failed the Balmoral test. A distant relation of the banking dynasty whose previous escorts had included Mick Jagger and

Jack Nicholson, she had fallen at the first hurdle. When she arrived at the castle, she went to sit down. As she was lowering her bottom, the Queen shouted: 'Don't sit there—that's Queen Victoria's chair!' She never recovered from that setback and the rest of the weekend, she remembered, was 'terrifying'. Charles stopped seeing her shortly afterwards.

Diana had avoided such faux pas. She had joined in the games of cards the royal family play after dinner, laughed at Prince Philip's jokes, got wet, fallen into bogs, said all the right things and passed with flying colours. It had brought her a magnificent engagement ring—an oval sapphire circled by diamonds.

Diana had selected it from a tray brought by Garrards, the royal jewellers. 'The Queen's eyes popped when I picked out the largest one,' she recalled. It cost £28,000, a fact which was known to everyone as the ring was displayed in the Garrard catalogue. 'The Queen paid for it,' Diana said.

What had been an exciting, playful game of courtship with a Prince as the quarry had suddenly turned deadly serious, however. Diana, young, naïve and dazzled by romantic ambition, had never really looked to the future and thought through what it entailed. The chase had been the thing. Now she was condemned to live with the consequences. She was given a police escort, moved out of her flat into the privacy of Clarence House and then, three days later, the few hundred yards down the Mall into Buckingham Palace.

'I trust that Diana will find living here less of a burden than expected,' the Queen wrote to a friend on Buckingham Palace headed notepaper from her sitting room on the first floor overlooking Constitution Hill. But a burden is exactly what Diana did find it. She arrived with just two suitcases and was taken to her suite on the second-floor nursery. On the way upstairs she lost her enthusiasm. Within a few days she also underwent a disturbing personality change.

The engagement had started off well enough with a short break at Balmoral before Charles left for an official tour of Australia and New Zealand. With Nicholas Soames and his then wife, Catherine, in attendance, they stayed at Craigowan, a small shooting lodge on the estate, and spent their days fishing on the Dee and barbecuing on its banks. In the evenings, dressed casually in corduroys and tweeds, they ate, not with silver, but with stainless steel knives and forks. It was relaxed and informal and Diana enjoyed herself. They did not share a bed; Charles slept in the Duke of Edinburgh's dressing room while Diana retired to the bedroom usually reserved for the Queen.

The absence of physical intimacy would soon come to trouble Diana, but then, once back in London, so did just about everything else. In Buckingham Palace she found herself cut off, lonely and alone. She was a young girl with time on her hands and no interests or ideas to fill it with. The Palace staff had been put at her disposal and the chefs were anxious to show off their skills but she rarely asked anyone in.

Diana went to tea with the Duchess of Gloucester and the Duchess of Kent. She also saw Princess Michael of Kent who told her: 'You are marrying the most important member of the royal family and I am married to the least important.' Her mother, Frances Shand Kydd, who had been conspicuous by her absence throughout most of her life, became a frequent visitor and took her shopping at the General Trading Company in Sloane Square or to the design studio of David and Elizabeth Emanuel, who were making the wedding dress. She swam every morning in the Palace pool and started tap dancing and exercising in the Bow Room with a teacher called Nellie Smith.

For much of the rest of her days, however, she simply mooched around, bored and increasingly irritable. She resented the efforts of the courtiers to show her the Palace ropes. Charles's private secretary Oliver Everett and Lady Susan Hussey, the Queen's most trusted lady-in-waiting, were given that thankless task and found her a most unwilling pupil.

On Prince Philip's insistence, his children had received no special training for the business of being royal. In keeping with his ideas of creating a 'modern monarchy,' he was of the opinion that osmosis would prove more effective than any rigid set of rules. That may have been fine for Charles and his siblings, brought up in palaces, cynosures since birth of the attentions of the public, but it left Diana out on a distant limb.

It would have been difficult for anyone, but Diana certainly didn't help her own situation. She took against Everett and Lady Susan and resented what she called their 'interference'. Lady Susan took her shopping and tried to befriend her but Diana never took to this funny and formidable lady who, like Diana, was the daughter of an earl.

Everett fared even worse. Slim and diffident, he gave her Georgina Battiscombe's biography of King Edward VII's wife, Queen Alexandra, and James Pope-Hennessy's life of King George V's wife, Queen Mary. Both had been consorts of future monarchs and the hope was that the books would give her an understanding of the demands of the role. Diana threw them on the floor the moment Everett left the room. 'If he thinks I'm going to read those silly, boring books he's got another thing coming. I don't need them—and I won't read them!' she shouted at a member of the Queen's staff.

The staff were more successful in their tutoring. She tried to make friends with them and was forever popping downstairs to chat to them as they went about their duties. In so doing she violated an unwritten rule of Palace conduct and after one unwelcome visit too many to the kitchen, the Yeoman of the Glass and China pointed at the door and told her firmly: 'Through there is *your* side of the house—and through here is *my* side of the house.' She fled, never to return. Diana, it turned out, knew a lot less about the ways of royalty than the royal family had presumed.

Her step-grandmother Barbara Cartland, whose saccharin romantic novelettes had helped form Diana's half-baked notions of how relations between a man and a woman should be conducted, shrewdly observed: 'My son-in-law had been equerry to the Queen but Diana was only a little girl at the time and he didn't teach her anything. She did not know the rules and regulations. It came as a shock to her and therefore she found it very difficult. Diana didn't know half the things she ought to have known.'

Diana starting filling her day by railing to the staff assigned to look after her against people she decided she did not like. Not surprisingly, Dame Barbara was high on her list. So was her stepmother, Dame Barbara's formidable daughter Raine. Diana called her 'a conniving woman'. Lady Susan and Oliver Everett also came in for their share of complaints, as did her own mother, whom she called a 'self-promoter'.

*   *   *

Pent up and lonely, Diana began making herself ill to relieve her frustration. It was the first manifestation of the eating disorder that was to dog her for the rest of her life. She began to visit the nursery kitchen at odd hours, where she would take a large glass fruit bowl emblazoned with the EIIR cypher, fill it with half a packet of Kellogg's Frosties, add caster sugar and slices of fruit and smother the lot in Windsor cream, a thick double cream from the Queen's Jersey herd at Home Farm, Windsor. Afterwards she would go to the bathroom and make herself sick. She would repeat the pattern three to four times a day. She ate her way through so many packets of what the Americans call Frosted Flakes that questions started to be asked in the Royal Pantry, the department responsible for the Palace stores. Eventually one of her footmen was called downstairs and accused of stealing the cereal. Diana had to go and confirm that they were all for her.

As her bulimia took a hold, her mood swings became ever-more unpredictable. Her sister Sarah, who had once suffered from the slimmers' disease anorexia nervosa, was one who was hurt by Diana's ill humour. After an afternoon out shopping together, the two

78

returned to the Palace. Sarah had two hours to wait before catching her train to the country. Diana decided she was not going to let her use her suite as a waiting room. She went out into the corridor, told a passing footman to order a taxi and to then go in and tell her sister that the future Princess of Wales had been called away on urgent business.

Sarah was duly shown the Palace door, much to the embarrassment of the footman who knew, as Sarah must have known, that Diana had absolutely nothing to do that afternoon.

Charles also came in for a tongue-lashing. Why, she kept asking, was he not there with her? It was explained to her that the Prince had a full schedule of engagements which had been arranged months before. That did not pacify her. She became convinced that he was neglecting her or, worse, that he was still seeing someone else. Anna Wallace was her first suspect. After she had asked him about his past love affairs and he had made the dreadful mistake of telling her, she switched her jealousy to Camilla Parker Bowles. She kept asking her new staff about her—what she was like, how she dressed, how close Charles had been to her—to the point of fixation.

Her fears were unfounded—the Prince at this stage simply did not have it in him to run two women. He had a profound sense of decorum and an almost pathological determination to do 'the right thing'. In that he was his mother's, rather than his father's, son. That was not the way Diana saw it, and she started taxing him on the subject of Camilla. He told her she was his friend and would remain one, but nothing more. Diana did not believe him. As later events proved, Diana was a passionate woman and for all her innocence she could not understand why her fiancé was not prepared to take their relationship beyond a squeeze of the hand or an occasional but decidedly chaste kiss. 'Was there someone else?' she kept asking her staff.

On the night of 2 June she tried to push matters along. Awoken by a thunder storm, she ran two-thirds of the length of Buckingham Palace from her own suite to Charles's bedroom and climbed into bed with him, saying she was 'scared'. Nothing untoward happened. As she confided to her staff afterwards, the Prince had offered her a protective arm, told her not to be frightened—and then gone back to sleep. To the Prince's way of thinking he had behaved in a decent and honourable manner, but it was not what Diana had either expected or hoped for, and it left her with the corroding thought that Camilla was providing him with more than just a friendly ear to talk to.

The Queen seems to have been unaware of the severity of the trouble bubbling up under her own roof. Diana would later complain at her treatment, at the way she was left to fend for herself and, by implication, at the Queen's apparent indifference to her plight, but it was a situation of her own imagining. While Charles was away in Australia, the Queen had entertained her at Windsor and made every effort to make the young woman feel at home in a castle it was presumed she would one day reside in. She was installed in the Principal Guest Suite off the Green Corridor which is usually reserved for visiting heads of state. On the Queen's instructions, fresh lilies were placed in the room and boxes of Bendicks bitter mints put on the table beside the bed. The two lunched and dined together every day and Diana accompanied the Queen when she went out to walk the dogs.

'The Queen made a big fuss over Diana,' a member of the household recalls. 'It was a getting-to-know-you session and the Queen was trying to show Diana that she was interested in her for herself and not just as an attachment to Prince Charles.'

The Queen was keen to further develop this amity when the Court moved back to Buckingham Palace. Diana, however, wasn't interested.

When the Queen was in residence and the affairs of state permitted, she liked and encouraged her children to join her for lunch or dinner—and since the engagement, she regarded Diana as very much one of the family. Every morning her page would telephone through to his opposite numbers in the Palace and ask: 'Any of you lot coming down today?' Mark Phillips before her and Fergie afterwards often availed themselves of these informal invitations, and spent many lunch hours and long evenings chatting amiably with their mother-in-law in her private dining room on the first floor.

Diana, however, refused to go. 'I'm not having dinner with Brenda on my own,' she declared. If this unwillingness to make the effort to get to know the Queen better or to enter into the routine of royal life was born partly out of shyness and partly out of youthful defiance, it also smacked of ill-manners. It was, after all, the Queen's house she was staying in, and referring to the Sovereign as 'Brenda', the name given her by the satirical magazine *Private Eye*, was at the very least disrespectful (later in the engagement period Diana amused herself by running up and down the Palace corridors, leaping on the antique sofas and shouting: 'I'm jumping on Brenda's sofas!').

The Queen chose to overlook her future daughter-in-law's behaviour. She can be intimidating (she has a lofty grandeur polished by a lifetime of practice) but with friends and family she can be engaging company. What she does not do, what her position has taught her never to do, is force herself on people. When

Diana failed to respond to her page's solicitations, the Queen broke with custom and telephoned Diana herself and asked her down to her apartment. After Diana had proffered yet another excuse about having to go shopping or seeing some non-existent friends, the Queen stopped calling. 'She doesn't want to come and have a stuffy old dinner with me,' she said. Diana, she concluded, needed time by herself to settle in.

* * *

Viewed from the censorious high ground of hindsight, the Queen's insensitivity to Diana's predicament looks almost callous. In the context of time, though, it is hard to see how else she could have reacted. In the early 1980s few people in Britain outside of the medical profession had heard of bulimia. The Buckingham Palace staff who were detailed to look after the troubled young woman certainly had not. Like their royal mistress, they attributed Diana's behaviour to a bad case of 'nerves', that old-fashioned catch-all which covered everything from a mild case of bashfulness to full-blown psychosis.

Despite what Diana thought, the Queen was sympathetic to her plight. There was a limit to the Queen's understanding, however. She had lived through the Second World War when stress and bereavement were a daily fact of life and she belonged to a generation which had been brought up to expect the rough as well as the smooth and to maintain a stiff upper lip when confronted by either. The royal rule was: Get on with the job—and don't think too much about yourself.

In years to come the royal family would be roundly criticized for their failure to take time out of their schedule to devote time to Diana, but in that, too, they were bound in by their backgrounds. Since the reign of George VI and with the atrocious example of his brother, the Duke of Windsor, louring over them, they had done all they could to avoid being labelled as frivolous, lackadaisical, capricious or unreliable. It was an uphill struggle. Too many weeks spent at Balmoral or too many days on *Britannia* led to charges of indolence at the expense of the taxpayer. By way of self-defence, they had forsaken the pleasures of fashion and folly which were the traditional prerogatives of royalty and become what the public wanted them to be: respectable, hard-working and dull. Their diaries were filled months in advance and it would have been unthinkable, had it ever occurred to them which it didn't, to rearrange or cancel their commitments to accommodate one young woman. It would have been better if they had. Instead they carried on with business as usual.

Even the upsets of Ascot week in June failed to sound the warning bells. Once again

Charles was away, this time in the United States, and Diana was left to struggle through on her own. It proved to be a trying time. Installed at Windsor Castle, she went upstairs to the top floor of the Queen's Tower where she encountered Princess Anne with her children. Still only a Lady, she dropped at deep curtsey to the Princess. It was the wrong thing to do. Anne dislikes pretension and unnecessary ceremony and, with a look of cold contempt, stared straight through her sister-in-law-to-be. In what was becoming something of a habit, Diana fled the room.

She managed to get through the carriage rides down the course without mishap, waving to the crowds and giving the photographers the 'Shy Di' look they had come to expect. When Charles arrived home on the last day, however, the tensions which had been building up got the better of her. She was waiting at the private 'dog door' of the castle to greet him but instead of the loving embrace of reunion she had been looking forward to, she got a quick peck on the cheek as Charles carried on upstairs to change for luncheon. There was no slight intended—Charles was jet-lagged and behind schedule—but Diana felt understandably humiliated and rushed to her room where she dissolved into tears. She emerged half an hour later and made the afternoon's carriage procession down the course, at her husband-to-be's side and with her smile back in place. By nightfall, however, her mood had swung again.

Using the excuse of Prince Andrew's twenty-first birthday which had actually taken place four months earlier, the Queen held a grand ball for a thousand people in the castle that night. Elton John provided the entertainment and the dancing continued until the early hours. Diana went wild. She danced with first one man and then another. The Queen said how nice it was to see Diana enjoying herself; Prince Charles gave up on his fiancée and went to bed early.

One by one the other guests drifted away until Diana was alone. In the half-light of dawn one of the household looked out of the window and saw Diana in the quadrangle, alone, but still swaying to the music which by then was playing only in her head. At 5.30 a.m. she got into her car and drove north to Althorp, her family home in Northamptonshire. When she got there she told her bewildered father that she intended to call off the engagement.

Earl Spencer had not fully recovered from the stroke he had suffered three years earlier and this was hardly the kind of stressful situation his doctors would have recommended. But with fatherly understanding he listened to his daughter as she poured out her heart, told her that she must do what she thought was right and then calmly advised her that it was probably just the pressure getting the better of her and that once she was married things would be a lot easier.

He succeeded in calming her down and by Sunday night Diana was back in Buckingham Palace and acting as if nothing had happened. A few sound words of advice were not going to eradicate the underlying problem, however, and there would be more scenes and more hysterics as Diana lurched unsteadily towards the altar in St Paul's Cathedral.

Her obsession with Camilla Parker Bowles increased and the weight continued to pour off her. Tears flowed at a polo match. And two days before the wedding when, according to Diana, Charles went off to say his goodbyes to his erstwhile mistress and present her with a gold bracelet bearing the entwined letters GF, she told her sisters: 'I can't marry him.'

Again her family talked her out of throwing in the towel—by pointing out that her face was already emblazoned on millions of souvenir tea towels.

The Prince did indeed see Camilla that day but it was no intimate tête-à-tête. Along with the Queen and the rest of the royal family she was a guest at Windsor for the christening of Princess Anne's daughter Zara. Camilla's husband, Brigadier Andrew Parker Bowles, was a godfather. Diana had been invited, and Charles had pleaded with her to go, but she had refused; Anne's Ascot put-down still smarted, and she had no desire to be in the same room as Camilla.

Charles saw Camilla again that night at the wedding party at Buckingham Palace. It was the most lavish royal ball in over half a century with a guest list which included just about every European royal, both major and minor, as well as America's First Lady Nancy Reagan. The champagne was vintage Krug and Princess Margaret became noticeably 'over-trained', an upper-class euphemism for someone who had drunk too much (when the Princess tried to order her daughter home, Sarah Armstrong-Jones remarked: '*She* needs to go home—I don't!').

Charles is alleged to have spent what remained of the night with Camilla. This is not true. Even if he had wanted to (and that is a presumption which takes no account of Charles's character), there simply wasn't the time or, more pertinently, the opportunity. There were footmen and maids in attendance on every floor, every room was full, and such was the pressure for accommodation that Princess Grace of Monaco was forced to share a sitting room with Crown Prince Harald of Norway and his wife, Sonja (Harald, the great-great-grandson of Queen Victoria, was thrilled; Grace, the granddaughter of a poor Irish immigrant, took spoilt umbrage at the arrangement).

From the Queen's point of view the evening was a great success. It was royal entertainment on a scale she had never before afforded herself. And as its centrepiece, there was her beloved son and heir with his beautiful bride-to-be, dancing closely, smiling into each other's faces, looking for all the world like the enchanted couple the world had decreed them to be.

Diana awoke the next morning in the best of spirits. There were no tantrums, no complaints. The waiting was almost at an end. The following day she would walk down the aisle of St Paul's Cathedral and become the Princess of Wales and that imminent prospect appeared to have lifted the gloom she had laboured under for the past five months.

The Queen, too, was in excellent humour. In mid-morning the two women met in the Queen's sitting room and sat down side by side on a low sofa. The Queen produced two red leather boxes, one flat, one almost square. From the smaller one she produced a necklace of emeralds, from the other a tiara of lovers' knots of diamonds from which hung nineteen drops of milk-white pearls.

Without pretence or ado, the Queen handed the boxes to Diana. This was more than just a sumptuous wedding gift. The jewels had once belonged to Queen Mary and, in giving them to Diana, the Queen was symbolically handing the future of the royal family over to a young woman who should one day be Queen herself.

So endowed, Diana went back upstairs to her rooms. She opened the boxes, showed them to her footman and told him 'how sweet' the Queen had been to her. Then she started chanting, in the manner of a child in the playground: 'I've got Brenda's rocks . . .'

CHAPTER THREE

FROM BALMORAL TO SANDRINGHAM

The sky was grey and overcast but the reception which greeted Diana when she arrived at Balmoral for the second leg of her honeymoon could not have been warmer or more open-hearted. She was being welcomed into the royal family and the whole estate turned out to greet her.

The couple crossed the ancient granite bridge over the River Dee and, just after four o'clock, drew up at the wrought iron gates, emblazoned with the cyphers of George V and Queen Mary, which guard the entrance to the castle grounds. The Queen was there, Prince Philip at her side; both beaming. Charles and Diana were ushered out of their Range Rover and into an old pony trap. Four strapping ghillies took hold of the ropes and, accompanied by much laughter and jest, the Prince and Princess were pulled up the long drive which was lined with over two hundred staff and estate workers, there with their waving wives and children.

The Queen, putting aside regal dignity, walked alongside, occasionally breaking into a little skip in her effort to keep up. Philip was in the best of spirits and on an old bicycle a couple of sizes too small, pedalling frantically, riding up beside the ghillies to offer good-humoured advice, then racing off ahead to ensure that he was there at the front door when the cart pulled up ten minutes later.

Diana appeared to be enjoying herself. She was dressed in a lightweight, fashionably cut tweed skirt with matching high-collared jacket. Her hair was highlighted and her skin tanned by the Mediterranean sun, and she looked fresh, beautiful and happy. She tugged at her husband's sleeve and nestled her head on his shoulder. When they arrived at the castle, she leapt out of the cart and turned to Charles and, without a trace of affectation or artifice, told him how wonderful it all was.

The Queen, panting up behind, looked at her son and his young bride and smiled with delight. They looked for all the world just as the world took them to be: a couple in love. Everyone who was there that day remarked on it—and how pleased the Queen looked. All her concerns about Charles's future appeared to have been resolved by his marriage to this captivating, stunning young woman who had walked across the hill and into their lives only a few short months before. Like everyone else, Prince Philip included, she was enchanted by Diana and said how sure she was that Britain's newest princess would make Charles a 'perfect wife'.

'It was a glorious afternoon,' one of the household recalled sadly. 'We cheered and we clapped and everything seemed so cheerful and bright.'

For the two people in the pony trap, however, a shadow more ominous than the skudding rain clouds rolling in from the mountains to the east had already settled over their relationship. Diana and Charles were only a few weeks into their marriage but Diana was already a woman in crisis, consumed by illness and burning jealousies which were as harmful as they were irrational. And part of the problem was where she was and who she had just become.

The Queen was at her most easygoing as she led the couple into the Ladies Drawing Room for the customary ritual of afternoon tea, but the veneer of formality which disguises her shyness can easily be mistaken for coldness. Diana was on her best behaviour but, as she half-listened to the drone of conversation of her in-laws, she felt her

92

confidence slipping away.

The royal family had gone out of their way to welcome her back to the castle which she had always professed to adore and which, it the fates had been kinder, would one day have become her home. But for the moment this was her mother-in-law's house, governed by her mother-in-law's rules, and instead of settling back and enjoying her good fortune, Diana felt like an outsider who was about to be swallowed up by a family which bewildered and soon overawed her. Her abiding memory of that day, she told me, was not one of exhilaration or joy, but of 'inadequacy'.

*   *   *

Charles was also deeply troubled. He had entered into what he fervently believed to be a lifetime's commitment. He was now stricken with the dawning realization that he had probably made the worst mistake of his life.

The Prince had been wary about entering into marriage. Uncertain in the company of women ('I don't know how the idea got about that I am amazingly successful with women—my constant battle is to escape,' he once remarked), and too inhibited to be driven by passion ('If I'm deciding on whom I want to live with for fifty years, well, that's the last decision on which I would want my head to be ruled by my heart'), he had to be pushed into it. His mother had let it be known how taken she was with Diana—and how irritated she was becoming with her son's deliberations—and her subtle promptings had been pivotal in persuading him to ask the dewy-eyed ingénue to be his wife. Left to his own devices he would most probably never have taken that fateful decision.

The ceremony itself, and the public enthusiasm it generated, had moved him deeply. 'I found we were carried along on a wave of enormous friendliness and enthusiasm,' he said. 'It was remarkable. And I kept telling myself to remember this for as long as I could because it was such a unique experience.'

On the balcony of Buckingham Palace, this most reserved of men had even been moved to respond to the urgings of the crowd gathered in the Mall below and kiss his bride in front of a worldwide television audience of 700 million people.

It was the moment when the needs of state and individual coalesced in a splendidly orchestrated rite of passage. Charles later observed: 'Inevitably these things don't always last very long, but I think it made one realize that underneath everything else, all the rowing and the bickering and disagreements that go on for the rest of the time, every now and then you get a reason for a celebration or a feeling of being a nation.'

To Diana, however, a state occasion, no matter how magnificent, did not constitute a marriage. The grandeur of the wedding had overwhelmed her and left her feeling flat and confused. But so had the intimacy which followed, and the honeymoon was an unmitigated disaster.

The couple still hardly knew each other, despite the months Diana had lived at the Palace. She had seen little of her fiancé, who refused to adjust his schedule of engagements. When they were together he treated her with a distant courtesy. Diana had tried to break through his reserve: all he had done that night in June, when she had climbed into his bed, was cuddle her, as she told her staff the following morning.

Charles doubtless believed he was acting decorously. Diana, however, was most upset by Charles's lack of ardour. 'She couldn't understand why he was so unromantic,' one of her staff recalled. 'She took it as rejection.'

Charles and Diana finally slept together for the first time on the first night of their honeymoon, in the same bed Prince Philip and the Queen had shared at the start of their own married life, thirty-four years before. It was the Tudor four-poster in the Portico Room at Broadlands, Earl Mountbatten's Hampshire home. On the wall there hung an eighteenth-century print bearing an inscription which, translated, reads: 'Consideration, tenderness, courtesy, all flows from this day.'

The Queen enjoyed herself. Philip told his cousin, the Marquis of Milford Haven, that it had been 'bliss'. Mountbatten's valet, Charles Smith, who had been seconded to royal duty, recalled how the following morning the couple had called down late for a breakfast of boiled eggs and grapefruit. There would be upsets in the days to come—the house was besieged by gaping onlookers and Prince Philip lost his temper, for what proved to be the first of many times, with the hordes of journalists who had descended on the house on the banks of the River Test, where the gentle art of dry fly-fishing was first perfected. But, by the end of their fortnight there, the couple were firmly established as man and wife.

Diana came away with no happy memories: she admitted that she found the whole experience 'grim'. She complained that Charles only wanted to go fishing and to read the books he had brought with him.

Sex had brought Philip and Elizabeth together. It did little to leaven the situation between Charles and Diana. Rather the contrary: in her inexperience, Diana found it bemusing and, at this stage in her life, unfulfilling. She later told her staff that the first time they made love she started giggling, which did nothing for her husband's *amour-propre* ('Frigid wasn't the word—Big F when it comes to that,' she recalled).

96

The situation deteriorated even further aboard the royal yacht which took them cruising through the Mediterranean on the next stage of their honeymoon. Most brides would have revelled in their good fortune and enjoyed this romantic interlude, before settling down to the more mundane routine of married life. Instead, Diana became violently ill with bulimia and decided that her husband was dreary. The days were punctuated by rows, bitter silences and moments of hysteria, while her nights were ruined by 'appalling' dreams and thoughts of Camilla Parker Bowles.

When the ill-starred couple made it up to Balmoral for the last leg of what was supposed to be their nuptial celebrations, the Prince became so disturbed by his wife's behaviour that he summoned a doctor to the castle. Diana introduced him saying, 'This is my psychiatrist.'

The doctor was to be the first of many who would be called in to try and help a young woman perilously close to losing her mental health—or worse.

'All the analysts and psychiatrists you could ever dream of came plodding in trying to sort me out,' she recalled.

They never did. The royal family had checked beforehand to make sure Diana was a virgin. They would have been better advised to check her psychological profile. In medical terms, Diana suffered from Borderline

Personality Disorder as defined in volume IV of the *Diagnostic and Statistical Manual for Mental Disorders.* It is a standard medical textbook, used around the world. In Britain, doctors treat perhaps one in every six women for the disorder. The condition is not certifiable, but the prisons contain a disproportionately high percentage of the total number of sufferers. The symptoms include unstable interpersonal relationships, a desperate fear, real or imagined, of abandonment, a tendency towards histrionic behaviour, a need for adoration, and mood swings. Bulimia is another manifestation. It has its root in the shocks of childhood and, according to the psychiatrists who tended her, Diana's was a classic case. As early as January 1983, Dr Thomas Holmes, the head of the Department of Psychiatry at Washington Medical School and the deviser of the Holmes-Rahe stress scale, was warning, 'The Princess of Wales stands an 80 per cent chance of becoming ill through the strains of royal life. An obsessive compulsive illness could definitely be a possibility.'

Keeping these symptoms in check proved extremely difficult. A psychoanalyst with knowledge of the case said: 'To ignore the condition is cruel, but to break through the barriers the patient builds around his or her self is almost impossible.'

The situation at Balmoral certainly did not

help. Any young bride would have found it a trial to spend her honeymoon with her in-laws. For Diana it was a trauma. All she wanted, as she declared over and over again, was to be loved—ostentatiously, wholeheartedly and, above all else, publicly.

What she singularly failed to grasp was that 'love' is not part of the royal vocabulary. This is not due to any inherent coldness (the Queen was deeply in love with Prince Philip when they married) but because, once promulgated, it sets a dangerous agenda for what is, in the final analysis, a union of state which is best preserved by being kept safely beyond the reach of the hurly-burly of human emotions. When that most modern and forthright of monarchs, King Juan Carlos of Spain, was asked on the day of his engagement to Princess Sofia of Greece, 'Are you in love?' a courtier promptly stepped forward and sternly informed the reporter that this was not a question Juan Carlos would answer.

No one came to Charles's aid when he was asked the same question. Taken aback by the presumption of the enquiry, all he managed to come out with was a stumbling, 'Whatever "in love" means.' It was a phrase which would haunt him for the rest of his marriage—and illustrates the practical good sense behind Juan Carlos's silence.

Still unfettered by regal constraints, Diana had responded with a positive 'Of course' when she was asked if she was 'in love' with her fiancé. She quickly discovered, however, that her definition of that most ill-defined of emotions did not fit in with the royal routine, even on honeymoon in a turreted castle in the picturesque remoteness of the Scottish Highlands. Everything she now did was governed by precedent, something she could not escape, even when she went to bed with her husband in the Victorian bed.

Their apartment was next to the Queen's rooms. And if that was not impediment enough, the names of previous royal honeymooners were scratched on the windowsill to remind her that she was now a cog in an institutional wheel. The signatures scored into the woodwork included Marina and George, the parents of Princess Alexandra and the Duke of Kent, and Edward VII's daughter Maud, who married King Haakon VII of Norway. They were people Diana had never heard of but whose ghostly presence she resented.

*   *   *

Just as Diana had feared she would be, she also found herself overpowered by her in-laws. In desperate need of attention, she found herself pushed down the pecking order as more and more of the family descended on the castle for their summer holidays. The Queen

Mother came to stay. So did Princess Margaret, who brought her children, David and Sarah. Prince Andrew and Prince Edward were already there. Diana was now 'Your Royal Highness', entitled to the curtseys and bows that go with the status, but this hardly marked her out in a claustrophobic world where everyone had a title of one kind or another, and where the two queens always took precedence. When Charles poured the early evening drinks he always served his mother, the Queen, and his grandmother, the Queen Mother, before he came to his wife, the Princess of Wales. Diana took umbrage and complained, 'I always thought it was the wife first—stupid thought!'

The protests of a twenty-year-old were not going to interrupt the courtesies of centuries, however. Nor were they allowed to disrupt the established customs of a family whose habits are cast in stone. They include the almost daily ritual of the lunchtime picnic and the evening barbecue, and regardless of the weather ('It rained and rained and rained,' Diana remembered), the whole clan would traipse out to eat on the windswept hills.

In her courting days Lady Diana had cheerfully joined in these Spartan gastronomic excursions. Within a week of her return as Princess of Wales, she was sulkily refusing to go.

'She just about managed to drag herself out

for the occasional picnic, but she would try everything to get out of the barbecues,' a member of the staff recalled.

This was considered extremely 'bad form'. The idea of the barbecues was to give the staff the evening off, and when the family set off at seven o'clock the curtains were drawn, the lights turned down and the castle closed for the night, leaving the maids and footmen and chefs free to go into the local town of Ballater or retire to their own bar in a hut at the back of the castle. This perk was infringed upon by Diana's determination to stay behind and eat alone.

'But I'm only having sausage and mash,' or 'I'm only having baked beans,' she would say, oblivious to the fact that in a royal household even the simplest meal requires someone to cook it, someone else to serve it, and yet another to clean up afterwards. Diana's eating habits were soon causing disaffection in the servants' hall.

The Queen, too, was becoming annoyed by her daughter-in-law's behaviour and the point was made to the young princess that if the Queen Mother, at her great age, was able to attend these alfresco meals, so could Diana.

Diana, however, stood her ground and in doing so won the unexpected support of Princess Margaret. In the years ahead, Margaret would become one of Diana's most implacable critics but at that time she showed considerable sympathy for the young woman who had joined their ranks so recently. The Princess, she said, was having difficulties adjusting to her new role and that was only to be expected.

'Let her do what she likes,' Margaret said. 'Leave her alone and she will be all right.' The Queen, never one to force an issue if it could be avoided, took her sister's advice.

The Queen could afford to take a detached view of Diana's behaviour. Her son, on the other hand, could not. He had to live with it. He tried to enthuse Diana for the rhythms of country life which are so important to him, taking her fishing and for long walks up to the peaks, where, while she worked on her needlepoint, he would sit and wonder at the views or read to her from the works of Jung and his friend and mentor, Sir Laurens van der Post.

It was to no avail. Diana found the walks tedious and her husband's metaphysical musings incomprehensible. She withdrew into herself and, instead of joining the rest of the house party on their shoots or her husband on his outings, she started driving to the sweet shop in Ballater in her silver Ford Escort with a footman at her side, and spending the rest of the afternoon seated on a tartan rug on a rock, munching candy and complaining about her lot. Charles was baffled and then exasperated and within days the rows had started up again.

According to a former member of the Balmoral staff, Charles in anger is a frightening sight. His voice rises by several octaves. Like his grandfather George VI before him, he will throw a cup or sweep clear his desk with one swipe. As a schoolboy at Gordonstoun he had had to control his rages out of a dread of being thumped by one or, as sometimes happened, by several of his contemporaries. As Prince of Wales he was able to shout and scream as loud as he liked without fear of reprimand. He never lost his self-control in front of his mother, however. 'He was in awe of Mummy,' Diana noted drily. A wife, however, proved to be a different matter, and the staff on night duty at Balmoral recalled hearing the arguments taking place behind the closed door of the couple's apartment.

Yet for all their fury, Charles's flashes of temper never lasted for more than a few moments, and when they passed he would become polite and conciliatory and a little embarrassed by his momentary loss of composure. Diana was very different. Tears would quickly turn into tantrums and Charles's mollifying pleadings only seemed to make matters worse. Like his mother, Charles has always backed away from emotional confrontations and their quarrels ended with the Prince walking out of the room. When he returned offering what he hoped would be a consoling word or an apology, the still-fuming

Diana would reignite the row.

It was a wretched state for two newlyweds to find themselves in and one Charles was not equipped to deal with. The mother and grandmother who had taken it in turns to raise him had been distant but when they were with him they were never anything other than warm and affectionate. Even his pugnacious sister, Anne, had deferred to his position as heir to the throne. As she explained: 'I've always accepted the role of being second in everything from quite an early age.'

Diana was completely different. She regarded Charles, not as a prince, but as a man—and not one, as she made it patently clear, whom she was ever going to allow to have the final say. The Prince had spent patient hours teaching her how to fish. She never became an enthusiast for the sport, once remarking to the ghillie when she let a salmon slip off the hook, 'Not to worry—I've already caught the biggest fish.' But she had grasped the technique well enough to reel in her husband almost at will.

One of her duties as a royal bride was to pose for the inevitable honeymoon photo call. At first she refused to have anything to do with it, loudly proclaiming that she wasn't going to be photographed and that no one, certainly not Charles, was going to make her do what she didn't want to do. Then, just as Charles was about to go outside and tell the waiting pressmen that the session would have to be postponed, she switched mood and appeared wearing the same tweed outfit she had worn when she arrived at the castle, set off by an enchanting smile. She took hold of her husband's hand and allowed the cameras to do the rest. In the photograph that duly made its way around the world the Princess looks happy and relaxed while the Prince, still simmering with anger, appears cold and disgruntled. It was an image—of a loving wife married to a cold and indifferent husband—which soon would fix itself in the public's imagination.

*   *   *

It was a harbinger of the troubles to come, for it was becoming ever-more apparent to the Prince that Diana was very unwell. The view from her rain-drenched bedroom window matched her emotional landscape: bleak and miserable, the horizon obscured by an enveloping mist which left her feeling hopeless and alone.

The royal family have always sought spiritual solace in the countryside, and in Scotland in particular. It is there they retreat to recharge their batteries and escape the goldfish bowl of their official lives. Charles once declared: 'I am a countryman. I can't stand cities.' Diana was the opposite. She missed the bustle and excitement of city life.

All that the remote quietude of the Highlands appeared to do was exacerbate her anxieties. Her bulimia had taken such a destructive hold that she found it all but impossible to keep down what little she did eat, and her once supple body was becoming skeletal. She resented the presence of the other members of the family and the guests they invited for a few days' shooting. Convinced that everyone was staring at her, she found it extremely difficult to make conversation at the drinks beforehand or the dinners she attended. Unable to deal with the problem himself, the Prince decided he had no alternative but to seek professional help.

The psychiatrist arrived by train and was collected at the station by the Prince's valet, Stephen Barry. He was found accommodation at a hotel in Ballater, from where he was collected at about 11 o'clock each morning by a chauffeur who drove him up to the castle, took him in by the Tower Door and up to the Waleses' sitting room. Over coffee, he would spend half an hour talking to Charles and Diana together before spending another half hour alone with the Princess.

While she talked and cried the doctor took notes. His preliminary diagnosis was similar to the one Princess Margaret had arrived at: that Diana was having trouble adjusting to her dramatic change in circumstances, and that given time and encouragement she would settle down to the role that marriage had given her. The doctor suggested that the presence of friends of her own age would help speed the process along and her old flatmate Carolyn Pride was invited to spend a few days at Balmoral. The move out of the castle and into the comparative privacy of Craigowan, a small shooting lodge on the estate where Diana would be free to set her own routine without forever looking over her shoulder to see what her mother-in-law was doing, was also deemed to be a step in the right direction.

At first the signs were encouraging and by the end of September the couple had drawn close enough for Diana to inform her husband that she was pregnant. The Prince told his family that he was 'thrilled'. So was the Queen, who delighted in the prospect of becoming a grandmother for the third time. She, and everyone else, thought that motherhood would close the chapter on what the family referred to as Diana's 'little difficulties'.

Their optimism proved woefully premature. Diana's pregnancy only added to the sickness induced by bulimia, her dreams became ever-more tortured and by the end of October, the Princess was in such a state that, as she admitted later, 'I was about to cut my wrists.'

Charles sought the counsel of Sir Laurens van der Post, who made what was becoming the well-worn trek north. The old mystic, however, could offer no cure. 'He didn't understand me,' Diana protested.

Once again medical advice was sought and Diana was dispatched to London to begin what would become an interminable shuttle from one doctor to another, lasting for the rest of her life. The doctors strived to keep her condition in check and prescribed a medicine cabinet of anti-depressants, and also Valium. She was not a good patient. She resented their efforts and complained, 'They were telling me, "Pills". That was going to keep them happy. They could go to bed at night knowing that the Princess of Wales wasn't going to stab anyone.'

And she never did, at least not in the literal sense, but a pattern of behaviour was being established which was to bring great unhappiness, not only to herself but to almost everyone who became intimately involved with her. It caused immense damage to the prestige and reputation of the royal family, dividing first the nation, and then a world watching vicariously through the media, into two rival and bitterly opposed camps. One would come to regard the Princess as manipulative and conniving, the other would condemn her husband as cruel and heartless.

The Queen never took sides, either in public or, more intriguingly, in private. She remained steadfastly even-handed throughout the Waleses' marriage, counselling caution, appealing to both parties to understand the views of the other, refusing to be bullied into siding with her husband who was soon infuriated by what he regarded as Diana's incessant whingeing, and always available to lend a sympathetic ear to her daughter-in-law's tearful pleadings and angry complaints.

As a mother keen not to interfere in the marriage of her eldest son, the Queen was determined not to become directly involved in the problem developing under her own roof. As Sovereign, however, with the future of her dynasty to worry about, it was her duty to know exactly what that problem was.

Diana was more than a daughter-in-law: she was also, God willing, the future Queen of England and a lot more of the world besides.

It was Charles who first told his mother of his wife's bulimia. She then made it her duty to find out more, but it took her a long while to fully comprehend the nature of Diana's ailment. The Queen had been brought up to judge people by the way they behave, not to wonder why they behaved in that particular way. It had to be explained to her that Diana's difficulties stemmed, not from anything the royal family had done (although, as the Queen willingly acknowledged, shouldering the responsibilities that came with being married to the heir to the throne would have taxed the mental resources of anyone, never mind a woman whose only experience of life up until then had been teaching infants in a nursery school), but from things that had taken place years before in childhood. She was told that the condition is all but incurable.

CHAPTER FOUR

CHILDHOOD COMPARISONS

Parents carve deep impressions on one's childhood memories and Diana's scored theirs down to her psychological bone. The wounds never properly healed and it was frighteningly easy to open them up again: all I had to do was mention her mother.

It was six weeks before her tragic, unexpected death and we were sitting drinking coffee in her drawing room at Kensington Palace. She appeared calm and collected.

'And what,' I asked, 'does your mother think about the way your life is going?'

Without preamble or warning, Diana's demeanour changed and she almost shouted back: 'I don't tell her anything—ever!'

I was stunned. There are moments in everyone's life when parents can be annoying and irritating, resented and feared. There might even be occasions when a child will turn his or her feelings inside out and possibly confuse love with hatred. It is part of the process of growing up, of learning how to identify, define and deal with different emotions, and most people come to realize this.

Diana clearly never had. She was then thirty-six years old and at an age when the tribulations of a distant past should have been softened and given context by time and experience. Yet the merest reference to Frances Shand Kydd had unleashed a flood of vitriol, as embarrassing as it was unexpected. But surely, I asked when the spate subsided, every woman needs a mother she can talk to?

'I don't,' she repeated. 'I have never told her anything—ever!'

In times past mother and daughter had in fact been quite close. They had shopped together and Diana had taken her sons to visit Mrs Shand Kydd at her remote cottage on the Isle of Seil off the west coast of Scotland. They had taken holidays together, including one to Italy. They went to Bologna to hear Pavarotti sing, and then to Venice, where they took a dawn ride through the canals in a gondola and where they were serenaded by Diana's detective, Ken Wharf, who has a fine baritone voice. He sang *O Sole Mio* as they passed under the Bridge of Sighs. It was, Diana recalled, 'one of those magical times'.

Such moments seemed to have been whitewashed from her memory when we met. Caught in the maze of her recollections, Diana suddenly switched her thoughts to her father, Earl Spencer, who had died five years previously. They, too, had had their disagreements, most memorably when he had criticized her lack of money sense. Diana responded by giving her father what her staff called 'Mrs Wales's big freeze'. Whenever he turned up at Kensington Palace, she would pretend not to be there.

Spencer had tried to smooth the situation by saying, 'There is not one family in Britain whose members have not, at one time or another, fallen out with each other, but most of them make it up.' Eventually they did, and Diana talked regularly to her father in the last years of his life. 'I miss him so much,' she told me.

She never made it up with her mother and did not speak to her at all in the last months of her life. A friend of Mrs Shand Kydd observed, 'Their relationship was based on love, but love and hate run very close together.'

The row which drove such a wedge between the mother and her youngest daughter was ostensibly over an interview Mrs Shand Kydd had given to *Hello!* magazine to raise money for a shrine she was building on the holy island of Iona in the Western Isles of Scotland. In it she made mention of her daughter's eating disorder, said that losing the title 'Her Royal Highness' was 'liberating' and refused to blame Charles for the breakdown of the marriage. Diana interpreted her mother's remarks as disloyal.

113

The real cause of their disagreement, however, was buried in Diana's childhood. It dated back to when she was six years old and her parents had parted amidst scenes of violent acrimony. In her mind she remained the little girl who believed she had been cruelly abandoned by her mother.

The truth, as her mother-in-law well knew, was far more complex than such a simple reading. The Queen had known Johnnie Spencer for the better part of her life. He belonged to one of the richest families in Britain, who had made its fortune out of sheep farming in the fifteenth century and had given dutiful service to the Crown for the next ten generations. He had served as her equerry for two years from 1952, having also been equerry to her father George VI for the two years before that; he had once dated the Queen's sister, Princess Margaret; he lived on her Norfolk estate in Park House, a ten-bedroom Victorian lodge which he rented from the Queen while waiting to inherit his own, stately Althorp House in Northamptonshire, from his father; moreover Park House is only 200 yards from Sandringham House, which made him the Queen's nearest neighbour. While she never walked across to borrow a cup of sugar, she had come to know him very well indeed.

*   *   *

To all appearances Diana's father was an aristocrat typical of his age and station; dependable, aloof, taciturn and as dull as the flatlands of East Anglia where he lived. But Johnnie Spencer (or Viscount Althorp, as he was then called) was more complicated than his curriculum vitae might have suggested. His father, the 7th Earl, the ironically named 'Jolly Jack', was a crude, unsociable and bad-tempered martinet, who opened the door armed with a shotgun, doused his cousin Sir Winston Churchill's cigar in a glass of water, and filled his coffee cup to the brim with sugar before, to the disgust of everyone else at the table, swallowing the contents in one gulp. He allowed Johnnie no say in the management of the 20,000-acre estate he was born to inherit. Relations between father and son were 'uneasy', as the present Earl Spencer recorded, and there was thus a disturbing thread of moroseness woven into Johnnie's character.

In 1954 he married Lord Fermoy's daughter, Frances, in a lavish ceremony attended by the Queen and eight other members of the royal family. It was followed by a reception for eight hundred guests at St James's Palace which the Sovereign had lent for the occasion. Frances was just eighteen at the time. There is an intriguing symmetry in the fact that she was twelve years Johnny's junior. Her mother, Ruth, Lady Fermoy, was twelve years younger than her husband—the same age gap as between her own daughter, Diana, and her husband, the Prince of Wales. Lady Fermoy's marriage survived. Diana's didn't. Nor did Frances's.

She bore her husband two daughters, Sarah and Jane, but when in 1960 the son they both wanted died at birth the marriage started to go badly wrong. 'It was a dreadful time for my parents,' their son, the present Earl, said. 'I don't think they ever got over it.'

Diana was born the following year, but it could not save a union which was already pulling at its silken seams. Frances was young, impetuous, unfulfilled—and utterly bored with her dour husband. In the summer of 1966 she met Peter Shand Kydd, the Edinburgh University-educated heir to a wallpaper fortune, and took him as her lover. Within a few months, Shand Kydd had left his wife and three children and Frances had moved out of Park House into a flat in Cadogan Place in Chelsea, taking her children with her.

It was a traumatic time for the young Spencers and especially for Diana. Convinced (probably rightly) that she would not have been born if her dead brother had lived, she now found herself caught in the middle between two warring parents. The Princess gave a poignant account of the distress this caused her—of listening to her brother, Charles, calling pathetically for their mother in the middle of the night, but being too frightened of the dark to get out of bed to comfort him; of her mother's tears and her father's rages and the terrible sense of worthlessness she felt as she was pulled first one way, then the other.

Spencer had never found it easy to keep his temper under control and in his frustration and anger at his wife's adultery their arguments sometimes ended in violence. Diana witnessed these calamitous marital scenes from her hiding place 'behind the drawing-room door'.

Frances went to court and sued for divorce on the grounds of her husband's 'cruelty', which under the law as it then stood, meant physical abuse. Johnnie cross-petitioned on the grounds of her adultery.

The Queen stood silent witness to these wretched scenes unfolding on her doorstep. She may have felt vague sympathy for Frances—she knew how difficult her former equerry could be, and that struck a deep chord in her own background—but her loyalty was to Viscount Althorp. The Sixties were a decade of radical change—the epoch of 'free love', the Pill and the Beatles, when a 'gospel of Self-Fulfillment' thrust itself to the fore and a classless 'meritocracy' began to displace the old aristocracy at the top of the social pile. In the insular world the Queen inhabited, however, certain taboos continued to hold fast and a woman's infidelity, no matter what provocation lay behind it, still weighed heavily against her—so heavily, indeed, that Frances' own mother, Lady Fermoy, gave evidence against her. In April 1969 Mr Justice Wrangham granted Johnnie a divorce on the grounds of Frances's adultery and awarded custody of her four children to Viscount Althorp.

The Queen abided by the judge's decision and Frances Shand Kydd, as she soon became, was banished from the royal circle. She could live with her social exclusion. To lose her children, however, was an insufferable burden for any mother to endure and the ensuing years were punctuated with bitter recriminations culminating in her conversion to Roman Catholicism and her arrest for driving while under the influence of alcohol.

The effect on her youngest daughter proved to be even more destructive. Diana would recall her mother packing her suitcase and walking out of the house, never to return. She remembered her parents berating each other and the sound of her mother's footsteps ringing out across the corridor for the last time. Sometimes she would blame her father for what happened; in the last years of her life she had switched the fault to her mother. Either way, it ensured that she had what she called 'a *very* unhappy childhood', and it condemned her to a lifetime of mental anguish.

This was not Diana's fault. Nor was it, necessarily, a sign of weakness. As Britain's foremost counsellor of abused women, Erin Pizzey was privy to the details of what lay behind the Althorp divorce. She said: 'Diana forcibly lost her mother when she was very young and this loss—of a good, warm, loving figure—would have had a major effect on her. If you don't resolve the damage you take it with you into adulthood where it can affect your relationships with men.'

*   *   *

Prince Philip, somewhat predictably, was inclined to dismiss the doctors' diagnosis of Borderline Personality Disorder as so much medical 'mumbo-jumbo'. A self-made man in every sense of the phrase, he had endured a childhood which had seen the nervous breakdown of his deaf mother when he was ten and his effeminate father being condemned to death for cowardice before deserting his family to live with a widowed actress in Monte Carlo. He had spent long years in exile in Paris living off the charity of expatriate Greeks. During the holidays he had been the unwanted package in a poignant game of pass-the-parcel, as he was shipped around from one uninterested relation to another. Yet he had risen above an unpromising beginning to become a well-respected Royal Navy officer who, had he not seized his dynastic opportunity and married the heir to the British throne, was widely tipped to rise to the highest rank (Admiral of the Fleet Lord Lewin, the Chief of the Defence Staff during the Falklands conflict, who served with Philip as a midshipman aboard HMS *Valiant* in the early days of the Second World War, was of the firm opinion that if he had stayed in the Navy, Philip would have made it to First Sea Lord). Ruthlessly single-minded himself, Philip was intolerant of weakness in others. To his way of thinking, obstacles were there to be overcome and he had little time for what he perceived as his eldest son's faintheartedness—and even less for Diana's emotional self-indulgence.

The Queen, on the other hand, was considerably more understanding of Diana's difficulties. She had known her all her life and while she had no way of knowing how profoundly affected Diana had been by her parents' squabbles, after the divorce she made sure that the little girl next door was invited over to 'the big house' during the holidays. She had looked kindly on her as a young woman when she met her on the hills above Balmoral a decade later. And when it was made clear to her just how unwell Diana was, it was the Queen who became her most steadfast and, given the circumstances, most unlikely supporter.

'I have the best mother-in-law in the world,'

the Princess told me, using words she never employed to describe her own mother. But she never quite succeeded in mastering the vague unease she felt in what Palace staff call 'the Presence' (very few people do), and theirs was never a tactile relationship. The Queen shies away from physical contact, even with her own children, and the closest she and Diana ever came was the occasional and always rather formal peck on the cheek.

Yet the Queen, for all her reserve, seemed to have a natural empathy with Diana which is surprising perhaps, when one considers their respective backgrounds: Diana's was troubled, whereas to all appearances the Queen enjoyed a childhood which has always been described as 'idyllic'.

In hard truth, it was never that.

*   *   *

The Queen Mother had laid down the ground rules for bringing up her daughters: 'To spend as long as possible in the open air, to enjoy to the full the pleasures of the country, to be able to dance and draw and appreciate music, to acquire good manners and perfect deportment, and to cultivate all the distinctly feminine graces'. She put it even more succinctly to her daughter's governess Marion Crawford, who duly wrote it down. Childhood, the Queen Mother said, was simply there to provide 'lots of pleasant memories stored up against the days that might come and, later, a happy marriage'.

Those childhood experiences were carefully vetted, however, and for all the Queen Mother's good intentions, she was not always able to carry them out. The Queen was born into a family which was a closed community ruled by her grandfather, George V. He had exercised autocratic and often brutal control over his own children and he continued to impose his authority on the next generation. The Duchess of York, as the Queen Mother was then, was not even allowed to choose the names of her own daughters. She had wanted to call her second child Ann Margaret, but 'Papa', as she obsequiously addressed the King, did not approve and the name was changed to Margaret Rose.

'The House of Hanover, like ducks, produce bad parents; they trample their young,' Sir Owen Morshead, the Royal Librarian at the time, observed drily. The King had once famously declared: 'My father was frightened of his mother, I was frightened of my father, and I am damned well going to see to it that my children are frightened of me,' and the Queen's surviving uncles and aunt all carried the imprint of his heavy hand through into adulthood.

The youngest, Prince John, had been locked away in Wood Farm on the Sandringham estate, where in 1919 he died of epilepsy at the age of thirteen, ignored and all but forgotten. The eldest, David, known by turn as Prince of Wales, Edward VIII and Duke of Windsor, rejected his patrimony for a twice-divorced American woman of uncertain morals. Like his great-nephew and namesake, the present Prince of Wales, he had a nervous habit of pulling at his cuffs and fiddling with his tie. He was also obsessed with his weight and by modern definition was probably anorexic.

George V's third son Henry, Duke of Gloucester, was regarded by many of his contemporaries as a drunken bully; his fourth, George, Duke of Kent, was a bisexual drug taker. His only daughter, Mary, Princess Royal, was so repressed that, as her son the 7th Earl of Harewood recalled, she was incapable of talking about love or affection, let alone showing it.

The King's children all had their good points but their faults far outweighed their virtues, and together they made a sorry catalogue of human failings. Without ever having to leave the family compound, the Queen had a wealth of case histories on hand to draw upon when it came to dealing with her errant daughter-in-law.

Her father, Bertie, the future George VI, also bore the stamp of his upbringing. Terrified of own father, he was equally frightened of the world beyond the Palace walls and sought refuge in the introspective, self-contained family unit he created for himself—his wife and their two daughters whom he referred to as 'We four'. It had no room for outsiders and Elizabeth was rarely allowed to mix with children of her own age. Her only proper playmate was her sister, Margaret, who was four years younger than herself. When she learnt to dance it was with her teacher. And when she and her sister were taken for their daily walks in Hyde Park they were not allowed to join the other children in their games.

'Other children always had an enormous fascination, like mystic beings from a different world, and the little girls used to smile shyly at those they liked the look of,' Crawford recalled. 'They would have loved to speak to them and make friends, but this was never encouraged. I often thought it a pity.'

So did the little Elizabeth. As a young girl, Diana had a menagerie of twenty stuffed animals which she took to bed with her at night. 'That was my family,' she said. Elizabeth, deprived of companionship, made her friends her collection of foot-high model horses on wheels. She had thirty of them, each with its own name, and she spent hours putting their saddles and bridles on and off, combing their manes and tails, and making sure they were given a tiny bucket of water at bedtime. The highlight of her day was being allowed to watch the brewer's dray, pulled by two horses, draw up outside 145 Piccadilly where the Yorks lived and where the Intercontinental Hotel now stands. Crawford wrote: 'The little girls, their faces pressed to the nursery window, would watch for them fondly, anxious if they were late. And many a weary little pony trotting home at the end of the day in its roster cart little dreamed of the wealth of royal sympathy it roused from that upper window . . .'

Margaret Elphinstone was one of the few children with whom Elizabeth was allowed to mix, and then only because she was 'family' (her mother, Lady Mary, was the Queen Mother's sister). She was her royal cousin's companion during the summer holidays at Balmoral. 'Life was very simple then,' Margaret recalled. 'When autumn came, we played the game of catching leaves, believing each one brought a happy day. We spent hours catching happy days.'

Elizabeth saw little of her parents. When she was only nine months old, her parents left her and went on a six-month tour of New Zealand and Australia. There were many other separations in the years ahead; it was an era when royal duties and responsibilities were deemed more important than parental ones.

Even when the Yorks happened to be at home, they only saw their children for fifteen minutes each morning and, if they had no dinner engagement that night, between 5.30

and 6.30 in the evening. Elizabeth's daily care was left in the hands of nannies.

So, of course, was Diana's. To replace their departed mother, Earl Spencer (he inherited the title when Diana was thirteen) employed a succession of young women to look after his youngest daughter and her brother, Charles. The door to Althorp House proved to be a revolving one, for no sooner had they arrived than they were usually on their way out again. 'My brother and I, if we didn't like them, we used to stick pins in their chairs and throw their clothes out of the window,' Diana recalled. Most handed in their notice within a few weeks.

Diana regaled the Queen with tales of these mischievous exploits and the Queen found them amusing. They had no mirror in her own life, however. Elizabeth was brought up by Clara (Allah) Knight, a no-nonsense Hertfordshire woman who had been the Queen Mother's nanny and believed that to spoil the child was to ruin the adult. What this meant in practice was that everything was done according to a strict routine and at an appointed hour, from breakfast at 7.30 a.m. through to bedtime at 7.15 p.m. Any misbehaviour was punished with a sharp slap across the back of the legs.

The rigours of this inflexible regime were alleviated somewhat by the arrival of a nursery maid, 22-year-old Margaret MacDonald whom

Elizabeth nicknamed Bobo. A generation younger than the formidable Allah and a lot more easygoing, she came to share Elizabeth's bedroom and remained her closest friend and confidante until her death in 1993.

There was only so far even Bobo and Allah were allowed to go, however, in their efforts to make Elizabeth's young life as pleasant as they could, for riding shotgun was her grandmother, Queen Mary. The nannies took their instructions, not from the Duchess but from George V's indomitable wife, who ordered that Elizabeth be taught to wave to crowds and smile for photographers. 'Teach that child not to fidget!' the Queen would bark. In return for the small reward of a biscuit, Elizabeth learnt how to control her bladder for hours on end. It is unfair to judge one generation by the standards of another but even by the criteria of her own era, Elizabeth's childhood was repressed, regimented and desperately lonely.

At the age of eighteen Diana had left home and had moved into her own flat in Colherne Court on the corner of London's Earl's Court Road, bought out of money left her by her American grandmother. She attended a cookery course in Wimbledon, and earnt money by working first as a daily cleaner for her sister Sarah's friends, then as a nursery school teacher, all the while fending off the advances of a succession of young men attracted by her gamine beauty.

When the Queen was eighteen she was still living at home, still being made to dress in clothes of the same cut and colour as her fourteen-year-old sister. She was also painfully timid. As her father's equerry (and her sister's future lover) Group Captain Peter Townsend observed, 'She was shy, occasionally to the point of gaucheness.'

She also had her father to contend with. Of all George V's children (the tragic John excepted), Bertie had suffered the most as a child. 'Sensitive and easily rebuffed', as his official biographer, John Wheeler-Bennett, noted, he had been mocked, shouted at and tormented by his father and left unconsoled by his mother, who hid her feelings beneath what her friend Mabell, Countess of Airlie, called 'a hard crust of inhibition'. He had been made to wear painful leg-braces to correct his knock-knee and, naturally left-handed, he had been beaten into writing with his right. By the time he was eight, he was stricken by an atrocious stammer which rendered him all but incapable of mouthing even the simplest of sentences. He also gave the impression of being mentally weak and physically fragile, and was seen as such an embarrassment that when his brother Edward VIII's abdication seemed inevitable, the Government seriously considered by-passing him and handing the throne to the cocaine-snorting Duke of Kent.

It could never have happened: if the Monarchy was to continue, the Crown had to pass to Bertie, the next in line. The prospect appalled him. Told that he was going to be King, he admitted that he 'broke down and sobbed like a child'. (Much to the anguish of his mother, Queen Mary, who remarked: 'Really! This might be Romania'.)

Elizabeth was ten and her parents did what they could to shield her—hiding the newspapers, and sending her out to play when her uncle, Edward VIII, came to call—but she was too old not to be affected by the terrible despondency engulfing her family. Told that her beloved uncle David was going away for a long time and perhaps forever and that she was going to live in Buckingham Palace, she blurted out in horror: 'What, *for always*?' She had seen her mother crumble under the strain (as the Abdication crisis approached its climax, the Duchess had taken to her bed), and had witnessed her father reduced to helpless misery. She had also seen his temper flare out of control—and would do so many times again.

Since he was a little boy, Bertie had been subject to sudden, unchecked flashes of anger—his 'gnashes' as they were called. They exploded without warning, just as do his grandson Prince Charles's. The smallest irritation could bring them on; a medal worn incorrectly, food served at the wrong temperature, a drive of pheasant poorly executed. He never succeeded in mastering them and his wife and daughters were not spared.

The public, taught to regard the royal family as the epitome of well-bred, decorous respectability, knew little of what really went on in Buckingham Palace but there are still courtiers old enough to recall the heated rows that raged between the King and his wife in those formative years of Elizabeth's life.

According to John Wheeler-Bennett, George VI was subject to morbidness and introspection and self-pity—a description which might equally apply to Diana's father, Earl Spencer. Like George VI, who could finish a bottle of whisky in one sitting, Spencer also drank heavily.

Yet in defiance of modern notions of child rearing, Elizabeth emerged from the traumas of her upbringing remarkably unscathed. Nevertheless she found it an ordeal to play the part birth had assigned her. Diana complained that she was forced into a role, but the Queen, too, had to be forced to play hers. 'I was terrified out of my tiny mind,' Diana recalled of her first public engagements. 'I felt so sick.' She continued: 'I didn't know whether your handbag should be in your left hand or your right hand.'

The Queen had once felt exactly the same. At the age of seventeen this painfully shy young woman was dispatched to undertake her first official duty. She had been made honorary colonel of the Grenadier Guards and drove to Salisbury Plain to perform her first grown-up inspection of the battalion.

'What shall I do with my handbag during the march past?' she kept asking of her mother's lady-in-waiting, Lady Della Peel. A stream of other questions followed.

As they drew nearer to their destination Elizabeth's face started to blanch as her nerves got the better of her. She was on the verge of actually being sick when Lady Della fished into her bag and produced a barley sugar. 'Munch this slowly,' the lady-in-waiting commanded. 'You will find it good for the stomach muscles.'

It worked and she managed to walk up and down the lines of soldiers as though she had been inspecting troops all her life. And when the whole battalion marched past twice, she stood stock-still, handbag at her side. Queen Mary's instructions never to fidget had paid off.

On the way back to Windsor Castle that evening she saw Stonehenge for the first time and asked if they could stop and have a look.

'No, we can't—it's not on the schedule,' replied Lady Della. Lady Della was the eldest daughter of the 6th Earl Spencer. It was by ironic coincidence, therefore, that it should fall to Diana's great-aunt to remind the Queen of the constraints that go with being royal. It was

131

a lesson the Queen failed to pass on to Lady Diana Spencer. Consumed with her own problems and unable to control herself, Diana lashed out at the restrictions and regulations she was now subjected to.

'My mother never understood what it was like to be in my situation,' Diana told me. 'She never knew what I was going through. How could she? She has never been in my position.'

But the Queen had and it gave her an insight into the troubled mind of the young woman to whose unsteady hands the future of the Windsor dynasty was now entrusted. The Queen is the product of her childhood, just as Diana was of hers. In one it created the appearance of coldness while the other is remembered as warm and open-hearted. Behind the disparate façades, however, there was a common bond. Diana tugged and jerked at it but each time the Queen would give her a little more slack, forever counselling more patience, more compassion and understanding when others urged her to cast Diana loose and leave her to her own devices. The tie held almost—but not quite—to the end of Diana's life.

CHAPTER FIVE

RIDING FOR A FALL

At 9.03 on 21 June 1982, ten days before her twenty-first birthday, the Princess of Wales gave birth to a boy in the private Lindo Wing of St Mary's Hospital, Paddington. He weighed in at 7 lbs, 1½ oz. He was the child the Queen believed would save his parents' marriage.

Prince Charles, playing the New Man he professed to be, was at the bedside to see his son and heir delivered. He told the crowd waiting outside, 'He has a wisp of fair hair, sort of blondish, and blue eyes.'

The Queen came to visit the following day, expressed herself 'delighted', and by way of an aside added: 'Thank goodness he hasn't got ears like his father.'

The boy was induced on the longest day and his arrival was the high point, the one spire of happiness in the bleak, careworn landscape of an otherwise quite dreadful year for the royal family.

Diana had spent most of the preceding six months in tears. She 'hated' (a word she used with disturbing regularity) the pressures of the role marriage had forced on her, resented her in-laws who she believed regarded her as 'a nuisance' and was becoming psychotically suspicious of her husband.

Her ordeal had begun the previous Christmas when the royal family moved en masse to Windsor Castle, then on to Sandringham for the New Year. This elongated seasonal holiday is an organized affair, run according to a strict timetable and the Queen can be an exacting hostess. To anyone unused to her ways it can be a nerve-racking experience full of unforeseen social pitfalls and Diana found the atmosphere stifling.

In her generosity Diana had spent time and money buying what she thought were presents appropriate to her new-found position. What she failed to realize, because no one had told her, was that in a family which has literally everything, small is beautiful—and the cheaper the better. Diana had splashed out on cashmere scarves and expensive bath oils from Floris in Jermyn Street in London's West End, only to discover that everyone else was handing out £3 woollen shooting socks and 50p bars of soap bought at country fairs. Diana's gifts were all carefully wrapped; some of her in-laws' were tied with odd lengths of old wool.

The presents were stacked on a trestle table in the Crimson Drawing Room and were opened on a nod from the Queen after afternoon tea on Christmas Eve. The guest list always included minor royals such as Princess

Alexandra, the Duke and Duchess of Gloucester and Prince and Princess Michael of Kent, as well as the ubiquitous Queen Mother and Princess Margaret. As one after another of the parcels was torn open, great roars of laughter would erupt as the family compared each other's shoddy offerings. The sport here was to see who had spent the least, not the most, and Diana's expensive gifts were received with the polite but withering condescension which the British upper classes reserve for anyone who does not play the social game according to their rules.

There were other obstacles to be overcome and Diana balked at every one. Fitting in with the Christmas rituals of someone else's family is a trial for many newlyweds—and no family comes with such a complete set of customs as the Windsors. She felt, she said, 'an outsider', terrified and 'so disappointed'. There was early morning church and pre-luncheon drinks and a formal lunch with chefs carving oversized birds on a great sideboard decorated with a boar's head. At 3 o'clock she had to sit in absolute silence and without comment and watch the Queen deliver her pre-recorded Christmas message on the television.

At dinner the Queen, who drew up the seating plan, placed Diana next to Prince Andrew one night, Prince Philip another, but never beside Charles—court etiquette does not allow husbands to sit next to their wives.

In a letter to a friend written on Boxing Day, Prince Charles said: 'We've had such a lovely Christmas—the two of us. It has been extraordinarily happy and cosy being able to share it together.'

The Prince was either being diplomatic or preposterously inattentive, because 'happy' Diana most certainly was not. She was in maternity clothes and feeling unattractive. She was also very unwell. Her bulimia was now exacerbated by acute morning sickness which carried on throughout the day and necessitated her constantly having to leave the dining table to be ill.

To compound her discomfort, she had inadvertently antagonized her sister-in-law when, on Charles's insistence, she had been put into the top floor of the Queen's Tower, rooms that Princess Anne had used for thirty years and which she understandably had come to regard as her own.

Diana wasn't the only person at Windsor that year who breathed a deep sigh of relief when this 'Festival of the Family', as George V called it in the very first royal Christmas address, came to an end the day after Boxing Day. Anne, annoyed and upset at the way she had been pushed down the pecking order, was glad to get out and on to Sandringham. The others were free to return home, but Diana was also required to move on with the Court to Sandringham. It was more than she could tolerate, and, only a few days into the New Year, she threw herself down the North End staircase at Sandringham.

Exactly what happened that January afternoon depends on who is doing the recounting. Some saw it as a desperate cry for help from a young woman three months pregnant, who had been driven to the verge of suicide by the indifference of her husband and his family. To others it was no more than an unfortunate accident. Even Diana's own accounts were often at variance with each other. She told her friend Elsa Bowker that she 'did not think it was worth living or having a baby'. She told Andrew Morton: 'I knew I wasn't going to lose the baby.'

According to members of the household who were there that day, what actually happened was that at 4.45 p.m. Diana was coming down the twenty or so steps of the green-painted North End staircase which leads to the Queen Mother's rooms and which the old lady was able to negotiate unassisted until she was well into her nineties. Afternoon tea was about to be served and the Queen Mother was at the foot of the stairs feeding her corgis, Geordie and Blackie. Suddenly there was a cry and the Princess of Wales came tumbling down, almost landing in the dogs' bowls. The dogs started barking and the Queen's page ran in, shouting: 'The Princess of Wales has fallen down the stairs!' Staff and family, including

137

the Queen, rushed to the staircase. Diana was quickly helped to her feet, then everyone turned to the Queen Mother, who had nearly fainted. In Diana's memory, 'The Queen comes out, absolutely horrified, shaking—she was so frightened.' But it was more out of concern for her aged mother than it was for her daughter-in-law, who was looking embarrassed and saying that she must have tripped. Diana apologized to the Queen Mother, all the time insisting that she herself was 'absolutely all right'. Just to make sure, the royal gynaecologist, George Pinker, was called, and he duly reported that both mother and child were unharmed. The excitement over, life in the 'big house' then settled back into its orderly routine. As far the Queen was concerned, the incident was closed.

Charles did not take such a benign view of his wife's behaviour. He accused Diana of crying 'wolf'. His mood did not lighten in the days to come.

His mother, always anxious to avoid confrontation and ever one to take a middle course, counselled patience. Diana, she said, was still adjusting. Charles replied: 'You don't have to live with her', forgetting the fact that Diana was living under the Queen's roof at that very moment.

A few weeks earlier, in an attempt to relieve the pressure on the young woman, the Queen had taken the unprecedented step of inviting the editors of the Fleet Street newspapers to Buckingham Palace and personally asking them to give Diana some breathing space. Kelvin MacKenzie of the *Sun* had refused to attend although for a short time he, along with the others, dampened down their coverage of Britain's newest Princess. It was never going to last, however. The public would roundly condemn the press for harassing Diana but every time her picture appeared on the front page, newspaper sales increased. She had become a huge commercial asset and the cameramen and reporters were soon back on her doorstep, recording her every move—even going to the ungentlemanly length of sneaking up on her on holiday in Eleuthera in the Bahamas, to snatch a photograph of her in a bikini on a beach (the Queen called it an 'unprecedented breach of privacy').

*   *   *

It was not only the attention of the press that was preying on Diana's mind, however. First and foremost was her absolute conviction that her husband had resumed his affair with Camilla Parker Bowles—if it had ever ceased, which Diana doubted. Charles denied it and insisted the affair was over. Diana remained unconvinced. If Charles was late home she persuaded herself that he had been seeing his old girlfriend. When he made a telephone call she was certain that he was calling the 'Rottweiler', as she came to refer to Mrs Parker Bowles. And at night she slept fitfully, dreaming of Camilla.

The Prince had never made an attempt to deny his affection for Camilla. It would have been better if he had, but Charles was too naïve, too unsophisticated, and too used to having his own way to appreciate that when it comes to past romances, utter discretion is undoubtedly the better part of valour.

But then he had never been particularly sure-footed in his dealings with women: James Bond he wasn't. He once recounted to me how, back in his courting days, he had taken a girl to a restaurant in London's Ebury Street. The restaurant was empty, the atmosphere was deathly and the entire staff of waiters swarmed all over the couple. Trying to impress her, Charles ordered a bottle of the the most expensive claret. 'I promptly knocked it over when it arrived,' Charles recounted. The evening was a complete disaster. 'I never had the courage to call her again,' he said.

Diana was a great deal more complex than even the most sophisticated French wine and had taken hysterical umbrage when she discovered, on the eve of her wedding, that Charles had bought Camilla a bracelet stamped with the initials GF. They stood for Girl Friday, Charles's nickname for Mrs Parker Bowles. Charles had insisted on his right to hand over the gift in person, later telling Diana that he had used the occasion to say a final farewell to his old flame but that did not placate his wife.

Charles certainly did not help his own case by continuing to see Camilla on the hunting field and occasionally speaking to her on the telephone. But if he saw nothing wrong in that, Diana most certainly did. She was newly wed and out of her depth, and she didn't have to be suffering from Borderline Personality Disorder to feel the pangs of jealousy and rejection. Most young women would have felt the same—just as any man of sense, intent on making a success of his marriage, would have responded to the obvious and ended all association with a former lover his wife had come to see as a threat and a rival.

What made the situation doubly sad was that Charles was telling the truth when he said his relationship with Camilla had ended. It could not have been otherwise: Charles was determined to make a success of his marriage. Like his grandfather, George VI, he was anxious to build a secure family unit in which he could be himself. 'I find it quite a challenge being who I am,' he once admitted. He was too conventional, too pedestrian in his outlook to jeopardize this by conducting an all-consuming love affair on the side.

One suspects that in the beginning, at least, the Princess of Wales did not really believe he was. Diana was inclined to change her story according to her mood, but when we discussed the early years of her marriage and I mentioned what I called 'the Camilla situation' she was quite emphatic in her reply.

'I loved Charles—and he loved me,' she told me. 'It is terribly hurtful when people say that he did not love me. He did. If one day anyone sees the letters we wrote to each other they will know how much we loved each other.' (These letters are now in the royal family's private archives.)

*   *   *

In the turmoil of that first year, however, Diana was incapable of viewing her situation with any rationality. She had got it into her mind that her husband was being unkind to her and that thought alone was enough to provoke another outburst of tears and temper.

She found little long-term sympathy from the other women in the family. Princess Margaret, self-obsessed herself, would weary of Diana's self-obsession; the Queen Mother was irked by what she called Diana's 'tiresome' behaviour; and Lady Fermoy turned against her granddaughter, just as she had turned against her daughter, Frances, before her ('My grandmother has done a good hatchet job on me,' the Princess of Wales would later complain).

142

The Queen was more tolerant, although she was becoming perturbed by Diana's endless complaints. It sometimes takes a while to adjust to married life, she explained. She spoke with the wisdom of personal experience. It had taken several years to smooth out the bumps in her own marriage. Never the most biddable of men, Philip had not responded well to the constraints of domesticity. Indeed, in the early years he acted as if he were still single.

*   *   *

Prince Philip joined the Thursday Club which met every week at Wheeler's restaurant in Soho for lunches that sometimes went on late into the night. Its raffish members included the urbane actor David Niven, who had once shared a Hollywood home with Errol Flynn, and Prince Alfonso von Hohenlohe, the founder of the Marbella Club, who in 1955 created an international scandal when he married fifteen-year-old Princess Ira von Fürstenberg. It was founded by the society photographer Baron who, as Eileen, the wife of Philip's aide-de-camp, Michael Parker, noted, 'was hardly known as a model of sexual propriety in the gossip columns, nor in the drawing rooms of Mayfair and Belgravia'. Another member was Stephen Ward, the society osteopath-cum-pimp. His call girls included Christine Keeler, whose liaison with War Minister John Profumo resulted in a spy and sex scandal which almost toppled Harold Macmillan's government.

In the evening Philip would often repair to the Grosvenor Square apartment of his cousin and best man, the Marquis of Milford Haven. On one occasion, Philip was so late home that he had to climb in over the locked gates of Clarence House where he and his wife were living. 'Serves him right,' the future Queen remarked.

These were not always all-male outings. Women frequently joined in the merrymaking. Secretly, of course, though the dam of discretion was nearly breached on at least a couple of occasions.

When a waitress at Fortnum and Mason was overheard regaling a friend with the details of her friendship with the Prince ('The poor thing, what an awful life he lives; he's like a caged animal,' she remarked), Farrar's, the royal solicitors, were called into action, statements were taken, and the woman was never seen at Fortnum's again. The allegation is that she was quietly paid off.

One clandestine assignation failed to take place when the go-between delivered the Prince's missive to the wrong address. Philip was very friendly with Douglas Fairbanks Jnr, whose name would feature prominently in the Profumo scandal and again in Margaret,

Duchess of Argyll's lurid divorce case. Charming and debonair, his *savour faire* usually got him out of the predicaments his sexual adventures sometimes got him into. (Approached during the height of the scandal by two reporters from the *Daily Express* and asked if he had ever attended parties at Cliveden, the house where the disgraced Profumo had romped in the swimming pool with Christine Keeler, Fairbanks suavely replied: 'Yes—I was taken by Sir Max Aitken.' Sir Max was the proprietor of the *Daily Express*. The story never appeared.)

His nonchalance could be unsettling for others, however. Fairbanks would take letters Philip had written, arranging a time and place for a covert meeting, and leave them with the porter at White's club for collection. On one occasion, he entrusted a note addressed to a woman called Ava to a new secretary. Not knowing one club from another, she delivered it, not to White's but to Boodle's. Clubland was highly amused by the mistake, but the story went no further.

The Prince dismissed such tales as calumnious nonsense. 'Have you ever stopped to think,' he asked, 'that for the past forty years I have never moved anywhere without a policeman accompanying me? So how the hell could I get away with anything like that?'

The answer is that his policemen indeed did know what he was doing—just as those assigned to Charles and Diana would come to know precisely what they, too, got up to. Royal Protection Officers are not chaperons, however. Nor are they in the business of writing revelatory memoirs. They are there to guard their charges, not tell them what they can or cannot do. As one of Diana's protection officers later told me: 'We were not there to make moral judgements.'

Such a responsibility lies with the Palace courtiers, that frequently maligned body of men (and now women) whose job it is to keep the wheels of state turning smoothly, avoiding the stir of sensation wherever possible. They quickly took against Philip, not least because of what Eileen Parker called 'his apparent desire to continue bachelor friendships'.

Lieutenant-General Sir Frederick 'Boy' Browning, hero of the Battle of Arnhem, husband of the writer Daphne du Maurier and the first comptroller of Elizabeth's household, initially disliked him. The Queen's first private secretary, Sir Alan Lascelles, whose cousin, the 6th Earl of Harewood, had married George V's daughter Mary, took a particularly jaundiced view of the future Queen's husband and confided to his friend, Harold Nicolson, that Philip was 'rough, uneducated and would probably not be faithful'. But however unpromising the material, he was now part of the royal family, and gradually they started to tighten their hold on this boisterous outsider.

Philip was made to give up his red convertible sports car in which he had driven to Windsor (sometimes by way of a ditch) when he was courting the King's daughter. And when he started to learn to fly helicopters, he was called in by Winston Churchill. The newly re-elected Prime Minister kept him standing for several minutes like a snotty-nosed schoolboy, before looking up over his glasses to growl: 'Is your objective the destruction of the whole royal family?' It requires no great leap of the imagination to envisage how Diana would have reacted if she had been called before Mrs Margaret Thatcher and given such a perfunctory dressing down.

There were further humiliations to follow. Philip was not allowed to see the state papers which are delivered to his wife in a red dispatch box each day, or to play any part in her decision making, as Queen Victoria's Consort Prince Albert had done. Most offensive of all, he was the only man in Britain forbidden to give his children his own name.

When Victoria married Albert, the royal family had taken his patronymic and become the House of Saxe-Coburg-Gotha. To placate the anti-German feelings generated by the First World War, George V had changed it to Windsor (thereby prompting his cousin, the Kaiser, to quip that Shakespeare's play would henceforth be called *The Merry Wives of Saxe-Coburg*).

147

Now, by the usual rules governing such matters, it should have changed again, this time to Mountbatten—the name Philip, who was born without a surname, had assumed a few weeks before his marriage. By way of a compromise, Philip would willingly have settled for Mountbatten-Windsor.

No one had actually given the matter much thought until his uncle, Earl Mountbatten, blurted out at a dinner party at Broadlands that the House of Windsor was no more and that 'It is now the House of Mountbatten.'

A guest at the table that night was Prince Ernst of Hanover, head of the house which had produced Kings George I, II, III, William IV and Queen Victoria. Had Salic law, which only allows the male to inherit, been in force in Britain, he would have himself been King of England. Ruffled by Mountbatten dynastic ambitions, he reported the remarks to Queen Mary, who was appalled at the thought. She enlisted the support of the Queen Mother, who was equally dismayed. The two queens went to see Churchill. He took their side, and the Queen was 'advised' by her Cabinet that the name of the royal family was Windsor—and would remain so.

Philip pleaded his case in a forthright memorandum. Churchill dismissed it out of hand. Philip's irate retort was: 'I feel like a bloody amoeba.' (The actual language he used was much stronger, but in the same way that

President Lyndon Johnson's observation that President Gerald Ford could not think and fart at the same time became 'think and chew gum', so Philip's remark was sanitized for public consumption.)

'He felt terribly frustrated,' observed the late Lord Charteris, who served the Queen, first as Assistant Private Secretary, then as Private Secretary, for twenty-five years. ' "What can I do?" he would say. "I'm a sailor." '

'If you look now, with hindsight, at the Coronation, it was unfair. If you are a woman and your husband becomes king, you get crowned, too. But if a woman becomes sovereign, her husband is not crowned beside her. Nowadays that looks absurd. I think it was unfair even then.'

Unfair or not, no impecunious interloper was going to be allowed to change the British system, and by their actions the Government and the Court were making it absolutely plain how they regarded the princeling who had a mere 2s.6d (12½p) in the bank when he married the heiress to the greatest throne on earth.

Even after the matter had been resolved and the Queen had proclaimed that 'she and her descendants should bear the family name of Windsor', Queen Mary continued to fume at what she regarded as Philip's impertinence. 'What the devil does that damned fool Edinburgh think that the family name has to with him,' she raged.

Philip could see very well what was happening. He is not quite the unfeeling boor, insensitive to the opinions of others, that he sometimes appears. He paints well and takes an interest in poetry, and there is no doubt that he was hurt by the way he was treated by the Establishment and the Palace strictures which he came to loathe just as much as Diana ever did. The difference lay in their reactions. The one thing Prince Philip isn't is a victim. The Queen has observed: 'He is someone who doesn't take easily to compliments.' She might have added that neither is he someone who takes much notice of criticism. A lesser man would have been submerged by the rebuffs and insults but instead of griping, Philip simply got on with the task of carving a life for himself out of what few areas of opportunity were left open to him, too proud to allow the mask of self-sufficiency to slip.

His mother-in-law did nothing to help him. As her opposition to the change in the family name made clear, the Queen Mother was not over-enamoured with the Mountbattens. She was distrustful of Lord Mountbatten and disapproving of his nephew, and would have much preferred it if Elizabeth had married an heir to a British dukedom (Johnny Dalkeith, now the Duke of Buccleuch, and Hugh Euston, the present Duke of Grafton, were considered suitable suitors). She found Philip by turns rude and abrasive. She did not appreciate his attempts to strip away the cobwebbed protocols of a court which she had been largely responsible for creating. With the memory of two world wars to draw upon, the Queen Mother was suspicious of his German ancestry (she called the Germans 'Huns' and when a group of Philip's relations came to stay at Balmoral she instructed her staff: 'You certainly don't curtsey to Germans').

She also harboured a mother's disapproval of the late night shenanigans of her daughter's husband which did not increase her liking for her son-in-law (they would frequently be observed passing each on a staircase without acknowledgement). Elizabeth had discussed her concerns with her mother. Most women grew away from their mother's influence. Elizabeth never did; whenever they were not under the same roof, the Queen spoke to her mother at least twice a day on the telephone and continued to be guided by her opinions. They were not always opinions it would have been wise to broadcast; the Queen Mother's conversation is peppered with remarks which, taken out of their social context, could be interpreted as prejudiced and highly reactionary.

However, the Queen Mother had never been able to address any personal drama which impinged on her almost beatific sense of well-being. She inhabited a mental fairyland

151

from which emotional turmoil was banished and, adopting the attitude that if a problem was ignored it would go away, had taken to her bed at the time of the Abdication, would do so again during the 'Townsend affair', as Princess Margaret's ill-starred love affair with Group Captain Peter Townsend was called, and declined to become involved in the furore of the Waleses' separation. When her eldest daughter began to wonder, as any wife would, exactly what it was her husband was up to, she was typically noncommittal, confining herself to remarks of the 'don't worry, everything will be all right' variety.

In this instance, however, her approach proved to be a sensible one. Elizabeth chose not to listen to the gossip which came her way, preferring to put her husband's late night wanderings down to high spirits. The policy paid off, and in November 1997 at the Guildhall luncheon held to honour their Golden Wedding, Prince Philip gave thanks to his wife for her forbearance. He said: 'The main lesson that we have learnt is that tolerance is the one essential ingredient of any happy marriage. It may not be quite so important when things are going well, but it is absolutely vital when the going gets difficult. You can take it from me that the Queen has the quality of tolerance in abundance.'

Underpinning this sentiment was a foundation of genuine affection. The couple continued to share a bed into old age and the Queen never lost her admiration for the handsome blond sailor she had first caught sight of when she was thirteen years old, and with whom she had instantly fallen in love. Her infatuation had mellowed with the passing of the years as it always does and the then Foreign Minister Anthony Crosland's wife, Susan, once heard the Queen say over dinner: 'Oh, Philip, do shut up—you don't know what you're talking about.' And once, when he got into a fierce row with a friend over lunch at Balmoral, the Queen leant across the table and said: 'Go on, you tell him. No one ever stands up to him.' But if the put-downs had edge, they were delivered without malice. As Lord Mountbatten's son-in-law, David Hicks said to me: 'She likes to get her say in, but it is touching the way the Queen is always amused by what he has to say.'

Even more poignant was the way she responded to his attentions. Her late dressmaker, Ian Thomas, recounted to me how the Queen had blushed with pleasure on the morning of Fergie's wedding when Prince Philip told her how beautiful she looked.

In her own Golden Wedding speech the Queen paid equally moving tribute to her husband when she said: 'He has, quite simply, been my strength and my stay all these years.' Despite half a century of rifts and rumours of extramarital transgressions which dogged

Philip into his seventies, the Queen's marriage has survived, enduring testimony to the virtue of forgiveness—and the practical benefits of Nelson's eye.

It is a praiseworthy achievement, due in no small measure to the Queen's knack for maintaining a sense of proportion. Her friend Mrs Rhodes, the Margaret Elphinstone that was, explained: 'She has this wonderful ability to shut off worries, putting them into one compartment and closing the door, so even if something pretty awful is happening, like the sadness of her children, she remains resilient, able to laugh and do her ordinary stuff.' Bill Clinton was accused of compartmentalizing his life; but what was deemed indecorous in a philandering president proved to be expedient in a devoted sovereign.

It was an ability the Princess of Wales singularly lacked. Her difficulties, real and imaginary, collided with each other in a vortex of depression. The Queen as a young wife had genuine cause for concern, but soldiered on. Diana, married to a man desperately keen to make his marriage work, became listless, sometimes sitting for hours with her head on her knees, oblivious to the entreaties of her husband and staff.

Diana claimed that, because no other woman in the royal family before had ever suffered from morning sickness, they had no comprehension of how she was feeling. 'I was "a problem" and they registered Diana as "A problem. She's different, she's doing everything we never did",' Diana told Andrew Morton.

In fact, the Queen had not had an easy time of it during her own first pregnancy. She, too, had suffered the discomforts of morning sickness and Prince Charles had had to be delivered by Caesarean section.

She had carried Anne and Andrew with more ease, but to help her through her last pregnancy at what was then considered the advanced age of thirty-seven, she sought the help of former nurse and midwife, Betty Parsons. White-haired and full of commonsense, Betty placed great emphasis on breathing, and during her private pre-natal classes the Queen was made to lie on the floor of her private sitting room and practise what Betty called, 'doggy, doggy, candle, candle' (pant, pant, blow, blow).

Betty gave detailed explanation of the emotional changes taking place in the mother, while at the same time involving the father as much as possible. But not Prince Philip—she never did persuade him to lie on the floor and pant like a dog. He was intrigued by her methods, however, liked her no-nonsense approach, and against the advice of the Queen's doctors who were sceptical of her 'alternative' techniques, personally ushered Betty into the delivery room which had been set up in the bathroom of the Belgium Suite at Buckingham Palace.

Betty was therefore at the Queen's side when Prince Edward was delivered on the evening of 10 March 1964. So was Prince Philip, who thereby became the first royal father in modern history to see his child born. It was a slow delivery and the anaesthetist Vernon Hall administered gas, oxygen and pethidine, a popular pain reliever of the time with properties similar to morphine. The Queen's gynaecologist, Sir John Peel, recalled how Philip helped ease the tension by quipping: 'It's a solemn thought that only a week ago General de Gaulle was having a bath in this very room.'

The Queen had found Betty Parson's techniques helpful and reassuring, and it was on her recommendation that Diana went to her for advice. This time the father proved more amenable and Charles avidly read and re-read her lighthearted but informative guide, *The Expectant Father*, which advised him how best to give support and encouragement to his wife.

Neither Betty's encouragement nor the move back to London at the end of January could lift Diana's spirits, however. When she did stir herself it was usually to go on frenetic shopping sprees which became the subject of much adverse comment.

In an effort to involve Diana in his life while at the same time underlining his commitment to their future together, Charles had put her in charge of refurbishing Highgrove, the Georgian house set in 410 Gloucestershire acres, which he had bought for £750,000 from former Prime Minister Harold Macmillan's alcoholic son, Maurice. On the advice of her mother Diana hired Dudley Poplak, the interior decorator Mrs Shand Kydd had employed to decorate her own London flat. Though Highgrove was small by royal standards, Diana nonetheless managed to spend over £100,000 on refurbishments. Charles had wanted a traditional English country home; Diana gave him what one friend dismissed as a 'Park Lane apartment fit for an Arab prince', with fitted carpets instead of polished wood floors, and *frou frou* frills on every cushion. Charles did not like the results. But then neither did Diana. Her heart was not in it. She wanted to move back to Park House, her childhood home which had come up for rent. 'I don't like Highgrove,' she kept saying. 'We're probably going to move.'

Nothing that Charles did or was interested in seemed to coincide with what Diana wanted. In what the Palace staff saw as a deliberate attempt to upset him, she flirted with the more handsome (and usually gay) footmen. She also refused to accompany him to the opera, preferring to stay at home and fume at what she regarded as his thoughtless insensitivity in going by himself and leaving her alone. When he returned he would be treated to another bout of door-banging hysteria.

Charles blamed himself for his wife's condition. The strain of being married to the heir to the throne, he told friends like Norton Knatchbull, was proving too much for her. And so it was. But there was more to it than that, as her psychiatrists were well aware. The drugs they prescribed calmed her down but only when she took them, which frequently she didn't. No one enjoys being unwell but it struck a number of people who were working for her at the time that she was making little effort to make herself better. It was a very sick woman, therefore, who started her labour on that midsummer weekend.

According to Diana, the baby was induced on a date that fitted in with Charles's polo schedule. Her unscheduled contractions actually started on the Sunday evening, and before dawn the following morning, Prince Charles drove from their new home at Kensington Palace to St Mary's hospital, Paddington.

Traditionally, royal children are born at home, but following the example of Princess Anne and at the urging of her doctor, the

Queen's surgeon-gynaecologist George Pinker, Diana was booked into the Lindo Wing. Betty Parsons agreed with the decision; if any complications arose, she told the Princess, a hospital was the best and safest place to be.

It proved to be sound advice. Like many first-time mothers, Diana wanted to have a 'natural' birth, but complications did indeed arise and the labour proved long and hard.

The Lindo Wing was not the grandest setting for a future king to make his entrance into the world. The Queen gave birth to Charles in the stately Buhl Room on the first floor of Buckingham Palace, which had a view out over the tree-lined Mall. Diana's end-of-corridor room was only fourteen feet by twelve, smaller than her dressing room at Kensington Palace. The wallpaper had an unappetizing floral design, the curtains were pink and frayed, there was no private bathroom, the metal bed was standard hospital issue, and the outlook from the small window was over the grimy rooftops of Paddington. But what St Mary's did have was a well-trained staff of maternity nurses and excellent medical equipment.

Diana, with Charles at her side, entered by a side door at the unearthly hour of 5 a.m. on the morning of Monday, 21 June 1982. Pinker and Parsons arrived soon afterwards. Diana had wanted to give birth without the aid of anaesthetic, but the pain was such that she voiced no protest when Pinker decided to give her an epidural injection. Diana was sick throughout and at one point Pinker was sufficiently worried to consider a Caesarean operation. In the end, Diana made it on her own and after sixteen agonizing hours of labour, she was delivered of a son. Prince Charles was at her bedside throughout, holding her hand, urging her on, joining in when Betty Parsons told her patient to push and breathe deeply and 'pick up your surfboard and ride it like a whale'.

Afterwards, Charles admitted that those sixteen stressful hours had been 'rather a shock to my system'. He did not regret being there, however. 'I think it is a very good thing for a husband to be with a mother when she is expecting a baby,' he said, and when the boy was born healthy he declared himself 'relieved, delighted, overwhelmed, over the moon'.

So was Diana. She was, she said, 'thrilled and excited' and her friend Carolyn Bartholomew noted a 'contentment about her'.

It was not to last. On top of all her other problems, Diana was soon overcome with post-natal depression which pulled her ever further into the psychological mire. Most worrying was her apparent lack of interest in any subject other than her own unhappiness.

Unlike the rest of the country which had been animated by a frenzy of atavistic nationalism, Diana had paid little attention to the Falklands conflict which erupted in April, when Argentina invaded that lonely remnant of the British Empire in the South Atlantic. She did not share the Queen's concern for the welfare of Prince Andrew who was serving with the Task Force as a helicopter pilot aboard HMS *Invincible*. Indeed, according to Prince Charles's authorized biographer, Jonathan Dimbleby, 'She seemed to resent the interest being shown in the Falklands rather than in her.'

Even Michael Fagan's break-in seemed to pass her by. Diana and Charles had only recently moved out of Buckingham Palace when the itinerant painter and decorator scaled the walls, made his way past the supposedly foolproof security system and let himself into the Queen's bedroom.

The date was 9 July, less than three weeks after the birth of her grandson, and the Queen was alone. Prince Philip, who would normally have been in the room, had slept the night in his dressing room so as not wake her when he left for an early morning appointment; Princess Anne was abroad; Capt. Mark Phillips had spent the night at the Palace but had left a few minutes earlier to return to Gatcombe Park, and the Queen's page, Paul Whybrow, was out in the Palace gardens taking the royal corgis for their morning walk. The Queen was dozing when Fagan burst in at 7.15 a.m., clutching a piece of glass from an ashtray he had smashed moments before in the Page's Vestibule next door. Fagan recalled: 'I opened the door and there's a little bundle in the bed. I thought, "This isn't the Queen, this is too small",' Fagan recalled.

He strode across the room and opened the curtains. The Queen sat bolt upright. Over the years, Prince Philip had helped exercise her voice to lower the pitch. In this moment of alarm, however, it rose two octaves as she shouted: 'What are you doing here? Get out! Get *out*!'

Fagan would later explain that he only wanted to tell the Queen of the troubles he was having in his marriage (his wife Christine had left him, taking their six children with her). The Queen was not prepared to listen. She grabbed her white telephone and shouted for help, 'then hopped out of bed, ran across the room and out of the door,' Fagan said. 'I was surprised how nimble she was. She ran like a girl. It was all over in thirty seconds. I felt really sad and disillusioned. It was a complete shock because the Queen wasn't what I had expected. I felt so badly let down. The conversation never took place. I just sat down on the bed crying my eyes out.'

The incident revealed the extraordinary inefficiency of the Palace's security arrangements: Fagan had been able to scale the wall undetected and walk around the Palace for fifteen minutes, and it was a full six minutes before anyone answered the Queen's call for assistance. In the meantime, Paul the page had returned, and on the Queen's instructions ushered Fagan into a pantry and given him a cigarette and a glass of whisky. When the police did finally arrive, Fagan was taken away and later tried and jailed for breaking and entering.

The Queen gave the firmest instructions that no word of what had happened should leak to the press. Keeping a secret of this magnitude was not possible, however, and news soon reached Fleet Street. First with the story was a Sunday paper, but when no official confirmation was forthcoming, the editor refused to publish. In time-honoured tradition, the paper's crime correspondent, certain of his information which had been given to him by a senior police officer, passed it on to a friend on the *Daily Express*. He also encountered a wall of silence but the *Express* had the huge advantage of still having on its payroll Percy Hoskins, the doyen of crime correspondents and founder of the Saints and Sinners dining club which Prince Charles has attended. Hoskins was well into his eighties but he still boasted the best contacts in the business. He made one call. His only remark when he came off the telephone was: 'Run it.' He never revealed who he had spoken to, but clearly it was someone of the highest authority, and on Hoskins's say-so the presses rolled.

In the accounts which followed, it was the Queen who was credited with coolly offering Fagan the cigarette and forests were felled to record how calmly the Queen had dealt with this astonishing threat to her safety. 'She said she met so many dotty people that one more made no difference. Mind you, I think she was making light of that,' recalled Margaret Rhodes.

Mrs Rhodes was right. The insouciance was feigned; the Queen had actually been profoundly unnerved by this violation of her person and privacy. Nothing like this had ever happened to her before, and it would take several months for her to recover her equilibrium. For the first time ever she needed professional assistance. Others might have sought medical help, but the Queen turned to someone she trusted, and once again Betty Parsons was summoned to the palace. Using breathing techniques similar to yoga, Betty taught her to drop her shoulders, inhale slowly and deeply, and empty her mind of all thoughts.

For someone as reserved as the Queen, talking about her fears and showing weakness did not come easily. As one crisis followed another, however, her inhibitions peeled away and she derived great comfort from her sessions with the sensible and down-to-earth Mrs Parsons.

A week after the Fagan break-in the Queen

went to hospital, ostensibly to have a wisdom tooth removed, but conveniently at the same time as her long-serving police officer, Commander Trestrail, of whom she was very fond, had to resign after it was revealed that he had been conducting a long-running affair with a male prostitute. Then, on 20 July 1982, an IRA bomb exploded in Hyde Park, murdering eleven soldiers of her Household Cavalry, injuring fifty others and killing seven horses. The Queen was distraught. Her seemingly safe world was being torn apart and for the first time anyone could remember she cancelled her annual visit to the Goodwood race meeting.

Where royalty is concerned, however, the show must go on and on 4 August the Queen, a smile firmly fixed on her face, attended the christening of her heir presumptive.

Diana was not her most supportive. Her mind was focused on her newborn son, not the difficulties his grandmother was having to contend with.

Diana had argued with her husband over the choice of name. Charles wanted to call the boy Arthur Albert. Diana refused point blank and the couple eventually compromised on William Arthur Philip Louis. This small victory did little to appease her, however, and she hated every minute of the baptism which took place in the Music Room at Buckingham Palace.

Diana objected to the chosen hour of 11 o'clock in the morning ('Nobody asked me when it was suitable for William—11 o'clock couldn't have been worse'). She complained that the Queen, Queen Mother, Charles and little William got all the attention. She said: 'I was excluded totally . . . I just blabbed my eyes out.'

The royal caravan still trundled serenely on, but the trusses and bindings were working loose and the Princess of Wales was perilously close to falling off.

CHAPTER SIX

ADULATION

No woman has ever been greeted so rapturously.

'She was welcomed like a deliverer,' wrote the political commentator Ben Pimlott of the newly crowned Queen Elizabeth II.

Tens of thousands lined the streets in crowds twenty-deep to catch a glimpse of her as she drove by in an open-topped car or stood on the steps of a town hall, resplendent in her designer clothes. Her husband, 'handsome and cheerful', was at her side, and they were the picture of a truly romantic couple. Together, the historian Philip Ziegler declared, they heralded 'a brighter and more successful future'.

The year was 1954, and Elizabeth was making her first visit to Australia.

In the cities, onlookers fainted in the crush, while out in the Bush, families waited for hours in the searing heat on roads usually empty to see her pass by.

Earl Mountbatten's daughter Lady Pamela Hicks, who was in the royal party, noted: 'She was very meticulous in the motorcades that the car should go slowly enough for people to get a proper view. She used to say, "What's the point in coming unless they can see me?"'

Sometimes she was forced to stop and make as many as six impromptu speeches a day, but her public demeanour never faltered. 'It's awful—I've got the kind of face that if I'm not smiling I look cross,' she said. 'But I'm not cross. If you try to smile for two hours continuously it gives you a nervous tick. But the moment I stop smiling somebody will see me and say, "Doesn't she look cross?"' So she smiled until her face hurt. Her reward was adulation.

Elizabeth was hailed as a divinity, and the country succumbed to the throes of what the historian Robert Hughes described as 'monarchist ecstasies'. Diana, too, would come to know what it was like to be adored but never to such an extent.

In 1983 when the Princess arrived in

Brisbane on her first tour, a quarter of a million people were waiting to wave her in. It was a staggering number, greater even than the crowd that had greeted the Beatles twenty years earlier, but it was as nothing compared to the scenes her mother-in-law had witnessed as a young woman of almost the same age. When the converted Shaw Savill liner *Gothic* on which she had journeyed sailed into Sydney Harbour the water was a carpet of small craft and a million people lined the shore. By the time the Queen ended her tour it is estimated that three quarters of Australia's entire population of 12 million had turned out to see her in person.

There were times when it was more than the Queen was able to handle. She came from a background as sheltered as they come and she was painfully shy. She was still only twenty-eight, in a distant land, and her children were half a world away. After one particularly gruelling twelve-hour day when she had shaken hands with more dignitaries than she could count in more towns than she could name, her composure nearly deserted her. She had been gaped at, waved at, cheered at, blinded by old-fashioned camera bulbs and had had her hand shaken until it ached. She was tired and overwrought, and her crowded schedule allowed her no privacy; when she went to what was euphemistically referred to as 'repairing her make-up' she had to do so in a public lavatory in front of an audience of the attendant and her friends. In a snatched moment alone with Prince Philip and on the verge of tears, she turned and in trembling, high pitched voice demanded: 'Why is everyone so boring, boring, boring . . .'

Diana, too, was overcome by the attention she received on tour. She wrote: 'Not a moment to breathe. I find the endless receptions quite difficult as people tend to ask extraordinarily personal questions.' Her solution was to take 'five deep breaths and plunge in'.

No matter how hard she tried, Diana never succeeded in getting rid of that implosive feeling of claustrophobia which pressed down on her whenever she was called upon to play the crowds. Almost at the end of her life she told me: 'I still feel really insecure about going out and meeting people I don't know. After all these years I've never really got over it.'

Remarkably, neither has the Queen. After half a century of practice she continues to find it hard to make light conversation with people she has never met and will never meet again. It was hard right from the outset, and there would be occasions on that Australian tour when she would wonder if it was worth the strain—and whether she was truly worthy of the homage bestowed on her. She had been Queen for only two years and the responsibility still terrified and confused her.

But she kept her misgivings to herself. She was the head of a great and venerable institution and by her way of thinking it would have been an egotistical abjuration of sacred obligation to surrender to self-doubt. After the tension had been released by that uncharacteristic outburst, she again took steel-willed control of herself and set off on her next round of engagements, her smile firmly in place.

Diana was unable to imitate what now seems a quaint approach to the problem. Her illness was too deeply embedded, her bulimia too debilitating for her to form an objective opinion of the extraordinary position she was in. The tour of Australia and New Zealand was her first foreign testing ground just as it had been the Queen's, and the journey and the heat and never-ending attention got the better of her. 'The whole world was focusing on my every day,' she recalled. 'I was on the front of the papers. I thought this was just so appalling. I hadn't done something specific like climb Everest or done something wonderful like that.' (By coincidence, the news that Sir Edmund Hillary had conquered Everest came through on the day before the Queen's Coronation). At the end of the first week she was in her room, crying her eyes out and complaining that nobody—and certainly not her husband—was giving her any help or support.

Social context as well as character

formulated the two women's different reactions to a remarkably similar situation. The Queen's outlook was forged in the inter-war years when, in defiance of the economic statistics, most Britons remained convinced that their country was still the world's pre-eminent power. They continued to believe in the Victorian ethic of work and personal virtue.

Diana, on the other hand, was a child of the Welfare State, brought up in the dependency culture of the Sixties and Seventies when private enterprise and individual responsibility were discouraged, and Britain's decline reached such a humiliating low that in 1976 it had to place its economic affairs under the direction of the International Monetary Fund. The Queen had been raised to get on with the job without complaint; Diana was forever making excuses and demanding the support of others. Without ever thinking about it, the two women were representative of the far-reaching changes which had taken place in Britain during the half century which divided them.

Charles's former private secretary Michael Colborne observed: 'Diana could not understand the requirements of duty.'

Prince Charles, more prosaically, blamed the media for his wife's condition. Sir Arthur Conan Doyle, creator of Sherlock Holmes, had once stated in 1900 that he considered the greatest danger confronting Britain in the new century was: 'an ill-balanced, excitable and sensation-mongering press'. In the Prince's opinion, Conan Doyle's dire prediction had come true. In a letter home to a friend he wrote: 'There is no twitch she can make without these ghastly, and, I'm quite convinced, mindless people photographing it. How can anyone, let alone a 21-year old, be expected to come out of all this obsessed and crazed attention unscathed?'

He was right, but not quite in the way he imagined. Diana was indeed confused by the press coverage she was receiving but Charles's friends, and members of the Royal Household, had already started to notice that, for all her protests, she nonetheless appeared to thrive on the attention. During her engagement she had rushed to the newspapers every morning and, ignoring everything else, had quickly turned the pages looking for photographs of herself. Sometimes she would scream in mock horror, 'I look hideous; I'm so fat; I'm so ugly!' But she never stopped looking, and on the morning when *The Times* finally capitulated and put her picture on its front page, she leapt up and down, chanting in the same singsong, child's voice she had used when the Queen presented her with her jewels: 'I've made *The Times . . .*' When media interest did fade, she discovered that a slight change of hairstyle or a new frock would fan it instantly back to life.

The Queen took several trunks of Norman

Hartnell outfits with her to Australia. She was pretty (at the time she was always called beautiful), blessed with a good figure and a 23-inch waist, and she took pleasure in dressing well. But decorum did not allow clothes to become a passion and she saw them as a tool of her trade more than did Diana. For the Princess of Wales they were a means of drawing attention to herself, and watching her wardrobe changes became a national pastime. But if the public enjoyed the spectacle, the Royal Household most definitely did not and they took grave exception when, in the middle of her tour, Diana contacted London and insisted on having a John Boyd hat specially flown out to Australia.

On a weightier note, the Palace courtiers were also becoming concerned at the way Diana was upstaging her husband. Initially this was not her doing. Without even trying, Diana had brought back the glamour which the royal family had divested itself of after the fiasco of Edward VIII's abdication. She had natural star quality and wherever she went people clamoured to see the princess who, to all outward appearance, looked as if she had been cut from the pages of a fairytale. Whenever the Prince and Princess of Wales got out of a car, a cheer would greet Diana while an audible groan would run through the crowd on Charles's side.

Later, her lover, James Hewitt, would

describe what many other people had felt. He attended Charles's fortieth birthday party at Buckingham Palace and recalled 'the incredible aura that just radiated from her, overpowering and almost eclipsing the presence of Charles and his parents'.

Diana had been quick to grasp that it was herself, and not her husband, that people wanted to see. Hewitt recalled: 'She told me that one of her "crimes" was that she got more attention than he did, most notably when they were on a visit to Australia. But there was nothing she could do about it.' It was, Diana said, only natural; whoever he had married would have been the cynosure of public interest. She was undoubtedly right. What concerned the royal advisers, however, was not the attention she was receiving but the way she appeared to be deliberately courting it.

Royalty works on a hierarchical principle which previous generations of royal spouses had been careful not to violate. Throughout their life together, the Queen Mother had made it her marital duty to push forward the timid King George VI, and then stand back and allow him to take the plaudits.

Even Prince Philip, who did not usually take kindly to court protocols, was prepared to go along with this rigid convention. On the Australia tour he kept himself in the background and avoided making the faux pas which would later come to distinguish his trips abroad. He kept his mouth shut, and amused himself by waving to the drunks hanging on to the lamp-posts outside the pubs and, as he drove by, watching as they collapsed on to the ground when they let go to wave back ('Stop being silly,' his wife would admonish him).

Theirs was not an example Diana was prepared to follow. She was too modern, too insecure, and far too needful of being noticed to walk three paces behind in her husband's shadow.

Charles tried to make light of it. 'I'm going to have to get used to looking at the backs of photographers,' he said. He was perceptive enough to appreciate the contribution that Diana was making to the image of the royal family and his letters were full of praise for the 'marvellous help' she gave him. There was no doubt, however, that the situation was starting to rankle. 'He was jealous,' Diana observed.

As heir to the throne, Charles had been brought up to command centre stage. Now his role was being usurped by a newcomer who was playing the part according to a script of her own writing. The Monarchy, as first his father and then Charles himself were fond of pointing out, needed updating if it was going to stay in touch with the changing world beyond the Palace walls. What had not crossed his mind was the possibility that this might be achieved by downgrading his own importance in the regal production.

What made it doubly trying was the unpredictability of Diana's behaviour. Calm and collected one day, she would be tense and tearful the next. Sometimes the mood swings happened in the space of a few minutes. The worst example of this occurred at the Festival of Remembrance four months before the Australian tour.

This grave and formal event, held to commemorate those who gave their lives in two world wars, is one of those occasions when the royal family is on duty to represent the nation. Just before they were scheduled to leave their home at Kensington Palace for the two-minute drive to the Royal Albert Hall, Diana informed Prince Charles that she didn't want to go and that nothing he could say would change her mind. Charles's increasingly desperate pleadings only seemed to increase her temper. Finally running out of time and patience, Charles left on his own, leaving his wife shouting abuse in his wake.

No sooner was he out of the door, however, than Diana's tantrum subsided and she turned to her bewildered hairdresser, Kevin Shanley, who had been summoned to style her hair for the event, and said: 'I'm exhausted, but how can I let people down?'

When he arrived at the Albert Hall, Charles had explained that his pregnant wife was not feeling well. His white lie was exposed when Diana rushed in a full fifteen minutes after the

176

Queen. 'This was an insult not only to the Sovereign, but, through her, to the memory of the dead.

She conducted herself with more propriety on her six-week visit of Australia and New Zealand. The presence of her little son undoubtedly helped. By royal tradition, children were always left at home while their parents went on their often tedious but always physically arduous flag-waving trips around the Empire and, later, the Commonwealth.

In 1927, the Queen Mother had entrusted the little Princess Elizabeth to the care of her nanny and grandmother, Queen Mary, when she accompanied her husband on her own six-month tour of New Zealand and Australia. She, too, had been given a tumultuous welcome (the women of the British royal family always did incredibly well in Australia despite the country's built-in antipathy to the 'Poms'), but that had not entirely assuaged her unhappiness at being parted for so long from her daughter, who was not yet nine months old when she left. The Queen Mother had cried when she kissed her goodbye at her parents' home in Bruton Street, Mayfair. She would miss seeing her first-born's first steps and her first words which were 'Let's pretend'. When she returned, the little Princess Elizabeth did not recognize her.

It never occurred to the Duchess of York (as the Queen Mother was then) not to go, however. The separation of children from their parents had been a part of British life for over a century. The Empire was run by bureaucrats and soldiers who routinely sent their children home to be educated and often did not see them again for years. Nor was it just the Empire-builders for whom parenting was a long-range occupation: during the Second World War hundreds of thousands of working-class children were parted from their families when they were evacuated from the bombed cities to the safety of the countryside. It was a heartbreaking business for all concerned, but no one raised a voice in protest. It was considered normal.

Attitudes were little changed when Charles was born in 1948. When he was eleven months old, his father, Prince Philip, then an officer in the Royal Navy, was posted to Malta, and his mother spent more of the next two years with her husband in the Mediterranean than she did with her son in England. Charles was not to see his father for almost a year and his mother only intermittently. No one objected; the future Queen, like her mother before her, was simply doing what was expected of her. Indeed, had Elizabeth chosen not to accompany her husband, her decision would have been regarded as a dereliction of wifely duty.

It established a pattern which was to be repeated throughout Charles's early years and he spent much of his infancy in the care of his grandmother and, while he was alive, his grandfather King George VI, who doted on the little boy. A nanny was always close at hand to take care of the menial chores.

This was not the way Diana wished to bring up her own child. 'There is no substitute for a mother's arms,' she declared. The obligations that went with her title had not completely passed her by, however, and on her own tour of Australia she prepared to fall into line and leave William behind. She did not have to. The Australian Prime Minister Malcolm Fraser, mindful of the upset such a separation was likely to cause to a contemporary mother, wrote to the Waleses and invited them to bring William with them.

Diana was thrilled. So was Prince Charles, who was revelling in parenthood and was unhappy at the thought of leaving his nine-month-old. He readily agreed to Fraser's proposal and used the opportunity to extend the tour by two weeks to include New Zealand. There were reports that the Queen was opposed to the idea but this was not the case. The Queen knew from her own experience how unsettling these partings were and raised not the slightest objection when Charles told her what he planned to do.

The programme was a full one and Diana and Charles were not able to spend nearly as much time with their son as they would have liked. But they did have the pleasure of seeing him learn to crawl 'at high speed knocking everything off the tables and causing unbelievable destruction,' as Charles wrote to a friend. Diana recalled: 'We were a family unit.' And that, she said, was 'great'.

*　　　*　　　*

Charles's upbringing had been very different. The Queen had been too preoccupied by her public duties and Prince Philip, because of his naval duties, had missed his son's first three birthdays. The affection he craved was given by his nannies, but that was only as dependable as their employers allowed. Charles was first put in the care of Helen Lightbody, who arrived on the recommendation of the Queen's aunt-in-law, Princess Marina, Duchess of Kent. She was 'prim and proper, awfully kind and terribly fair', Eileen Parker, the wife of Michael Parker, Prince Philip's private secretary, recalled, but she was too old fashioned and set in her ways for Prince Philip's liking. In 1957, Charles was sent as a boarder to Cheam preparatory school. When he came back on holiday he discovered, to his immense distress, that Nana, as he called her, had been 'retired'.

He was then entrusted to Nanny Lightbody's deputy, Mabel Anderson, who had the good sense never to question Philip's authority openly as her predecessor had done. Charles grew very fond of Mabel, but it was still love at second-hand. As Princess Anne said: 'Nanny was always nanny, never some sort of surrogate parent.'

For all this, his mother and father were shadowy and somewhat intimidating figures, and it was the nannies who had day-to-day charge of his life, just as they had done when his mother was young.

Like his mother before him, Charles also had little contact with children of his own age. With only her own childhood to draw upon, the Queen continued the policy of raising the heir to the throne in splendid but lonely isolation. She vetoed the suggestion that other children be allowed to join him in his classroom on Buckingham Palace's second floor, where Princess Anne now has her office. Charles, she decided, was too timid to face the competition of other children, his sister included. Majesty had to be nurtured in isolation, or so the argument went.

Charles would later say that his mother's decisions concerning his education had been the right ones but others were not so sure. His governess, Catherine Peebles, called him a 'vague' child. Dermot Morrah, the Arundel Herald Extraordinary at the College of Heralds which oversees the granting of coats of arms, went further. He wrote an authorized account of Charles's early years in which he described Charles as 'a child who had only a vague relationship to the external world'.

The Queen's approach to motherhood had mellowed somewhat when Andrew and then Edward arrived in the family a decade later. She had become an avid reader of women's magazines, which by then were devoting an increasing number of their pages to the subject of good parenting. The ideas were usually American and all rejected the old notion that children should be seen and not heard. The emphasis now was on the importance of 'bonding' and with now two small children, the Queen set about putting theory into practice.

Nannies still played an important role in the upbringing of their charges, but the Queen now played a more hands-on role. On the rare occasions she had visited Charles at bathtime, a liveried footman brought in a gilt chair and everyone had to stand until the Queen took her seat to watch as nanny applied the soap. With Andrew and Edward, she rolled up her sleeves and got her own arms wet. And as a youngster, Edward was allowed to toddle around in his mother's study while she read the state papers—a privilege which would have been out the question in Charles's day.

Prince Philip also starred taking a more relaxed approach. Like many fathers, he had been determined to mould his first-born son in his own image. It was an ambition doomed to failure. Whereas Philip was confident and forceful, Charles was meek, uncertain and frightened of the demands his father made of him. He was scared of water and was slow learning to swim. His father's barked commands did not speed up his progress or increase his confidence. One morning, in exasperation, Philip picked him up and threw him into the Buckingham Palace pool.

'Philip tolerated Charles but I don't think he was a loving father,' Eileen Parker observed. 'I think Charles was frightened of him.'

He was less impulsive and a lot more understanding with Andrew and Edward. As he explained at the time: 'It's no good saying do this, do that, don't do this, don't do that. It's very easy when children want to do something to say no immediately. I think it's quite important not to give an unequivocal answer at once. Much better to think it over. Then, if you eventually say no they really accept it.'

His younger brothers' education was also more enlightened than Charles's had been. Lessons were still held in the Palace, but this time round, the Queen decreed that other children of the same age should be there; Andrew and Edward were joined by their cousins, Princess Alexandra's son James Ogilvy, Princess Margaret's daughter Lady Sarah Armstrong-Jones, Princess Tania of Hanover, the granddaughter of one of Prince

Philip's sisters, and, on a less socially exalted level, any offspring of the household who were of the same age. Their teacher was Lavinia Keppel, a relation of King Edward VII's mistress Alice Keppel, who was the great-grandmother of Prince Charles's mistress, Camilla Parker Bowles.

When her children were of the age to be sent to boarding school, the Queen chose Heatherdown, not so much for its academic reputation as for the fact that it was conveniently close to Windsor Castle. The headmaster James Edwards told me: 'She knew their faults and their shortcomings; she really did know them terribly well. She knew how they behaved. Some parents who give their children over to nannies sometimes hardly know their children at all. But she did.'

She took a close interest in their activities and drove them back to school at the end of half-term and holidays in her green Vauxhall station wagon. 'She came to every single show, sports day, play and carol service that we had,' said Edwards. 'She only missed one, and that was when Edward was playing the part of Saul in *The Boy David* and she was on tour in Australia on a state visit. And over nine years that is pretty good.'

The school saw less of Prince Philip. Recalled Edwards: 'He appeared, but not as much as the Queen. She determined and controlled their early schooling. I discussed their school reports with her rather than him.'

In Edwards's estimation, both the princes were well-adjusted. 'I was expecting when I got the first one that they would expect much more than the average child expected. In other words, possibly spoilt, brought up to have much higher expectations of creature comforts. This was very far from the truth. This isn't sycophancy, but I was staggered how marvellously well brought up they were.'

Royal duty would sometimes impinge on their lives, as it was bound to do, but the Queen brought a motherly touch to such occasions. In 1969, just a few weeks before Charles's Investiture as Prince of Wales, there was an outbreak of mumps at Heatherdown and the school was placed in quarantine. Andrew had been scheduled to go to Windsor Castle to be fitted for the kilt he was to wear at that elaborate ceremony at Caernarvon Castle, but because Charles had not had mumps, the Queen went to Andrew to measure him up herself in the headmaster's drawing room.

'I went into the room and the Queen was on her knees with one end of the measuring tape in her mouth,' said Edwards. 'She turned round to me and said, "This son of mine has the most villainous taste—he wants a purple jersey to go with the grey Balmoral tartan!"' Andrew got his way.

What the Queen as a mother never did was involve her four children in any of her personal problems. Her embrace of the new ideas of parenting only went so far and her offspring never saw her tearful or distressed. Whatever her private concerns may have been, she took the determinedly old-fashioned view that her children should not be affected by them.

*   *   *

The Queen and her daughter-in-law had very different views on how to bring up their children. As a mother, the Queen had been affectionate but distant. Diana insisted on involving her sons in everything she did. In one generation, the royal family's approach to bringing up children had lurched from one extreme to another and Charles was bemused and at times concerned by Diana's emotionally suffocating relationship with William and Harry.

'The only arguments they had were over the children,' the Queen's former press secretary Michael Shea told me.

Diana laid out her parental agenda soon after William's birth when she declared, 'A child's stability arises mainly from the affection received from his parents, and there is no substitute for affection.' Nannies were employed, but only as glorified nursery maids, not as mother substitutes. 'A mother's arms are so much more comforting,' the Princess said, harking back to her own unhappy childhood experiences.

Charles went along with his wife. He said: 'Although the whole attitude has changed towards women and what women are expected to do, I still feel, all the same, at the risk of sticking my neck out, that one of the most important roles any woman could ever perform is to be a mother. And nobody should denigrate that role. How children grow up, what attitudes they have, are absolutely vital both from the social point of view and for the future. And all this stems so much from the role the mother performs. I know it's awfully difficult nowadays because women want to work and have to do so, to earn enough. But the role of mother is so terribly important.'

At first the couple seemed to derive a joint pleasure from William and then from Harry who was born two years later. They laughed at William's boisterousness and called him the Mini Tornado. Diana noted with pleasure how Charles involved himself in the ritual of bathtime. One evening, when they were due at an engagement, her husband went missing. She found him in the bath with their eldest son. 'They were having a great time. There was soap and water everywhere,' Diana said.

It was an attractive image and one that played to excellent reviews. The public, generally unaware of the difficulties Charles and Diana were having, responded enthusiastically to the sight of the newlyweds apparently settling down so well to parenthood, and assumed that whatever problems they might have had were now behind them. The press, keen to provide its readers with information to fuel this popular belief, gamely reported how well the couple were getting on. There was even some truth in it; according to Diana, the weeks leading up to Harry's birth on 15 September 1984 were when they were at their closest.

It was not long, however, before the smooth and glistening surface was disturbed by the currents flowing underneath. Diana called the period between the birth of William and Harry a time of 'total darkness—I can't remember much, I've blotted it out, it was such pain'.

She began to resent Charles's involvement and, even more, his views on how William should be brought up. He said: 'It isn't only a woman's job to bring children up, it's a man's job as well.' To which she irritably responded: 'Charles knows so much about rearing children that I've suggested he has the next one and I'll sit back and give advice.'

She became annoyed by his Laurens van der Post-like musing. Forever seeking a metaphysical explanation to life, he observed: 'Suddenly you find that your child is not a malleable being or an offprint of you: it is the culmination of heaven knows how many thousands of years of genetic traits of your ancestors.'

William certainly had enough of those. The genealogists worked out that his forebears included, on his father's side and along with the requisite litter of kings and queens, an Arab sheik called Musa ibn Naseir, who was born in Mecca in 660; Charlemagne, the first Holy Roman Emperor; Peter Checke, a sixteenth-century Essex innkeeper; and Vlad the Impaler, who provided the model for Dracula.

Diana also was richly endowed with antecedents including George Washington, and Queen Anne's lesbian lover, Sarah, Duchess of Marlborough. She was much more interested, however, in the new branches, rather than the old roots, of the family tree.

The British aristocracy of which she was a part attaches great importance to bloodlines. Not Diana. William looked like her and as far as she was concerned, that was all that mattered. It was also a matter of approach, and in this debate she placed her faith in nurture, not nature, and Charles's genealogical musing both bored and irked her.

But then, so it seemed, did everything else about her husband, and the rows which had so blighted their first months together flared up again. One continuing disagreement was over the nannies and what their role should be. The Prince had wanted to re-employ his old nurse, Mabel Anderson, but Diana refused to countenance the suggestion. Too old and too traditional, she said. Charles gave way, as he usually did, and allowed her to select a woman of her own choice. The nanny she chose was Barbara Barnes, the daughter of a forestry worker who came to Kensington Palace on the recommendation of Lord Glenconner, whose wife Anne was one of Princess Margaret's ladies-in-waiting. 'She is a natural with children,' Glenconner said. 'She has a genius for bringing out the best in them. They're never bored. She has all the traditional values to the highest degree but is perfectly up to date.'

'I'm here to help the Princess, not to take over,' Barbara said diplomatically.

Barbara proved herself too efficient for Diana's liking, however. The boys responded well to her and that inevitably set her on a collision course with her volatile employer and on 15 January 1987, after almost five years of employment, it was announced that Barbara Barnes would be leaving Kensington Palace. In an attempt to avoid any adverse publicity, the statement was timed to coincide with Prince William's first day at his new school.

'I thought no one would notice,' Diana said, 'but I was wrong, wasn't I.'

She was. Barnes's departure made the front pages of the newspapers; William's first day at Wetherby pre-preparatory in West London was relegated to the inside.

Barbara, who was given a grace and favour home on the Duchy of Cornwall's London estate in Kennington, has never given a public explanation of the circumstances which led up to her departure, and for a long while it was assumed that Charles had prompted it. He was annoyed, so the theory went, with the jet-set lifestyle she enjoyed during her time off work, and in particular by the pictures which appeared of her hobnobbing with the likes of actress Raquel Welch and Mick Jagger's wife, Jerry Hall, at Glenconner's sixtieth birthday party on Mustique, his private island in the Caribbean.

In fact, it was Diana who wanted the change and the nanny did not again see the boys whose young lives she had helped shape until William's confirmation. 'Difficult', is how Barbara, in an unguarded moment, described the Princess.

She was not alone in her sentiment. When she had first moved into Buckingham Palace, Diana had been anxious to the point of embarrassment to make friends with the staff. Once installed as Princess of Wales she swung in the opposite direction, and by 1985 some forty royal servants had been 'let go' on the Princess's instructions. This enforced exodus included footmen, police officers and chauffeurs. A maid was dismissed on the totally unfounded charge that she was a lesbian.

One of the first to be frozen out was Charles's valet, Stephen Barry. 'Diana was beastly to him,' one of the household recalled. 'When she saw him coming down a corridor she would dive into the nearest room so that she wouldn't have to speak to him. It was very childish but it hurt Stephen enormously.'

Oliver Everett, who had given Diana the books which he felt would help her understand her new role, was rewarded for his presumption by being moved out. Colborne, Prince Charles's own private secretary, tendered his resignation. So did Edward Adeane, the Prince and Princess of Wales's joint private secretary.

Adeane's was the most notable departure of them all. He came from the very highest echelon of royal servants, where service is seen as a lifelong vocation. His father, Sir Michael, later Lord Adeane, had been principal private secretary to the Queen. His great-grandfather Lord Stamfordham had been private secretary to Queen Victoria and to the Duke of York, later King George V. A man with a precise and practical mind, he had found the intellectually erratic prince hard enough to deal with. Diana, he found impossible. He regarded her as ill-educated and took exception to the way she would go around after him, picking up his cigar butts and holding them gingerly in her fingertips by way of a silent ticking-off. On more than one occasion Charles had to intervene to smooth his ruffled feathers. He eventually decided that he could stand no more and left.

Diana's brother, Charles Spencer, stepped in to defend his sister. All she was doing, he said, was 'getting rid of the hangers-on who surrounded Charles'. To pass comment, however well-intentioned, on how others choose to order their domestic affairs is regarded in aristocratic circles as impertinence. To do so about the head of state's family, was regarded by the Palace as nothing short of gross bad manners. One can only imagine what Queen Mary, who had been so scathing about Prince Philip's justifiable wish to have his children bear his surname, would have had to say about such insolence from the son of a former equerry.

The Queen chose not to interfere in the bloodletting taking place below stairs, on the well-mannered grounds that how her daughter-in-law ran her household was her business. She most certainly did not approve, however. Her relations with her own staff were always cordial. She tolerated their eccentricities, overlooked their sometimes unorthodox sexual tastes, and turned a blind eye to their drinking habits which often veered towards the excessive. At one luncheon during Ascot Week a footman was so 'over-served' (Palace-speak for drunk) that he dropped the silver tray laden with crystal glasses of drinks for the guests. The Queen batted not an eyelid. Ignoring the commotion, she merely indicated that it was time to go through to the dining table. The footman was not dismissed: a lifetime's employ was considered flair recompense for long hours and low wages. She paid for another footman to go to a drying out clinic. And when yet another became embroiled in an unfortunate love affair with a girl, she paid for his psychiatric treatment.

Diana took a more abrasive attitude to what is still condescendingly called 'the servant problem' and it offended the Queen's sense of propriety.

Particularly worrying was the turnover in nannies. When Barbara Barnes left, Diana 'poached' Ruth Wallace, nanny to her Kensington Palace neighbour, Princess Michael of Kent. Princess Michael was furious with Diana. As the old joke went, a bounder may steal a man's wife but never his butler and Princess Michael took much the same view about the woman who helped look after her two children, Freddie, born in 1979, and Gabriella who was two years younger.

Wallace was a nurse who had trained at Bart's Hospital before working for the husband of Diana's former flatmate, Carolyn Bartholomew, running a discotheque in a hotel near Heathrow airport. She then took charge of the disco at Raffles nightclub in London's King's Road before answering an advertisement in *The Lady* and going to work for the Kents. She stayed with the Waleses for three years—'I found the press attention very difficult', she recalled—and left to go on an expedition up the Amazon.

She was replaced by Jessie Webb who had worked for fifteen years with the internationally renowned interior decorator Nina Campbell, who had done the decor at Annabel's, Diana's favourite nightclub in Berkeley Square in the heart of London.

The Queen firmly believed that changing nannies would disrupt the nursery routine, and not even Prince Philip's dislike of Mabel Anderson's growing authority (in protest he refused to invite her down to lunch with the children when he was eating alone, as he did the relief nanny) had been enough to persuade her to look for someone else. Diana's household was far less settled. Having declared so forcefully that she was going to look after her children herself, she had come to realize that she needed help in order to fulfil her duties. What she seemed unable to do, however, was give her nannies the trust they required to do their job properly. In the effort to keep her sons for herself, she was inadvertently subjecting them to exactly the same instability she herself had suffered as a child.

'I hug my children to death and get into bed with them at night, hug them and say: "Who loves you most in the world?" and they always say "Mummy",' she said. 'I always feed them love and affection—it's so important. I want to bring them security.'

It was security of the smothering kind, and Charles worried about the inconsistency in her methods.

As a child, he had been smacked on the bottom or across the back of the legs by his nanny or his mother when he threw an infantile rage or was rude to a footman. The Palace had received a number of letters calling for an end to these spankings but they continued up to the age when he was sent away to school. There was nothing unusual in that; in the Fifties most parents, and all but the most 'progressive' schools, used corporal punishment as a means of enforcing discipline. The sensitive Charles disapproved of such tactics and was reluctant to employ them on his own sons, believing that being banished to their room was a more effective punishment.

Diana was more spontaneous, more instinctive. When William kicked the leg of a footman as he was about to step into a carriage in the Palace's Royal Mews, she immediately whacked him across his backside. William burst into tears. Overcome with guilt, Diana took him in her arms and covered him in kisses, thereby negating the punishment she had just administered.

She was equally erratic when it came to the

matter of presents. Her own parents had given her gifts as a substitute for their time and attention. She had been given a catalogue from Hamley's toy shop and told to tick the items she wanted. 'It makes you very materialistic,' her brother Charles said. Diana was determined not to spoil her own sons in that manner and told her friends to give them books instead of toys. She raised no objection, however, when the singer Barry Manilow gave Harry a valuable antique baby piano, or Jaguar presented William with a miniature car. To Charles that all smacked of disquieting inconstancy.

Initially, the couple had tried to present a united front to their children. Whereas Prince Philip had rarely bothered to attend his sons' birthday parties, Charles always made the effort to be there. When ex-King Constantine of Greece threw a cowboys and Indians party at his North London home for William, Diana went as a cowgirl and Charles wore a stetson hat. 'They both joined in all the games like running with a plate of water, and appeared to be thoroughly enjoying themselves,' recalled Smarty Arty, the children's entertainer that afternoon.

It was all part of Diana's avowed intention to bring her sons up in as 'ordinary' a way as possible. They were allowed to mix with other children, to visit their homes and to have them back for tea at Kensington Palace. They were taken to the zoo, abroad skiing, and to popular amusement parks were they were photographed with their mother screaming with laughter as they came splashing down the water shoots.

Diana was right to give 'my boys', as she called them, a glimpse of life beyond the Palace walls and in this she had the support of the Queen, who was astute enough to appreciate that the days when princes had to be brought up in the aspic of regal isolation were long past. It was agreed that William and Harry would have an 'ordinary' education, albeit of a rareified kind (only 14 per cent of British children are educated privately and only a tiny fraction of these attend the elitist schools which the princes were sent to).

They started, not with a governess, but at Miss Mynors's nursery school across the road from Kensington Palace in Notting Hill. Wetherby's came next and from there they went on to Ludgrove, a preparatory boarding school in Berkshire. On the day William left home for Ludgrove, Diana wrote to a friend how she 'dived into the Kleenex box'. It would not be the last time the Princess needed tissues but on this occasion she fetched them herself.

By family tradition, they should then have gone on to Gordonstoun, the Spartan establishment in the north of Scotland where first Prince Philip and then Charles, Andrew, Edward and Princess Anne's children, Peter and Zara, had all been educated. Charles, however, had had a thoroughly miserable time at the school where he had been bullied and teased. On Diana's prompting, it was decided to send them instead to Eton, Britain's most exclusive public school which is conveniently situated on the opposite bank of the River Thames to Windsor Castle.

The Queen approved of the choice. It was where she had wanted to send Charles, in the firm belief that he would meet and make friends with young men from a more appropriate social background than the one those who attended Gordonstoun were drawn from. (One of Charles's teachers described Gordonstoun as a place 'for the idiot sons of the local lairds', and if that was overly harsh, the school was certainly a great deal tougher and a lot less refined than Eton.)

For all Diana's good intentions, however, what she could not change was the destiny of their birth. Harry was a prince. His brother was born to be king and there was nothing 'ordinary' about that. It is a job that requires training. Nanny Barnes observed to a member of the household: 'William needs to be treated differently because he is different. It's no good Diana pretending he can have a completely normal life, because he can't.' Jessie Webb, another highly regarded nanny, who subsequently worked for Viscount Linley and his wife Serena, put it more candidly when she told the Highgrove housekeeper Wendy Berry: 'Those boys are going to need a lot of help if they are not going to end up as barking as their mum and dad.'

Miss Mynors would say of William: 'His classmates hardly know who he is', but that was not true because the eldest son of the heir to the throne knew very well who he was, and was soon informing the other children: 'My daddy's a real prince.' In one playground brawl he threatened his adversary with all the Queen's horses and all the Queen's men. The Queen in question, of course, was his grandmother.

There was also the ever-present security to remind him of who he was. As one member of the household observed: 'There is nothing normal about those children; there is nothing normal about having two back-up cars wherever they go.'

Even Eton failed to give the princes the anonymity their mother sought, for herself as much as for them. 'The parents there are so difficult,' Diana told me. 'They are always pointing and staring at me. They just stare . . .'

This may have been impolite, but it was hardly unexpected. No one had pointed at the Queen when she visited Heatherdown or drove over from Balmoral to Gordonstoun to see Charles, Andrew or Edward. Diana was different. The Queen, as Sovereign, was entitled to the respect due her position. Diana, on the other hand, had acquired the image of an international soap star, and a notorious one at that. Eton is the favoured school of Britain's aristocracy (Diana's father and brother went there), most of whom had come to regard Diana with something akin to disdain. It is an intriguing commentary on her life that while she enjoyed great popularity with the general public, those of her own class saw her as spoilt, wilful, irresponsible and a threat to the institution she had married into—and treated her accordingly. It was no wonder, therefore, that she felt uncomfortable when she came under their scrutiny.

Time and again, Diana would insist that it was not her intention, and never had been, to damage the crown her eldest son was born to inherit. Even if this were true, it still left the problem of how best to prepare William, not just for the responsibilities, but the ever-more intrusive interest his position generates.

Diana was aware of the difficulties. She told me: 'William hates the attention. But he is just going to have to adjust to it.'

She did not always do as much to aid her son as she might have done, however. She was in a foul mood when she took William to Wetherby on his first day. As she approached the battery of photographers she whispered to her son: 'Don't you dare smile at the cameras.' She put her hand on his back and physically pushed him past the cameramen. Shy and

201

nervous, he clutched at his mother's legs. As he shambled up the school steps, having first shaken hands with the headmistress, Miss Blair-Turner, the photographers called out: 'William, William.' Unable to help himself, he gave a shy grin and half-hearted wave.

When he came out again at lunchtime his mother was not there and William was again the confident little boy the cameraman had come to know.

The accompanying policemen had been taken aback by the Princess's extraordinary instruction. Smiling for the cameras is a royal duty and one the Queen was taught to do from a very early age. One Royal Protection Officer recalled: 'William hardly knew what she was talking about. But he learnt quick enough. It is all her fault that he is so reticent now. She has left her legacy there.'

Royal life has changed greatly since Charles was a little boy, and beyond all measure from the days when Victoria reigned from high on a pedestal of deference. The one aspect which has changed most radically is the approach to childhood. The aim, however, remains the same—to instil a deep sense of responsibility, to repay homage with duty, and the trappings of majesty with a commitment to hard work. As Prince Michael of Kent explained to me: 'If you have privilege, which in my case you were born with, you have no option. You can't have all the perks without pulling your weight. You can't have it without some kind of obligation.'

Charles agreed. He said: 'I would like to try and bring up our children to be well-mannered, to think of other people, to put themselves in other people's positions, to do unto others as they would have done unto them.' In other words, to be royal in the broadest definition of the word. This requires training and discipline. You can't simply walk into the role—as Diana discovered, to her great personal cost. It has to be drummed in from an early age.

Like the Queen, Diana had paid close attention to her sons' development and reached her own conclusion as to their strengths and weaknesses.

William, she told me, 'is the intellectual one. Harry is more easy-going, artistic and sporty. He takes everything in his stride.'

Trying to reconcile their sons' individual needs with the requirements of royalty was never easy, however, as that bizarre scene at Wetherby illustrated. As the marriage disintegrated, so the arguments over the boys' upbringing increased.

The Queen and Prince Philip had had their disagreements. On one occasion, Philip shouted at his wife to stop being 'such a bloody fool'. When she had flinched at the reckless way he was driving her to Broadlands, Philip had turned round and shouted: 'Do that once more and I'll put you out.'

The Queen was not to be trampled over, however, and refused to be brow-beaten by his outbursts. If she didn't like what he was doing or saying, she told him so. 'Shut up!' she would shout. Nor was Philip the kind of man to back away from a row with his wife, even if she did happen to be Queen. But their squabbles were rarely more than the kind which enliven most marriages and like those of most married couples, they quickly blew over.

The Waleses' quarrels were conducted on a much more vicious level which left Charles 'drained and exhausted', as he put it. His friends advised him to take a firmer hand but that was all but impossible for someone who preferred retreat to confrontation. When he did try and stand up for himself, Diana simply shouted him down. Unable to cope, he started spending more and more time away from home with the inevitable result that he found himself forced on to the periphery of his family's life.

If he wanted to take his sons to polo, Diana would insist on taking them back to London. If he wanted the family to picnic out of doors under the trees at Highgrove, she would insist they ate in the kitchen. When Charles suggested he take his sons shooting which they both love, Diana would say that she had already arranged an outing of her own.

'She actually seemed to enjoy rowing,' one member of staff recalled.

It was inevitable that the Queen would be drawn into this domestic maelstrom, not because she wanted to be (her attitude towards other people's marital problems was to leave them to sort out their own mess), but because the Princess insisted on involving her.

Diana would later deny that she sought the Queen's counsel. 'I kept myself to myself—I didn't ask her advice,' the Princess said. She was being selective with her memories. During her engagement, it is true that she hardly had a word to say to the older woman. When her marriage started curdling, however, she began calling round at Buckingham Palace with ever-greater frequency to ask her mother-in-law's advice or, more usually, just to moan.

The Queen took a tolerant view of these unscheduled intrusions on her work day. She always got on better with Fergie who shared her rural interests, but she nonetheless quite enjoyed Diana's company. She also seemed to be able to calm Diana down.

'She was usually in a lot better mood when she left than she was when she arrived,' one of her staff recalled.

To show her support and try and help her along, the Queen issued an official statement of encouragement in the April of 1984. Her spokesman announced: 'The Queen could not be more pleased with her daughter-in-law. She is very proud of the Princess's activities around the world and at home.'

It was never more than a holding operation, however. There was a limit to what the Queen could do. She was not a trained psychiatrist or psychotherapist and those who were, had singularly failed to restore order in Diana's troubled mind. It was in 1984 that she had reluctantly drawn the conclusion that her daughter-in-law was unlikely ever to be truly well. Diana would insist that her bulimia was a symptom of her marital problems. The Queen, on medical advice, recognized it for what it was; the outward manifestation of an incurable condition which would put enormous strain on any relationship Diana was involved in.

The one relationship where this was most telling was her marriage, and when Charles and Diana returned to Australia for the bicentennial celebrations in 1988, the couple were in open conflict. The crowds were out in force, just as they had been on that first royal tour five years before. However, this time they came to gaze, not at a princess in love, but a couple in discord. They got what they were looking for in Melbourne.

On a visit to a music college, Charles met his old cello master from Geelong Grammar School which he had attended twenty-two years earlier. Charles was invited to play his instrument in front of a class of young musicians and the accompanying press pack of photographers and reporters. The moment Charles began to play Diana stood up, walked across to the grand piano in the corner, sat down, lifted the lid, and played the opening bars of Rachmaninov's second piano concerto. The cameras followed her, leaving Charles marooned in embarrassment.

'I sometimes play in the evenings to entertain the Queen,' she coyly explained.

The look on the Prince of Wales's face told a different story. He knew that his wife was deliberately upstaging him in the most humiliating way.

It did not signify the beginning of the end, however. That had come the day Prince Harry was born—on that day, Diana was to say, 'It just went bang, our marriage, the whole thing went down the drain.'

CHAPTER SEVEN

DOUBLE STANDARDS

Since 1982, the year of the Michael Fagan Palace break-in, the responsibility for protecting the royal family has lain with the Deputy Assistant Commissioner in charge of the Royal and Diplomatic Protection Department of the Metropolitan Police. He is directly responsible to the Commissioner, who in turn reports to the Home Secretary.

At the beginning of the chain are the armed

detectives whose job it is to safeguard the lives of the Queen and her family. Charles has his own rota of officers, as did Diana.

All the Waleses' official engagements were entered into the police records. All the private visits they made were carefully entered in the individual notes each officer is required to keep. Many of the assignations they logged were arranged by the officers themselves. It is these intimate records which give a detailed account of where Charles and Diana went, whom they saw, how long they stayed—and what they did while they were there. These logs are kept for the very good reason that were anything to go amiss, the police would have to know whom their charges had been seeing, and when.

They show that between his marriage in 1981 and its 'irretrievable breakdown' in 1986, Prince Charles did not spend any significant time alone with Camilla Parker Bowles.

They reveal that in 1985 Princess Diana was often behind closed doors, and alone with a man who was not her husband.

By the winter of 1986 she had formed another close, extramarital relationship. This, too, was recorded in the logs of the Personal Protection Officers (PPOs).

The first suitor was Sergeant Barry Mannakee, who was one of Diana's own Protection Officers. The second was Captain James Hewitt.

Prince Charles was informed of what was happening, often under his own roof, by his detective, Senior Protection Officer Colin Trimming. It was then that he resumed his friendship with Mrs Parker Bowles.

The Queen was advised of these unhappy developments but declined to become involved. In 1986, Diana went to see the Queen and demanded she order Charles to stop seeing Mrs Parker Bowles. The Queen, fully aware of Diana's own marital transgressions, refused to mediate.

Once again, Diana felt badly let down by the royal family and felt that she was not getting the support she was entitled to.

The Queen took the more prosaic opinion that it was not her job to embroil herself in the conjugal affairs of her 37-year-old son and his 25-year-old wife, who was set on her own course of extramarital action.

She had made it her business to know what lay behind her daughter-in-law's visit, however, just as she always made it her business to know what was going on in her family. The Queen can be most inquisitive, and as she goes round the bedrooms of her homes switching off lights (and tut-tutting as she does so) she often takes the opportunity to have a quick tidy-up although she would never disturb anything private.

She also has her own highly efficient Byzantine intelligence network to keep her informed. It is composed of private secretaries and ladies-in-waiting and, on a more gossipy but by no means less reliable level, footmen and pages, many of whom have been with her all their working lives.

She learnt very quickly, for instance, of her daughter Anne's liaison in 1982 with her PPO, Peter Cross. Usually so supportive of those in her service, she did not intervene when the matter came to the attention of Commander Michael Trestrail, the then head of the Royal Protection Squad, who summarily dismissed the detective from his post (and himself shortly afterwards when it was revealed that he was involved in a homosexual relationship with a rent boy).

Nor did she come to the aid of Barry Mannakee when he was similarly discharged in 1986 for overstepping the mark of propriety in his dealings with another princess.

Taking a stern moral line with policemen who had exceeded their duties set no precedent when it came to dealing with affairs of a different social order, however.

Camilla was the wife of Brigadier Andrew Parker Bowles, Silver Stick-in-Waiting and Colonel Commanding the Household Cavalry, 'the Sovereign's own troops'. Diana's latest paramour was Captain James Hewitt, an officer in the elite Life Guards which forms part of the Household Cavalry and therefore came under Brigadier Parker Bowles's command.

Neither were hired hands, to be cast into outer darkness at the nod of a regal head. Both were members of the inner corps of men and women that surrounds and supports the Crown (though in Hewitt's case, only just), and are left to conduct their lives without any heavy-handed interference from the Sovereign. There was a large dollop of snobbish hypocrisy in this, but then no one has ever suggested that the Monarchy is an egalitarian institution.

In the 1950s, the Court had been run on more stringent moral lines. As a divorcee, King George VI's equerry Peter Townsend was considered an unsuitable consort for Princess Margaret, and when his bid to make her his wife was overruled by the government, he was forced into foreign exile. By the time Charles and Diana started going their separate ways, however, the authority of the Court had weakened considerably and its attitudes had softened commensurately.

The Queen knew all about Anne's dalliance with Major Hugh Lindsay who had taken up where Cross had left off. She was accordingly somewhat taken aback when, in 1985, Lindsay announced his engagement to Sarah Brennan, who worked in the Buckingham Palace press office, and remarked, 'I thought I knew what was going on.' She had certainly not approved of her daughter's illicit romance. But Lindsay was one of her equerries, and the Queen did not intercede.

The Queen remained equally uninvolved when Anne took up with yet another of her equerries, Commander Tim Laurence. Her view was that these matters were best left to run their course. In this instance it led to Anne's divorce from Captain Mark Phillips (Anne would later marry Laurence). The Queen accepted the situation with sad resignation, but said little.

It was not only the Queen who applied double standards. So did Diana. The Princess was infuriated when she learnt that one of her nannies was having a clandestine affair with one of her PPOs, and let her go soon afterwards. It was not uncommon among Diana's set to take umbrage at the sexual shenanigans of their nannies if they were taking place 'on the premises'. What was unusual in this case was that Diana herself had by then become a great deal closer in her own home than decorum dictated, to another of her police officers, a married man with two small children.

Diana's friendship with Sergeant Mannakee was an unlikely one. He was plump, with thinning hair, and none of the social sheen of some of the other detectives seconded to look after the royal family. She had always been attracted by good looks and glamour, and the rough-edged Mannakee had neither. But he made her laugh, and that was no mean achievement at a time when Diana spent many of her days in tears. Their friendship was forged on the long drives up and down the M4 motorway to Highgrove, 'M4 chats' as they were called, the same route along which Princess Anne had got to know Sergeant Peter Cross so well on her way home to Gatcombe Park.

The royal policemen are in a difficult position. Because of the long hours they spend in the company of their charges, close friendships often develop. They play with their children (Ken Wharf had pillow fights with Prince William), come to know their habits and weaknesses, help with the cooking and the tidying up, join them on exotic holidays, are on duty throughout the night, and are sometimes called upon to give emotional support (Diana had thrown herself into Mannakee's arms before one public engagement, crying that she couldn't go on). They are kitted out by the Met with dinner jackets, white tie and tails and morning suits, to allow them to mingle easily at state banquets and such less onerous occasions like Royal Ascot. Yet they are expected to keep a professional distance at all times. As the Met says: 'Strict protocol is followed, as it is important that officers do not let themselves become so familiar with the situation that they cease to concentrate on their work as guards. This means they must maintain a distance, even from younger royals who may wish to relax into greater informality.'

It is a hard balancing act to perform but most succeed. Cross did not. Neither did Mannakee. He gave Diana a brown teddy bear which she installed in pride of place on her bed. When Hewitt later observed that it was rather an intimate present to receive from a bodyguard, Diana replied: 'He was my lover.'

Other policemen on royal duty had reached the same realization. Mannakee had taken up his post in the spring of 1985. In July of the following year he was called before Trimming, told that he had become 'too close' to the Princess, and transferred.

At this stage, the Waleses were still managing to keep up appearances, and the November 1985 issue of *Time* magazine put them on its front cover, proclaiming them 'the most glamorous couple' in the world.

The reality was that they were no longer sharing the same bed. Diana complained that she was being physically and emotionally rejected; Charles told friends that he could no longer bear his wife's rages, tantrums, tears and mood swings, and her ceaseless accusation that he was having an affair with Mrs Parker Bowles. The Prince wrote: 'How awful incompatibility is, and how dreadfully destructive it can be for the players in this extraordinary drama.'

His patience and sympathy exhausted, he

214

stopped trying to prop up his wife. What he did not do, however, was go out of his way to enquire too deeply into what his wife was doing on the ever-more frequent occasions they were apart. In a private letter dated 11 February 1987, he wrote: 'I don't want to spy on her or interfere in her life in any way.'

It was an approach his mother shared. She had once likened Diana to a 'nervy race horse' who needed careful handling, not the harsh bit of discipline. Despite the mounting evidence, she convinced herself that if Diana's rope was given the slack of independence which she claimed she needed, her self-assurance would increase, and she would eventually settle down. What the Queen most certainly did not grasp, when Diana came to see her in her first-floor study overlooking Buckingham Palace gardens that morning in 1986 to ask her to tell Charles to stop seeing Camilla, was that the marriage was heading for the rocks.

Neither, at this stage, did Charles or Diana. Diana tearfully told friends that she was condemned to a life sentence. Charles wrote: 'I feel I'm in a kind of cage, pacing up and down in it and longing to be free.'

Divorce, however, simply wasn't contemplated. An ever-increasing number of the Queen's subjects were choosing to bring their own marriages to a legal end, but the royal family, by allowing itself to be presented as the epitome of familial virtue, had painted itself into a corner. The Victorian constitutionalist, Walter Bagehot, had warned against such a thing. His book, *The English Constitution*, was regarded as the essential primer for royalty, and the Queen, like her father, George VI, and grandfather, George V, before her, had been made to study it. In it Bagehot had warned that while 'we have come to regard the Crown as the head of our *morality* . . . a little experience and less thought show that royalty cannot take credit for domestic excellence'. So it proved: while the rest of Britain were free to discard the restraints of the past, the Windsors continued to be judged—and condemned—according to the standards of the 1930s. As Charles wrote, 'That is the total *agony* of the situation.'

*   *   *

Charles blamed himself. As Prince of Wales, he succeeded in carving out a role for himself, most notably with the Prince's Trust, his charity set up in 1976 to help young disadvantaged people set up businesses of their own, which was both worthwhile and stimulating. As heir to the throne, however, his only real obligation was to secure the succession. That required a marriage which, by the precepts the royal family had set themselves, was expected to be unto death. And in that, he had been a manifest failure.

'How *could* I have got it all so wrong?' he asked.

In later years, the Queen also would come to wonder if she had failed in her duty. Looking back on the litter of her children's broken marriages, she asked of a lady-in-waiting, 'Where did we go wrong?'

To her former private secretary Lord Charteris, she sadly remarked: 'And I thought I had brought them up so well.'

Some would lay the blame on their upbringing, which had prepared them for the relentless, soulless round of official engagements and gruelling foreign tours, but left them so inhibited as to render them incapable of dealing with personal upheaval. Others, more charitably, have suggested that once the mantle of deference had been stripped away by the changes in social priorities that came with the restructuring of Britain's commercial and industrial base, the royal family was placed in an insupportable position. Most of the Court, and many of her own caste, simply blamed Diana.

The late Earl Mountbatten must take some of the responsibility for the fiasco of his great-nephew's marriage. He undoubtedly had a formative influence on Charles. Complex and contrary, Mountbatten had risen to the position of Supreme Allied Commander in South-East Asia during World War Two, yet he placed almost pathological store on his own fanciful bloodline. He was by turns ruthless and charming, hard-working and dilettantish, but never anything other than vain (he had advised that, as Charles had a cupboard full of uniforms and medals, he should wear them at every opportunity, as he himself always did). The two spent long summer days together alone at Windsor, stretched out on sun loungers beside the pool in the Orangery, drinking lemon refresher, rubbing suntan lotions into each other's back, and discussing the royal role.

As a young man, Charles was rather a lost soul. He had never settled at Gordonstoun where his lack of both athletic ability and robust social skills had set him apart from his contemporaries. He had found it hard to make friends, and could not have avoided the nagging thought that he had been made Guardian (head boy) only because of who, rather than what, he was. He was not helped by an insensitive housemaster, Bob Whitby, whose theories on education were those of a particularly insensitive drill sergeant (when Charles had wanted to take up the trumpet, Whitby had shouted: 'You're not going to play that thing around *my* house!'). His only cultural succour was provided by the art master, Bob Waddell, and by Eric Anderson, who taught English and drama.

Waddell cut a novel figure among the tweed-clad hearties in the staff common room.

Aesthetic, well-dressed (one of Charles's contemporaries remembered him flaunting a long silk scarf) and slightly precious, he drove an ancient open-topped silver touring car in defiance of the Scottish weather, and looked as if he would have been much more at home in the salons of Chelsea than on the windswept coast of the Moray Firth. He took the unhappy Prince under his wing, encouraged his interest in pottery, took delight in showing him the *objets* he had picked up in the London sales rooms, and spent many evenings discussing art with him over cups of coffee in his bachelor quarters in the Round Square, Gordonstoun's oldest building where the Guardian also had his quarters (a circular stable block, it was built in the eighteenth century by an owner who did not want to be cornered by the Devil).

In the longer term, however, it was Anderson who would play the greater part, not just in Charles's life but in the future of Britain. One of the most influential educationalists of his generation, he left Gordonstoun to become a housemaster at Fettes, the Scottish public school 007 James Bond is supposed to have attended. One of his pupils there was Tony Blair, the future Prime Minister. Blair has called the tall, donnish Anderson his schoolboy inspiration.

Anderson eventually became headmaster of Eton, which he had restored to its academic pre-eminence by the time Prince William and

Prince Harry arrived there. He is now the College's Provost. It has therefore fallen to one brilliant career to have a substantial say in the shaping of two future kings and one Prime Minister, an unprecedented commission.

It was during his spell at Gordonstoun that Anderson found a means of drawing Charles out of the shell into which he had retreated. He gave him the part of the Duke of Exeter in his alfresco Round Square production of Shakespeare's *Henry V.* Charles was not the best actor at the school (that honour belonged to David Gwillim, who left for the Royal Academy of Dramatic Art at the end of that term and went on to play the title role in the BBC's prestigious production of the same play), but he was certainly good enough to fully warrant Anderson's faith in his talent when he was cast as Macbeth the following year. In playing someone else, Charles at last started to find the confidence to play himself.

Anderson's motivational powers extended beyond the stage. In the weekly discussion groups he organized for certain favoured boys, he enabled Charles to think beyond the preconceptions of his background. He also passed on his own love of Shakespearean English and introduced the Prince to the concepts of courtly morality as expounded by his favourite author, Sir Walter Scott, whose novels contained the template for the gentlemen of America's Deep South.

Opening up the Prince's mind was easy enough, but persuading him to place his trust in his own opinions proved a much harder task. Unsure of his own judgement, Charles continued to look to others for guidance, reassurance and direction long after he left school. Laurens van der Post was one of his 'gurus'. The other was Earl Mountbatten.

The Queen did not approve. Like her mother and her husband, she was often irritated by the way Mountbatten tried to dictate to his royal relations. He was a difficult man to resist, however. He was charming, forceful and unrelenting, and it was on his urging that Charles, instead of dividing his time between the three services, joined the Royal Navy. 'Your father, grandfather, and both your great-grandfathers had a distinguished career in the Royal Navy,' the Admiral of the Fleet wrote sententiously. 'If you follow in their footsteps this would be very popular.'

It turned out to be a bad choice. The British navy prides itself on its ruthless qualities of seamanship which the Prince found hard to emulate. As one fellow officer observed, he couldn't dock the minesweeper he eventually came to command 'without risk of crashing into the wharf'.

This might have given a more mature, less impressionable man food for thought, but Charles was in thrall of the charismatic, dynamic war leader and former Chief of the Defence Staff who was paying him such flattering attention. Everything he said sounded like music to ears which Mountbatten had once advised him to have 'fixed—you can't possibly be King with ears like that'. He called him 'elderly wise uncle' and awarded him the title of 'honorary grandpapa'.

Some of the older man's ideas were fresh and forward-thinking, and it was Mountbatten who stirred Charles's interest in such diverse projects as the United World Colleges and the plans to raise Henry VIII's flagship, the *Mary Rose*, from the bed of the Solent where it had lain for over four hundred years.

On the question of women, however, his advice was rather more suspect. He was married to Edwina, the granddaughter of the financier Sir Ernest Cassell and the richest heiress of her generation, who gave him two daughters. It was nonetheless a union blighted by gossip. She was widely believed to have had affairs with the black American singer, Paul Robeson, and Pandit Nehru, the first Prime Minister of India where Mountbatten had served as Britain's last Viceroy. At the same time, he never quite managed shake off the rumours of bisexuality which haunted him throughout his career.

It was Mountbatten who wrote to Charles: 'For a wife [you] should choose a suitable, attractive and sweet-charactered girl before she has met anyone else she might fall for. I think it is disturbing for women to have experiences if they have to remain on a pedestal after marriage.' In the meantime, he advised Charles to 'sow his wild oats and have as many affairs as he could before settling down'. He gave Charles the run of Broadlands to pursue his romantic adventures, and one of the young women he entertained there was Camilla Shand, who had been introduced to him by Lucia Santa Cruz, the daughter of the Chilean ambassador to London who had played the first memorable role in his sexual education. Lucia described Camilla to the Prince as 'just the girl'.

Mountbatten did not agree. He still nursed ambitions to see his grandaughter, Amanda, married to the Prince. But even if he didn't, Camilla did not fit his definition of what made a royal wife. She had had other boyfriends, and to Mountbatten's crude way of thinking this gave her 'a past' which made her an unsuitable future queen. More ludicrously, Mountbatten also objected to the fact that Camilla happened to be a year older than the Prince. Faced with his honorary grandpapa's facile opposition, Charles dithered and Camilla, growing tired of life out on a limb, eventually went off, and in 1973 married Andrew Parker Bowles whom she had known and liked from before.

Charles's relationship with Camilla was not

extinguished by her defection, however. While Parker Bowles spent much of his time in London where he maintained old friendships (he continued to see a lot of Princess Anne), his wife remained in the country looking after their two young children, Tom and Laura. There was always enough time left over to see Charles.

These unconventional couplings were at embarrassing variance with the royal family's popular image as paragons of virtue and there were occasions when the complications of reconciling private appetites with public duty threatened to tumble out from under the bed covers and into public view.

In 1979, Parker Bowles had been posted to Rhodesia as ADC to the Governor-General, Sir Winston Churchill's son-in-law Lord Soames. There he made the acquaintance of Louise Gubb, a blonde photographer working for the Associated Press. Shortly before Rhodesia was handed over to black majority rule and became Zimbabwe, Soames and his wife Mary hosted a dinner party which Prince Charles flew in to attend. Parker Bowles was invited. So was Miss Gubb. The cosy arrangement was disturbed three days before the dinner when Camilla telephoned to announce that she would be flying in, too.

Mary Soames was momentarily disconcerted. So was just about everyone else in the governor's entourage. Who, they wanted to know, was Mrs Parker Bowles coming to see—her husband, or the Prince?

The one thing the British are good at, however, is hiding their feelings behind a veil of good manners. In a scene part-*Carry On*, part-Merchant-Ivory, Lady Soames remarked to her husband, 'Pray God the claret be good.' It was, and the dinner party was deemed a great success by everyone—everyone, that is, except the unfortunate Miss Gubb who did not know how to play the game by such devious rules. 'She was very upset,' one of her press colleagues recalled. None of the British journalists there wrote the story, and Miss Gubb moved to South Africa soon afterwards, defeated by a system she neither understood nor liked.

There were those in the Palace who also worried about the Prince's peculiar arrangements. Their concerns were not wounded feelings but the potentially damaging consequences of Charles's continued association with Mrs Parker Bowles. The Queen was one of them, and the Prince was alerted to the harm his liaison would cause if it became public knowledge. The warnings obviously were not delivered forcefully enough because Charles continued to see the woman he called 'my girl Friday' and 'my touchstone'.

In fact, the Queen herself was rather taken with Mrs Parker Bowles and her husband. They became frequent guests at Windsor and, during the shooting season, at Sandringham and Balmoral. Despite her brief flirtations with some of the faster members of the Chelsea set, Camilla is a countrywoman and would spend long hours talking knowledgeably to the Queen about horses and dogs and farm prices, subjects which Diana had not the slightest interest in.

Indeed, there were times when the Queen wondered, as any mother might, whether her son had not allowed his best chance for a happy marriage to slip away. If she blamed anyone— and in the years to come everyone would start blaming everyone else for the calamity which threatened to consume the royal family—it was Lord Mountbatten, for filling Charles's young and impressionable mind with his woolly, outmoded and thoroughly patronizing notions on women and marriage.

Given the distance between Charles and his father (Philip communicates with his son by scribbled note, even when they are both under the same roof) and the Prince's urgent need for an older man to confide in, it was perhaps inevitable that Mountbatten should come to hold such sway. Advice was always a thing Mountbatten was prepared to dispense, and in a way that someone as unsure of himself as Charles found irresistible.

The Queen took a more detached approach towards her children. She made it a point not to impose herself on them, and refrained from passing any overt judgement on their behaviour. As she herself acknowledged in that remark to her lady-in-waiting, it might have been better for all concerned if she hadn't.

*   *   *

It was not in the Queen's nature to become a participant in other people's troubles. She found it hard enough dealing with her own and, like her mother before her, preferred to overlook a problem rather than confront it, in the belief that if she ignored it long enough it would go away.

It was the policy she applied in her own marriage. Philip's early restlessness did not abate, and by the mid-Fifties, their marriage came under scathing scrutiny when he went on a four-month tour of the Commonwealth aboard the royal yacht *Britannia*. The catalyst which unleashed this unwelcome attention was the decision by Eileen Parker to divorce her husband, Michael, Philip's aide-de-camp and boon companion.

Eileen had finally grown tired of the long separations. 'How can one maintain a deep, lasting relationship with someone who hardly ever is present in the home except perhaps to change his clothes?' she asked.

On the advice of the Queen's usually tight-lipped press secretary, Commander Richard

227

Colville, she agreed to delay the announcement until *Britannia* was safely back in home waters. A leak to the *Sunday Pictorial*, however, put paid to the Palace's attempt at news manipulation, and when the royal yacht arrived in Gibraltar the story was front-page news. Parker promptly resigned. It did no good. He was Philip's closest friend and a member of the notorious Thursday Club, and his own marital difficulties provided an excuse to exhume the rumours, some wild, others perilously close to the truth, about the state of the royal marriage.

The name of Pat Kirkwood, the musical star with legs whom the late theatre critic Kenneth Tynan described as 'the eighth wonder of the world', was dragged into the frame.

Philip had been introduced to her by the photographer Baron at a dinner party at Les Ambassadeurs gambling club in Park Lane in 1948, a month before the Queen gave birth to Charles. They danced, to the anger of King George VI who was 'outraged' at his son-in-law's behaviour. It was generally assumed in theatrical circles that the 'dancing' had continued long after the club closed for the night and continued for many years to come.

Other names bandied about included Helene Cordet, Philip's childhood friend from Paris, who had arrived in London to run the capital's first discotheque, the Saddle Room, and Merle Oberon, the beautiful Anglo-Indian actress who became a Hollywood star.

When Commander Colville made the misguided decision to break with decades of stone-faced silence and announce: 'It is quite untrue that there is any rift between the Queen and the Duke', he only succeeded in inflaming the situation. One American newspaper declared in banner headlines, 'London Hushes Royal Rift'.

To add fuel to the allegations of infidelity, a close examination of the Court Circular revealed that Philip spent more time away from his wife and his son and daughter than he did with them. And why, so his critics wanted to know, did he feel it necessary to spend 124 days and 5 hours—someone worked that out, too—on a jolly with a gang of male companions?

In his traditional end-of-tour speech at the Guildhall, Philip tried to dampen down the situation by saying: 'I believe there are things for which it is worthwhile making some personal sacrifice, and I believe that the British Commonwealth is one of these.'

He had started in Melbourne where he opened the 1956 Olympic Games. *Britannia* then took him to New Zealand, Ceylon, the Gambia and, less impressively, the sparsely populated Galapagos and Falklands, as well as the empty ice wastes of Antarctica, which presumably would have survived without the benefit of a royal visit. It did not aid his case that Britain had invaded the Suez Canal zone in the middle of his trip and the royal yacht should have been on active service as a hospital ship, for which purpose it had ostensibly been built. Though as it turned out, *Britannia* was not needed: the United States refused to support Britain's action, British forces were ignominiously withdrawn and the government of Sir Anthony Eden fell.

The Parkers were divorced on 28 February 1957, on the grounds of Michael Parker's adultery with a Mrs Mary Alexandra Thompson. It was not her real name, but her true identity was never revealed. Philip would continue to see Parker in the ensuing years but he never saw or spoke again to Eileen, the one truly innocent party in the whole sorry mess.

The Queen remained calm throughout. She even managed to make light of the situation. During his time away Philip had grown a beard which he only shaved off when the royal yacht sailed from Gibraltar to Portugal. The Queen flew out to join him there for the commencement of their official visit to Britain's oldest ally. When he boarded the aeroplane which brought his wife to Montijo military air base just outside Lisbon, he found everyone on board wearing false beards—the Queen included. Once again her ability to lock her problems away in separate compartments was used to face-saving effect.

To underline her support of her husband,

the Queen agreed on the day of his return that he be created a Prince of the United Kingdom. He had been born a prince of Greece, but had surrendered the title when he married Elizabeth. Since then he had been known as the Duke of Edinburgh. Now he was Prince Philip again. It was a neat ending to the stories of a royal rift—but not to the rumours which had spawned them.

The Thursday Club was disbanded (it had in any case already lost much of its zest, and Baron, who had been its driving force, had died shortly before he was due to accompany Philip on his long seaborne trip). Never again would Philip be observed in an expensive nightclub dancing cheek-to-cheek with a showgirl.

The cloak of silence which had once protected the upper classes, and the royal family in particular, had worn thin by the end of the Sixties, however, and what had once been unmentionable gradually became the stuff of common gossip. The list of the Prince's alleged conquests includes a princess who is one of his wife's relations, a duchess, a couple of countesses, sundry other titled ladies, and the aforementioned waitress. Old age has not stilled the chatter: he kept his figure and his vigour and in his mid-seventies he was even being linked with Penny Romsey, the beautiful wife of his much younger cousin, Norton, heir to the Mountbatten earldom. A dance floor again played its part, not in the West End this time, but in the usually guarded environs of the royal yacht squadron on the Isle of Wight, where members attending the annual ball at the end of Cowes Regatta Week noted how the Prince and Lady Romsey spent most of the night dancing together. They later came to share a mutual interest in carriage driving.

Any mention of this infuriated the Prince who was angered by what he insisted was a gross misrepresentation of his interests and activities. In his defence he pointed to the police officers who keep a watchful eye on him wherever he goes. 'I have become a caricature,' he complained. 'That is the trouble when the media give you a reputation.'

It is not only the Prince who has to live with it. So must his wife. She dealt with it well, better than many younger women would have been able to. She accepted his love for what it was, continued to share her bed with him, valued his advice and support, and dosed her ears to the calumnies that sometimes came her way (one lady-in-waiting was dismissed when she over-stepped the unspoken parameters of their long friendship and tried to feed the Queen the latest over-ripe titbit of gossip involving Philip). It required single-minded commitment.

*   *   *

When Elizabeth was growing up, it was quite commonplace still for married members of the grander families, some of whom became her friends, others to whom she was related, to go their separate ways once the children were born. It was the Edwardian answer to the age-old problem of faltering sexual interest which is often a by-product of marital familiarity. To modern minds, it reeks of callous hypocrisy and emotional betrayal. It also favoured the men, which is no recommendation in a post-feminist age. But unlike the serial monogamy which replaced it, it kept the divorce rate down, held families and their properties together, and ensured that the children were brought up in a settled environment. The only cardinal axiom was absolute discretion. As the Edwardian actress and ironist Mrs Patrick Campbell pithily put it, it didn't matter what you did 'as long as you don't do it in the street and frighten the horses'.

It nonetheless required a fair amount of emotional detachment to deal with the frailties of human nature in such a worldly way. Something the Queen certainly has. Elizabeth and her sister Margaret had been brought up in exactly the same way, to the extent that they wore the same clothes until late in their teens. The end product could not have been more different, suggesting that for all Diana's beliefs to the contrary, genetic inheritance does have a lot to do with how a person turns out.

Margaret grew up to be wilful, self-indulgent and unchaste. She drank and smoked, liked staying up until the early hours and took lovers including the comedian Peter Sellers, nightclub pianist Robin Douglas-Home and a young trainee gardener seventeen years her junior called Roddy Llewellyn. Diana intriguingly 'adored' her.

The Queen, aware of the underlying unhappiness which drove her sister on, had good cause to wonder whether she might have done more to help. In 1955, in face of the unbending opposition of the government and the established Church of England, Margaret was forced to end her relationship with Group Captain Peter Townsend. The couple had hoped to marry, but Townsend was a divorcee. The fact that he had been the innocent party mattered not a jot. When it was ruled that the only way the two would be allowed to wed was if Margaret gave up her royal position, the romance came to its sorrowful end. Townsend went into exile in Belgium, and five years later Margaret married the photographer Anthony Armstrong-Jones who was created Earl of Snowdon.

The Queen could have intervened on behalf of Townsend. This she had categorically refused to do, giving not so much as a whisper of support for her stricken sister, preferring to allow the government and her own advisers to shoulder the blame.

It set the pattern for her reign. It was the portent of how she would behave when called upon to involve herself in the marital woes of her son and heir.

By way of justification of her inaction in the Townsend affair, her courtiers pointed out that the decision had been Margaret's alone. The excuse rang hollow. The Queen liked Townsend and thought him an eminently suitable suitor for her sister. Had she let it be known that she approved of the match, she might very well have swung opinion in its favour. After all, by the mid-Fifties, divorce was not the anathema it had once been. Indeed, her Prime Minister at the time, Sir Anthony Eden, had himself been the innocent party in a divorce case.

Instead, she took refuge in the moot argument that she could not go against the wishes of Parliament, the Cabinet, the Church of England and the Commonwealth. It was an essential part of her psychological make-up. She believed her role was to fulfil her duty, not to define what that duty should be.

On the occasion of her twenty-first birthday, while on tour of South Africa with her parents, she made an oath to the Commonwealth. Over a crackling radio link she said: 'I declare before you all that my whole life, whether it he long or short, shall be devoted to your service and the service of our great imperial family to which we all belong.'

The Empire is long gone and the institution she pledged her life to is no longer even the *British* Commonwealth, but simply the Commonwealth, a rag-tag body of independent nations whose links with the 'mother country' are ever-more tenuous. But the Queen has kept her vow. She has sat through countless state banquets and listened to corrupt dictators ramble on for hours; she has met more civic dignitaries than she can remember; she has opened so many factories, schools, hospitals and welfare centres that they merge into a grey blur. It is the mind-boggling boring routine of her reign, yet she has always managed to look interested and involved. She never complains. And the smile is still in place. It is as if the shadow of the old Queen Mary is forever louring over her, ordering her not to fidget, and to keep her hands out of her pockets with nothing more than the promise of a biscuit at the end of it.

'There will never he anyone like her again,' one of Elizabeth's senior ladies-in-waiting has observed.

She may very well be right, and that is a cause for worry where the the Monarchy is concerned. As one senior courtier has remarked: 'Will the Prince of Wales be able to carry it off?'

The Queen has privately admitted that she is sometimes 'mystified' by her son's interest in the metaphysical. Prince Philip, ever the sailor, called it a lack of a sense of reality. The one who harboured the greatest misgivings, however, was Princess Anne. Her brother, she has observed, has little understanding of everyday life. Something which shows in his lifestyle, which is grand in the extreme.

When the Waleses moved into Highgrove, Anne threw a party for them at her home at nearby Gatcombe so that they could meet 'the locals'. The Duke of Beaufort was among the fifty or so guests. So, inevitably, were Andrew and Camilla Parker Bowles. It was a black tie affair, but the dinner was a help-yourself buffet with dancing afterwards, and Anne did the cancan in the hall. Charles and Diana did not join in the merriment. While all around them were enjoying themselves, they sat stiffly on the sofa, hardly speaking to anyone. They left at 10.30 p.m., just as the party was getting underway. After they had gone, Anne remarked: 'I really resent that. My brother came to *my* house—and treated *my* party like an official engagement!'

The Queen and Prince Philip appreciated the informality of Gatcombe, and were always delighted to join in the rough-and-ready shoots Mark Phillips organized. Charles did not. One autumn when a guest had cancelled, and it was suggested that Charles be invited to take his place, Phillips said: 'No, that would never do. It's not smart enough here for Prince Charles.'

Such grandeur is not what is expected of the modern monarchy. For the production to work, feelings have to be contained, emotions suppressed—and dignity must never cross the line to haughtiness. Behaviour and tastes must be tailored to meet the requirements of an increasingly critical public. For any intelligent person the self-sacrifice involved is enormous. It may prove to be beyond Charles. It was certainly beyond his wife.

'After all I've done for this family . . .' Diana once remarked (expletives deleted). She was complaining about the way she felt she was being treated. But what she had done was not what the Queen would have wished—and most certainly not what she would ever have contemplated doing herself. By a great effort of will the Queen has kept to the course she set herself. While others fell by the moral wayside or took advantage of their royal positions, she soldiered on, avoiding so much as a breath of personal scandal.

But if her own life is without blemish, experience has given her an insight into the weaknesses of others and it was with compassion that she listened to her daughter-in-law as she gave tearful account for the umpteenth time of her troubles and fears. Diana made no mention of her own transgressions. Instead, she made endless complaint of Charles's behaviour. The Queen, aware of the broader picture, did what she always did and counselled patience. She told Diana: 'Just wait and see what happens.'

The implication of that remark was that, given time, everything would sort itself out. The Queen had misjudged the situation. The old maxims no longer applied. Diana had thrown away the rule book.

CHAPTER EIGHT

CRIES FOR HELP

Monarchy is not supposed to be a popularity contest. The Sovereign is not supposed to compete for attention. No one is meant to upstage the Crown even if, as is the case in a constitutional monarchy, the authority it represents is more symbolic than actual. It is there to be looked up to, and the system is as old as human history.

The precepts of the past were of little interest to Diana. History did not concern her. Had she not thrown away the books Oliver Everett had given her to help her understand her role as Princess of Wales? She needed attention in much the same way a drowning man needs air, and she pushed aside the restraints of both common sense and court protocols in her frantic attempts to get it.

She had demanded it of her husband,

sometimes to an embarrassing extent. One morning at Sandringham, early in their marriage, she had rushed out on to the forecourt as Charles was getting into his car. He was dressed in uniform and was on his way to one of the offical military luncheons which are the lot of his working life. She was in her nightdress.

The house party were just getting ready to go out for the day's shooting. They watched, stunned, as Diana wrenched at the car door and then threw herself, first on to the bonnet of the car, then finally on to the gravel, crying and pleading: 'If you love me you won't leave me, you won't go.'

Caught between a hysterical wife and his royal obligation, Charles chose the latter. He drove off, leaving the tearful Diana prostrate on the ground and his guests shuffling with discomfiture.

Diana later described such scenes as a desperate cry for help. Charles saw them in a different light. He had soon come to the conclusion that his wife's demands were illogical and impractical. There was also an element of jealousy in his thinking: as heir to the throne he had been brought up to be the centre of attention, and he did not like being upstaged—this was precisely what Diana had been doing almost from the first day of their marriage.

Diana said that Charles should have taken

pride in her achievements; that he should have encouraged her more and congratulated her on the way she was handling herself instead of cold-shouldering her successes. And so he should. But Diana also wanted him to be what she called 'a father figure' and that was not a role Charles was capable of performing for a young woman whose needs were so consuming. He also suspected that she was deliberately trying to poach his limelight. And so she was—and she did it brilliantly.

If stealing a husband's thunder was one thing, outshining the Queen was quite another, however. It ran against all constitutional precedents. But it gave Diana the attention she craved, and once she had discovered how easy it was, it became her modus operandi. By the end of her life it was possible to read through the calendar of forthcoming events, pick out the important ones and predict with near certainty that Diana would do or say something on the day which would guarantee her the headlines at the expense of anyone else, the Queen included.

The first occasion on which Diana exercised her fearsome media power was at the State Opening of Parliament in November 1984. This formal ritual is when the Sovereign, in full regalia, reads out the agenda for the new parliamentary session. It is when she exercises her theoretical political authority. Diana turned it into a photo opportunity.

When her hairdresser Kevin Shanley called at Kensington Palace that morning, she asked him to put her hair, which she had hitherto worn in her trademark peck-a-boo 'Shy Di' style, up into a classic chignon known as the Royal Roll. Shanley refused. 'I knew it wouldn't suit her—her hair wasn't long enough,' he explained.

Diana was insistent. 'I want my hair up. I really want my hair up for the State Opening of Parliament,' she said. Shanley was still unpersuaded—'It will make you look old,' he countered—and left it to his assistant Richard Dalton to carry out her instructions.

The style did not suit ('Di-saster' was one headline), but that was never the point. The next day it was Diana's new hairdo which dominated the front pages. The Queen, wearing the Imperial State Crown, was relegated to the subtext.

Prince Philip was incensed. 'It's the Queen's day, not yours,' he caustically informed his daughter-in-law afterwards.

Princess Margaret was equally irate and said to the Queen: 'How *could* you let her make such a *fool* of you?'

The Queen said and did nothing. Worried by Diana's fragile state of health, and wary of adding to her manifest problems by taking her to task for her behaviour, she preferred to give her daughter-in-law the benefit of the doubt. There was probably little that could have been done to make Diana toe a more settled line. Her actions were too impulsive, too unthought-out to be kept in check by a simple ticking-off. She reacted badly to criticism and would doubtless have taken any rebuke by the Queen as yet another instance of the family, whose ways she found so incomprehensible, ganging up against her. Yet by doing nothing, and allowing her to disregard the constraints of convention which keep the Monarchy in place, the Queen was unwittingly allowing her to establish a dangerous precedent.

*   *   *

The Eighties were not the best of times for the Queen. Society was changing rapidly, the old certainties were eroding and the Monarchy was finding itself increasingly out of step with the hopes and aspirations of a growing number of its subjects.

On the political front, the Queen continually found herself at loggerheads with her government over the question of the Commonwealth. As Princess Elizabeth, she had dedicated her life to the organization which had replaced the old empire (and to a large extent had been invented to disguise its passing). Throughout her reign she remained deeply committed to its welfare and concerned by the poverty of many of its members.

Her ministers took a more pragmatic view.

Prime Minister Edward Heath regarded most of its leaders with barely disguised contempt. So did Margaret Thatcher, and at one juncture the issue of South African sanctions, and the refusal of successive British governments to impose them, threatened to break up the organization.

The situation spilled over into controversy in July 1986 when the *Sunday Times*, in what it billed as an 'unprecedented disclosure of the Monarch's political views', carried the story that the Queen was profoundly troubled by the direction in which the country was headed. According to the *Sunday Times*, she regarded as 'uncaring, confrontational and divisive' Mrs Thatcher's radical reforms which threatened to undermine 'the consensus in British politics which she thinks has served the country well since the Second World War'. She was said to be disturbed at the state of race relations and inner city decay, to have objected to the way the bitter, year-long miners' strike of 1984 had been handled, and to the decision to allow American bombers to use British airbases to strike at Libya in 1986. Above all, she was 'concerned that nothing detracts from the Commonwealth'.

The source of this explosive insight into the Queen's purported thinking was revealed to be Michael Shea, her Gordonstoun-educated press secretary who promptly denied that she had ever said any such things. The Queen's private secretary, Sir William Heseltine, weighed in with a letter to *The Times* in which he stated that it was 'preposterous' to suggest that the Queen, after thirty-four years on the throne, would suddenly make such a dramatic departure from her policy of unbiased impartiality to go against the government of the day.

Nor would she have. As a previous prime minister, James Callaghan, observed: 'Prime ministers get a great deal of understanding of their problems—without the Queen sharing them, since she is outside politics.'

The Queen, he added, 'doesn't offer advice . . . she's pretty detached on all that.'

However, in answering the *Sunday Times*'s question,—'Is the Queen concerned about the Commonwealth?'—in the way he did—'The Queen is always concerned about the Commonwealth'—Shea had given flesh to the bones of speculation which surrounded the Sovereign's relations with her first woman prime minister.

Although they were the same age, the Queen had been brought up in comfort to enjoy the soft rhythms of the countryside, while Mrs Thatcher was born over a shop and had had to make her own way in life. She disliked the country, much preferring the adrenalin pump of Westminster to the driving rain of Balmoral, which she was always impatient to leave. Their differences carried through into politics: whereas the Queen believed wholeheartedly in compromise and concession, Mrs Thatcher was guided by the incandescent light of zeal which brooked no opposition.

There was never any personal animosity between the two, however. Mrs Thatcher was too deferential of the institution of monarchy (she always greeted the Queen with a deep curtsey of respect); the Queen too aware of her constitutional limitations, for either to allow their differences to come between a sovereign and her prime minister.

But for all the denials, Shea did work for the Queen. He saw her several times a week to discuss a wide range of issues. And while he could fairly claim that words had been put in his mouth, he had absorbed the Palace ethos which most definitely was not in tune with Mrs Thatcher's confrontational style of government.

The Court and its head had ample reason to be apprehensive. Mrs Thatcher was excavating the sand of post-war complacency without regard for the tremors that this sent through the institutions built on it. She disliked the Commonwealth and despised the established Church of England, both of which the Queen is head of.

Her assertiveness was controversial, and at times extremely painful for those caught in its blast but it reflected the mood of an electorate which had grown impatient of having their lives dictated by the conceptions which had seen Britain spiral into economic and political decline.

The Monarchy, wrapped in what one critic called its 'glamour of backwardness', could not escape the onslaught, and barbed questions started to be asked about the royal finances. The issue had been a rumbling complaint since the early Seventies, when a Select Committee appointed by Prime Minister Harold Wilson had issued a damning report on what it decided was regal extravagance. It concluded that the Crown's demand for more money 'represented the most insensitive and brazen pay claim made in the last two hundred years'.

By the time the report was issued, Wilson was out of power and the Heath government neatly swept its recommendations under the carpet of parliamentary procedure and upped the Queen's Civil List from £475,000 to £980,000 a year, with corresponding increases for the rest of her family. Inflation was no respecter of royal personages, however, and the Eighties were marked with endless unedifying arguments about money.

The crux of this problem was the fact that the Queen did not pay tax on the income from her substantial private fortune. This was no hallowed tradition protected by precedent (and such was the feeling at the time that it is unlikely to have made much difference, even if it had been). Queen Victoria had paid income tax, and in 1901 her successor Edward VII had been 'advised' by the government that he could not avoid his commitment to do the same.

No one likes handing over money to the revenue collectors, however, and when the Queen's grandfather George V came to the throne in 1910, the royal advisers took the initiative and got income tax removed from the Civil List, the movies paid by the government to maintain the Head of State in an appropriate style. In 1933 he got the same exemption on his income from the Duchy of Lancaster.

He did continue to pay tax on his income from his private investments, and this was deducted at source as most of it came from dividends on goverment stocks and company shares. After more backroom negotiations, the Treasury informed the Palace that because of his special position the King was allowed to reclaim such deductions. George V did not take up this concession; with the nation in the grip of the Great Depression and with millions unemployed, he kept his fiscal head down and continued to pay tax which by the end of his reign stood at 22.5 per cent in the pound.

His son was not so open handed. Within three weeks of coming to the Throne, George VI was asking if he had to pay any income tax at all. More secret talks were held and it was agreed with the government that he could reclaim the tax which was being deducted at source—and pay nothing at all on his other investments.

This remarkable arrangement, which placed the Crown beyond the laws which applied to ordinary people, was never publicly explained. Nor is it ever likely to be—in 1991 it was revealed that the key file which was listed at the Public Records Office had been 'withheld by the Treasury' and mysteriously destroyed in 1977.

In the early years of her reign, the Queen took full advantage of the deal and was able to add considerably to her private fortune without having to account to the tax authorities. In the obsequious Fifties this did not matter and anyone foolhardy enough to question this intriguing compact between the Sovereign and her government was accused of scabrous and, most probably, Communist-inspired disloyalty.

The cultural revolution of the Sixties had broken through that protective barrier. The aristocracy had come down off its gilded perch to mingle with rock stars from Liverpool and the suburbs of London; the gossip columnists were writing about a new breed of untitled celebrities; the military uniforms of the kind the royal family wore on state occasions had been turned into an iconoclastic fashion sold in the boutiques of Chelsea; the self-made started enjoying a kudos which had once been the prerequisite of the well-born, while successive Labour governments mounted a series of concerted assaults on inherited wealth which was represented as a social evil.

The royal family, forever marching several years behind social trends, had been typically slow to react and during the Eighties, found themselves buffeted by an increasingly acrimonious condemnation of their financial arrangements which was exacerbated by every review of the Civil List. In 1989, the American magazine *Fortune* estimated the Queen's personal fortune at £7 billion, which would have made her the fourth richest person in the world.

Her defenders tried to claim that most of her assets were not hers to dispose of (for example, Windsor Castle and Buckingham Palace), or were held in trust for the nation (the fabulous royal collection of pictures). Prince Charles weighed in and said: 'The royal family must have money. If they have to look to the state for everything, they become nothing more than puppets and prisoners in their own country.'

The Queen found an unexpected ally in Mrs Thatcher, who in 1990 took the Civil List out of the political arena by setting it at £7.9 million a year for the next decade, thereby avoiding the annual Budget Day rows. The argument over tax was not so easily quashed, however. Provocative headlines proclaimed that the Queen's exemption was costing the

Exchequer £200 million a year, 'enough for a dozen hospitals'. In 1989, when Britain was again in recession with an unemployment figure rivalling that of the Thirties, the *People* declared: 'The chill wind of recession won't be blowing under the carpets of Buckingham Palace, not when you're saving more than £256 million on tax!'

When, two years later, the Palace leaked the story that if the Queen had to pay tax she would be forced to sell Balmoral because she would no longer be able to afford the upkeep of £1 million a year, the claim was greeted with derision. Whichever way you looked at it and regardless of the figures being bandied around, the Queen was a very rich woman indeed with a private fortune which Philip Hall, who had made a detailed study of the subject, put at £341 million. It was a long way short of £7 billion, but still quite enough to pay for the upkeep of her private Scottish castle out of the interest alone, with plenty left over. If the Queen couldn't make ends meet, the general feeling was that it was her own fault and it was high time she got her house in order.

The royal family finally bowed to the inevitable in 1993, when the Queen 'voluntarily' agreed to pay tax. It was in fact a resounding defeat for the old guard and the old order. Her accountant, Michael Peat of KPMG Peat Marwick, acknowledged as much when he said: 'The Queen is a very pragmatic person. She appreciates that there is a general feeling that she should pay tax.'

It wasn't just money which accounted for this striking swing in public opinion against a reigning house which only a few years earlier had been so venerated. It was a symptom of a deeper disquiet at the way the royal family was managing its affairs and, specifically, at the increasingly erratic behaviour of the 'young' royals whose conduct was deemed most unbecoming.

Bagehot had cautioned that 'a *family* on the throne . . . brings down the pride of sovereignty to the level of petty life.' It went a lot lower than this and came to resemble the kind of television serial Diana was so addicted to, embracing all the classic features of the genre—extravagance, malice, feuds, immorality, infidelity.

'The media have turned us into a soap opera,' Prince Philip complained.

In blaming the press, the Prince was attempting to avoid the altogether more unpalatable truth that it was his own children and their respective spouses and assorted partners who were the instigators of the damage.

*   *   *

It was shortly after Diana and Charles's marriage that the carefully woven image of a decorous family united by a sense of duty began to unravel. Diana's shopping sprees were soon provoking unfavourable comment, and within a few months the first rumours that all was not as it should be between the Prince and his young bride started to leak out.

Next it was Prince Andrew's turn. He fought with distinction in the Falklands conflict and in so doing had stirred the envy of his elder brother, who regretfully admitted: 'I never had that chance to test myself. It is terribly important to see how you react, to be tested.'

Shortly after Andrew's return to a hero's welcome at Portsmouth it was revealed that he was involved with a beautiful American actress named Koo Stark. Andrew took her up to Balmoral and introduced her to his mother who took to her immediately. Quiet, demure and with an ability to make polite conversation with just about anyone, she would sit for hours chatting to the Queen. Diana called her 'sweet Koo' and said she 'adored' her. Princess Margaret, who was inclined to be offhand with people she did not know or who failed to amuse her, called her 'one of the nicest girls I have ever met'.

In addition, she also appeared to be truly in love in a simple, uncomplicated way with the Prince the Canadians had dubbed Randy Andy. A mutual friend recalled: 'She could talk him out of his moods. She never shouted at him, never tried to bully him. She treated him very gently and that worked.' In that she was very different to Diana. Unlike the Princess, however, Koo was a woman with what Lord Mountbatten would have called 'a past'. She had appeared in a titillating film made by the Earl of Pembroke entitled *The Adventures of Emily*. In it, she had revealed enough of her body to be labelled a 'soft porn actress' and this was no recommendation on the CV of a prospective wife for the son of a Queen. The couple tried to brazen it out and went on holiday together to Mustique, only to find themselves besieged by pursuing photographers. The romance fizzled out under Palace pressure and Andrew retreated to Barbados—into the even less suitable arms of Vicki Hodge.

The daughter of a baronet and the sister-in-law of press magnate Lord Beaverbrook's grandson, Vicki had been a successful model in the Sixties. Even by the standards of that uninhibited decade, Vicki was a wild one whose amours had included Ringo Starr and George Lazenby, who played James Bond in *On Her Majesty's Secret Service*. Her fling with Prince Andrew under a palm tree on the edge of a Caribbean beach made fascinating reading and Vicki, never one to hide the light of her sexual exploits under a bushel of discretion, made sure that millions did read, by telling all to a Sunday newspaper (and she would have told a lot more if her hair-raising memoirs had ever found a publisher).

In the company of friends and family Andrew can be rather dull. 'Solid, unexciting, easily bored, doesn't like a row, sometimes a little too grand', is how one of his best friends described him. By his choice of a 'soft porn actress' and a Sixties playgirl, however, he had forged an impression of himself as a latter-day Errol Flynn with a title. The Queen was displeased. She once said she liked a good gossip, but not if it was about her own family. With his wife's agreement, Philip sternly informed his son that this was no way for a prince of the blood to be carrying on. The royal family, he said, had to remember their position and look to their duty. That should have been axiomatic but the message was no longer getting through to some of them.

*   *   *

Like Charles and Andrew before him, it was decided that the Queen's youngest son should follow his brothers into the military. Edward opted for the Royal Marines. It was not a fortuitous choice. As Edward's commanding officer Major Ewen Southby-Tailyour observed, 'In the Navy, the Army and the Air Force there are areas where a royal prince cannot serve, but he can easily pass those by with no stigma whatsoever. But there are no gaps in the Royal Marines career structure through which a royal prince can pass without comment.'

The Marines are a crack fighting unit, and when Edward joined there had only been one year since the end of the Second World War when they had not been on active duty somewhere in the world. And that, said Colonel Ian Moore, the commanding officer at the Commando Training Centre at Lympstone in Devon where Edward went for training, 'is something we pride ourselves on'.

As a prince, however, it would have been impossible for Edward to serve in Northern Ireland. He may also have been excluded from action elsewhere. Even on basic training he had a detective with him, which irritated his contemporaries who gruffly pointed out that the Prince was never going to be safer than when he was surrounded by armed marines. The Queen's advisers were not persuaded and insisted that his Police Protection Officer accompany him everywhere. When Edward came to realize that, no matter how hard he tried, he was never going to be a wholly integrated member of what is a very small corps of some 7,000 men, his enthusiasm started to 'wobble', as the marines put it.

There were those in the Marines who had queried whether the Prince was 'heterosexual enough' for the force. His senior officers, however, were of the firm opinion that he had the physical and the mental qualities to make a first-class officer. He was never put to that test. In January 1986, Edward quit before he had completed his training. He told me: 'Maybe I was becoming too aware of myself, or maybe people were becoming too aware of who I was, but it was getting more and more difficult and I didn't see really the way it was going to work. I was never going to fit very neatly in the way I had envisaged it and that, more than anything, decided me.'

His sister Anne had spent the Christmas break trying to make him change his mind, thought she had, and nearly drove her car into a ditch when she heard the announcement a few days later on the radio.

Prince Philip took it in his stride. Adam Wise, Edward's former private secretary, said: 'The first person he went to when he really had had enough of the Marines was Prince Philip, and he was extremely understanding about the whole thing. He was very reasonable and gave him very sensible advice. He did not get on his high horse at all.'

The Queen Mother, on the other hand, was angered. So was the Queen. To their way of thinking, Edward's decision to walk out on the Marines smacked of dereliction of duty, an unconscionable offence. Edward told me that all his family were supportive. According to members of the household, the Queen was icy-cold with her son for some time afterwards.

The Queen's displeasure was based on

sound reasoning. As Bagehot had written and she had read, placing a 'family on the throne' required the exemplary behaviour of all concerned. This, he argued, was a burden which took little account of the vagaries of human nature and should therefore be treated with caution. 'We have come to believe,' he wrote, 'that it is natural to have a virtuous sovereign . . . but a little experience and less thought show that royalty cannot take credit for domestic excellence.'

It was a warning that had been wilfully ignored for the better part of the century. As Prince Philip said, 'Monarchy involves the whole family, which means that different age groups are part of it. There are people who can look, for instance, at the Queen Mother and identify with that generation, or with us, or with our children.'

This was all very well, provided everyone was on their best behaviour. Should any member fail to live up to expectations, however, everyone else was affected by the fall-out. And when that happened Philip's own definition started sounding more like a television producer's outline for a soap opera than the blueprint for a modern monarchy.

It had taken great courage on Edward's part to resign from the Marines, and opinion polls suggested that most people were sympathetic. No matter what gloss the Palace tried to apply to events, however, large cracks were appearing in the royal edifice. Philip was Captain-General of the Royal Marines and it did not reflect well that his son lacked the commitment to join the force his own father was honorary head of. Once the masters of appearances, it was unavoidable that the royal family should be judged by them when they slipped.

*   *   *

The situation looked to have taken an upturn for the better when Prince Andrew, his wild oats sown, married Sarah Ferguson in the summer of 1986. Weddings were what the royal family did best, and in Sarah they appeared to have acquired a vibrant new member.

Her maternal grandmother was a cousin of the wife of the Queen's uncle, the Duke of Gloucester, and the genealogists worked out that she could trace her ancestry back to King Charles II. Like Diana, Sarah was related to the Queen's private secretary, Sir Robert Fellowes. Diana's brother, Charles, added an extra twist by claiming that her father, Major Ronald, had once proposed marriage to his mother, Mrs Shand Kydd ('Utter rubbish,' the Major retorted. The Major did hint, though, that Prince Philip had once been closer to Sarah's mother, Susan Barrantes, than he considered proper).

It was her exuberance rather than her spurious royal connections which made Fergie, as she became known, such an enchanting prospect. Here was a modern career girl (she had worked in PR) who knew something of the world (she had spent time in South America and had lived in Switzerland). The fact that she had what was still called 'a past' did not count against her; in the five years since Diana had married, the royal family had gone some way towards catching up with the change in social mores. Instead of being regarded as a blemish, her relationship with the millionaire motor racing impresario Paddy McNally was seen as an advantage; she was a mature woman of experience who knew her own mind and wouldn't be crushed by the Palace system. Or so the thinking went.

On top of that, she got on very well with the Queen and took enthusiastic delight in her royal ' role. Diana, trapped in a web of depression, was overawed and remarked: 'The energy of this creature is unbelievable.'

Diana had known Fergic since adolescence. Their mothers had been at school together, and in the year leading up to Diana's wedding they met for lunch every week or so. Without a deep pool of friends to draw from, Diana had invited Sarah to the wedding and given her a seat in St Paul's Cathedral. They had continued to see each other afterwards, and it was Diana who had engineered the romance between Sarah and her brother-in-law.

In the summer of 1985 the Queen had asked Diana whom of her friends she would like to invite to the annual Ascot house party at Windsor. Diana had put Sarah's name forward, and a heavy envelope bearing the Buckingham Palace postmark and containing the invitation written by Lieutenant-Colonel Blair Stewart-Wilson, Deputy Master of the Royal Household, was duly delivered to the extremely modest apartment in Clapham, south London, which Fergie shared with a girlfriend. She accepted, and was driven to the castle on the appropriate day by McNally, whose own relationship with Sarah was almost at an end.

She was seated next to Andrew at luncheon. She already knew him from childhood and, on a different level, from a weekend they had spent recently at Floors Castle, the Duke of Roxburghe's home on the Scottish borders, where they had bumped into each other at the breakfast buffet and she had impulsively kissed him on the cheek. The Prince was not slow on the uptake, Sarah was quick to respond, and by the end of Ascot week the couple had become extremely close.

Afterwards, Fergie went back to McNally and spent much of the summer in Ibiza with her old gang of friends. With Diana's connivance, however, Andrew kept in touch. She teased him and egged him on and reported what he said back to Fergie. Flowers were sent to Clapham and Fergie paid secret visits to the Palace when Andrew was on leave from his naval duties. She was invited to spend New Year with the royal family at Sandringham.

The Queen Mother had liked her at once. 'She is so English,' she said, and, in deliberate contradiction of Mountbatten's injunction against any princely involvement with a woman of experience, declared that any modern 26-year-old was bound to have had previous boyfriends, that it was only natural, and that Sarah and Andrew were ideal for each other.

Prince Philip went so far as to declare: 'I think Sarah will be a great asset.'

Prince Charles agreed. He said: 'I think she'll be a great asset to Andrew and the rest of us.'

Andrew proposed on bended knee the following February when the couple were once more the guests of the Duke and Duchess of Roxburghe at Floors. He informed his mother on her return from a tour of Australia and New Zealand. She was, he said, 'overjoyed. Very pleased, and beyond that what else is there? Just that of a delighted parent'. Andrew had always been her favourite, and she felt that in Fergie he had found someone who suited him well.

As far as the tens of thousands lining the

streets around Westminster Abbey and the millions more watching on television could see, the wedding on 23 July was a royal triumph. It was a typically lavish royal production involving the full panoply of gilded carriages and soldiers and flags and parades, bishops and princes, and a spectacular bridal gown. To the critical eye of the Queen, however, all was not quite as it should have been.

'Did you see William?' Diana asked afterwards. 'I'm glad he behaved himself because he can be a bit of a prankster. It was terribly hot in the Abbey, but he did very well considering he is only four.'

In fact he had fidgeted and jiggled right from the start. Dressed in his page boy sailor outfit, he had tried to outpace the bride and almost tripped over her 17½-foot train. Halfway through the ceremony boredom had set in, and after an enormous yawn which he didn't cover, he began fiddling with his hat cord, scratching his head and fingering the mini knife which was fortuitously firmly sewn into his outfit. By the time he left the Abbey, his hat was hanging off the back of his head.

The Queen was not amused. William was only four, but as far as she was concerned, that was no excuse. As a child of three she had had her pocket sewn up to stop her fiddling. Yet here was her grandson behaving like an ill-disciplined street urchin. So worried was she by his behaviour, that before the ceremony the Palace had 'requested' that the BBC cameras did not dwell on the antics of William.

Diana, the Queen had concluded, was an over-indulgent mother. Afterwards, in a rare break from her policy of non-interference, she sternly informed Charles and Diana that their son's conduct simply wasn't up to the standards expected of a boy who would one day be king.

She had another, more substantive cause for concern. By then it had become patently clear to everyone in the household that the Waleses' marriage was in serious trouble. Both were seeking comfort elsewhere and Diana was still racked by bulimia and prone to bouts of hysteria.

In the autumn of 1984, Diana had written to a friend from Balmoral: 'Depression is a disease like cancer—only in so many ways worse because it so so often misunderstood and the battle against it is so lonely.'

It was loneliness of the mind. Imprisoned in her own despondency, she claimed that no one understood her or did anything to assist. But that is not the way her royal relations, with whom she spent so much time, remembered it. 'We all went out of our way to be as friendly and helpful to her as we could, certainly at the beginning,' one member of the family recalled.

Such is the nature of Borderline Personality Disorder, that it had proved all but impossible to get through Diana's defences. The doctors who attended her included the Jungian psychotherapist and friend of van der Post, Dr Allan McGlashan, who had concentrated on analysing her dreams; David Mitchell who had concentrated on her relationship with her husband; and Maurice Lipsedge of Guy's Hospital in London who tried to treat her bulimia. None of them was able to offer an optimistic prognosis, and the pills they fed her did little more than dampen down the symptoms without getting to its root cause. Words of comfort from the Queen did not make any difference and the family gatherings which had been the highlight of the Queen's calendar had become fraught with tension.

It was to Fergie that the Queen now looked for support in dealing with a troubled woman whose difficulties had slipped beyond the reach of the royal family. She was hopeful that Diana would respond to a friend of her own age who was now also a member of the family, and therefore one with whom she would be able to share her problems. Fergie might provide her with the companionship she was always complaining she didn't have. She told members of the household that she believed Fergie would be 'good' for Diana.

The Queen got that prediction totally wrong. Instead of aiding each other, they goaded each other on.

The high jinks started a week before the

wedding on the night of Andrew's stag party. With the prince out of the way, Sarah and Diana went to the Belgravia home of the Duchess of Roxburghe for a picnic feast of smoked chicken, honey-glazed ham and cold beef, to be followed by strawberries and cream. They were joined by Sarah's friend, Jules Dodd-Noble, and Catherine Soames, the then wife of Sir Winston Churchill's grandson, Nicholas.

Their humour enhanced by lashings of champagne, they decided to try and disrupt the dinner at Aubrey House in Holland Park where Andrew's guests included the Prince of Wales, comedian Billy Connolly, singer Elton John and the television presenter David Frost.

But how to gain entrance? The answer was provided by Connolly's wife, Pamela Stephenson, who arrived after supper with Elton's wife Renate, dressed in a policewoman's uniform, complete down to regulation lace-up shoes. They had brought two spare uniforms and, amidst a great deal of giggling, Sarah and Diana put them on.

At 10.30 p.m. they set out. Having decided that Aubrey House was impregnable (it had only one gate which was guarded by real policemen), they headed off to Annabel's in Berkeley Square, where they installed themselves in the outer bar and ordered a round of drinks as if it was the most natural thing for four giggling policewomen to do.

One reveller offered to buy them a glass of champagne and orange juice. 'I don't drink on duty,' the Princess of Wales replied.

An American came up to the Princess and said: 'Gee, you policewomen—I suppose you're here because of the IRA.'

The joke over, Diana headed back up the stairs and waddled across the street in a Charlie Chaplin walk to her waiting car.

Twenty-four hours later the story was on the front pages of the newspapers. The Queen was aghast. She demanded to know what on earth the future Queen of England thought she was doing, disguising herself as a policewoman and going into a nightclub. Diana said she didn't think that she had done anything wrong, that she was simply having a little bit of innocent fun.

In matters of royal behaviour the Queen's views still carried great weight, but only when she elected to exert it. Instead of admonishing Diana, she accepted her excuse and put the incident down to youthful high spirits, thereby sacrificing another opportunity to the misguided belief that, given time, Diana would eventually come into line.

This was where the Queen wanted Fergie to come in. As the older and presumably wiser of the two, she was supposed to set an example. She did, but not of the kind the Queen would have wished.

For all her undoubted qualities, Fergie had

two flaws. One was avarice; the other was a heart that easily wandered. Together they would ruin her reputation and destroy her marriage.

The household had at first been delighted at the way she had settled in at Buckingham Palace where she had made a welcome contrast to the Princess of Wales. Diana had spent her early days there moping around the corridors or eating herself sick. She rarely entertained, and the cooks placed at her disposal complained that they had nothing to do. Fergie was the complete opposite. Every day friends were invited in to eat the excellent food brought up from the kitchens and drink the champagne and wines that came with it. 'It was a party almost every day,' one of the household recalled.

When she wasn't doing the entertaining herself, she would join the Queen in her first-floor dining room for lunch and an hour's amiable chat.

It wasn't long, however, before the household noticed the first signs of what they called 'red carpet fever'. The trappings of royalty are immense but the trick which those born into the purple had been taught from childhood was to treat them as part of the natural order, to be used only when needed. Fergie revelled in them. She gave the impression that she couldn't get enough of everything and anything that was suddenly on offer and the truth was she couldn't.

Despite their well-born connections, the Fergusons were not particularly well-off. Sarah's father, Major Ronald, had a farm in Hampshire, but it never showed any great profit. The allowance he gave his daughter was, he told me, 'a very small one', and as a young woman Sarah was very much dependent on her own modest wages or the generosity of whichever boyfriend she happened to be with. This put her at a distinct disadvantage in the fast moving set she had fallen in with when she moved to Switzerland to work as a chalet girl and, later, as a nanny. She was competing there against other girls, some a lot richer and many a great deal prettier. Her personality, combined with eager-to-please willingness to take on the chores others shunned, partly made up for that. When it came to jewellery and clothes, however, Sarah was always the poor relation.

Now she was a Royal Highness, to be addressed as 'ma'am' by the people who had regarded her with indifference, with access to a treasure trove of 'goodies', as she called them, and which she began flaunting with mindless ostentation.

'It was champagne all the way with Fergie,' one member of the household remembered. It led, not to the admiration she wanted, but into the cul-de-sac of condemnation. She was ridiculed for her dress sense, admonished for her spending sprees, attacked for the way she availed herself of every free first-class airline flight to any trashy jet-set gathering.

The uninhibited heartiness which had made such a refreshing change from the musty reserve of her in-laws started looking like boorishness. On a tour of the United States, an onlooker shouted, 'We love you, Fergie.' Sarah shouted back, 'I'll see you later.' The Americans loved it; the Palace cringed. The *Sunday Times* described her as 'an international embarrassment'. The Queen's former private secretary, Martin Charteris, called her 'vulgar'.

Major Ferguson blamed her husband for allowing his daughter to career off the tracks. 'To a certain extent becoming Duchess of York did go to her head,' he admitted. 'She didn't read the rule book properly. In the royal family certain privileges are there for the taking but there have to be limits.' Andrew, he said, 'should have been strong enough to guide and advise her'.

Fergie blamed the Palace. Like Diana before her, she accused them of not giving her the support she felt she deserved. What she got instead, she complained, was sarcastic comments. She told me how her first cousin, Sir Robert Fellowes, would call by her apartment in what had been Andrew's bachelor quarters, wave the day's press clippings at her and say, 'We haven't done very well this morning, have we, ma'am?'

Fellowes's exasperation was understandable. It was his job to act as the liaison between the Sovereign and her government, to advise on matters of policy and ensure that the Queen's schedule was precisely organized. Instead, he found himself having to spend more and more time trying to deal with two wayward women, both of whom he was closely related to, who had scant regard for the demands of their respective positions. His attempts to enforce some kind of order usually came to nothing; whenever he issued an instruction, they went behind his back to the Queen who almost invariably gave in to their demands.

Driven to distraction, Fellowes sometimes lost his temper. Fergie nicknamed him Bellows. Diana started calling him that, too. It was a joke they shared before Sarah became one herself and the Princess started distancing herself from her sister-in-law.

The split, when it came, was all but inevitable. They had been friends but in the closed world they had married into they soon came to see each other as rivals.

When Fergie was first married, Charles had compared her with Diana and found his wife wanting. 'Why can't you be more like Fergie?' he asked of Diana. 'Why can't you be more jolly?' It was not a kind question, but by the mid-Eighties, whatever empathy had existed between the couple had been eroded on the

271

grindstone of argument. It was enough to sow the seeds of resentment. 'I got terribly jealous and she got jealous of me,' Diana admitted. Always in need of attention, she was irritated by the coverage Fergie attracted, even when it was bad.

The reaction to *It's a Royal Knockout* in 1987 was certainly that. The brainchild of Prince Edward, it involved Fergie, Prince Andrew and Princess Anne in a maniacal television game where the contestants battled each other with giant whoopee cushions and rode ice cream cartons over models of the Victoria Falls.

Diana had wanted to take part, and was furious when Charles for once put his foot down and insisted she stay home with the children. She complained that he was trying to dominate her and another furious argument ensued. What he was actually doing was saving her from making an utter fool of herself on a programme which did untold damage to the Monarchy.

The royal family had never quite come to terms with the power of television or appreciated its need to reduce its subject matter to the level of a sound bite. When Prince Philip agreed in 1969 to open the royal doors for the landmark documentary, *The Royal Family*, David Attenborough, the distinguished maker of wildlife programmes, told its producer-director, Richard Cawston: 'You're killing the

Monarchy, you know, with this film you're making. The whole institution depends on mystique and the tribal chief in his hut. If any member of the tribe ever sees inside the hut, then the whole of system of the tribal chiefdom is damaged and the tribe eventually disintegrates.'

It was a warning which was ignored, and in retrospect the programme came to be seen to have given fateful encouragement to exactly the kind of intrusive interest in their lives which the royal family were at such pains to avoid. But if the consequences were dire, the programme was at least of a quality befitting its subject. The same could not be said of *It's a Royal Knockout.* This was mass televison at its most trivial which reduced what has been called the royal 'pageant of virtue' to the level of slapstick. The four royals each led a team of such celebrities as the *Carry On* actress Barbara Windsor, Superman actor Christopher Reeve, rock singer Meat Loaf and John Travolta.

Princess Anne managed to keep her dignity. The others did not. Fergie disported herself with all the grace of a braying donkey; Prince Andrew grinned inanely; Prince Edward was dressed as a medieval joker in yellow tights which made him look, as *The Times* drolly remarked, 'like one of Shakespeare's lesser jesters'.

It was one of the kinder remarks. Andrew

273

Morton, who was covering the filming at the Alton Towers amusement park for the *Star* newspaper said: 'We were just observers at the royal family's self-destruction.' Morton would soon make his own contribution to that process, but Edward certainly gave it a mighty push.

That is not something the Prince cared to dwell on, however. When I mentioned it to him some years later and called it 'disastrous', he rounded on me. 'It wasn't disastrous,' he insisted. 'How can you call something "disastrous" that raised over a million pounds for charity and is still raising money?'

The Queen Mother did not share her grandson's opinions. She was incensed by the programme and afterwards called in Andrew, Edward and Anne and told them: 'The King (George VI) and I spent years building up the reputation of the Monarchy and you, in one evening, destroy it.'

The Queen was just as upset. As her confidant, the Right Reverend Michael Mann, former Dean of Windsor, explained: 'For the best reasons in the world the younger members of the royal family wanted to make the Monarchy more approachable. I think the supreme example of that was when they all participated in *It's a Knockout*. It was making it a soap opera.'

It was certainly not a production the Queen wished to star in, but she had allowed the business of the Monarchy to slip out of her control. She was still the Sovereign, but she no longer commanded the stage. It had been taken over by younger players who had dispensed with the dowdy rituals of the past to create a crowd-pulling, free-flowing show full of tantalizing sub-plots and laden with gaudy passion. And it was Diana who now had the limelight.

CHAPTER NINE

ANNUS HORRIBILIS

Nothing in her life had prepared the Queen for the troubles which overwhelmed her family in the years leading up to the denouement of her *annus horribilis.*

She had dealt with bereavements, the suicide threats her sister had made during the breakdown of her marriage to Tony Armstrong-Jones, and her husband's alleged infidelities. She had sat in counsel with nine prime ministers and visited most of the world's countries. Over the span of half a century she had met nearly all the great leaders of the age, some good, many bad, a few utterly deranged, and handled them all with grace and finesse.

In that time she had shown herself to be a woman of will determined to carry out her duties in her own way and according to her own beliefs. She had seen the power of the Monarchy eroded, but had steadfastly maintained her personal authority. When in 1961, the British government, concerned for her safety, had tried to prevent her visiting Ghana, she had exerted her prerogative so forcefully that Prime Minister Harold Macmillan wrote nervously in his diary: 'If she is pressed too hard and if the Government and people here are determined to restrict her activities (including taking reasonably acceptable risks), I think she might be tempted to throw in her hand.' Faced with what he interpreted as the hint of abdication, Macmillan promptly backed down and the Queen went to West Africa.

'She means to be a Queen and not a puppet,' Macmillan noted.

She was just as quick to put Prime Minister Tony Blair in his place when, on a visit to Balmoral in 1999, he said to his sovereign that, with only three years to go, it was time to start making plans 'for the Golden Jubilee'. The Queen interpreted this as an attempt to hijack the arrangements. She sternly reminded him: '*My* Golden Jubilee, Mr Blair.'

She was also physically brave. When, at Trooping the Colour in 1981, someone had fired blank shots at her, she calmly continued with the ceremony and appeared unaffected by it (unlike Prince Charles, who was ashen-faced at the drinks in the Palace afterwards).

In person she is small and reticent, polite and, at first sight, unimposing. But she exudes what can best be called majesty, and when her staff go to see her they talk about going into 'The Presence'. It is an apt description, for in her presence even diehard republicans find themselves tongue-tied by atavistic deference. No one shouts at the Queen.

There was one person she never learnt to handle, however. That was Diana. Neither patience nor the silent, steely eyed displeasure she had learnt to deploy with such withering effect made any impression. Princess Michael of Kent called Diana 'the Media Queen' and warned, 'She's a time bomb.'

Eventually the Queen came to fear her daughter-in-law. 'The Queen was petrified of Diana. Not as a person, but because of her popularity. She wanted to do something about her but couldn't. She was trapped by Diana's popularity,' observed a member of the household.

In public, the Princess presented a captivating image of beauty and compassion. She was the only member of the royal family who could kneel down to comfort a sick child and look as if she meant it. And so she did. Her sympathy for the ill and troubled was genuine, and it plainly showed.

'I understand people's suffering, people's pain more than you will ever know,' she told the Bishop of Norwich.

The Bishop said, 'That's obvious by what you are doing for Aids.' Diana replied: 'It's not only Aids—it is anyone who suffers. I can smell them a mile away.'

Her stepmother, Raine Spencer, whose relationship with Diana was sometimes fraught to the point of violence, acknowledged her qualities. She once told me: 'I don't think Diana would have been so wonderful if she had not been so unhappy herself. It enabled her to relate to people.'

Simone Simmons, an 'energy healer' who was one of the Princess's many alternative therapists, agreed with Raine's analysis. 'Through memory of her own pain and suffering Diana was able genuinely to empathize with the trials and wounds of others. There was nothing artificial about these concerns, and those who have suggested that she had set out to sanctify herself were mistaken. No one forced her to work as hard as she did for her charities, and much of this work was accomplished privately.'

This public image did not always mirror the Diana who now arrived with such regularity in the Queen's Buckingham Palace sitting room. As the threads of her marriage started to unravel, the Princess became an ever-more frequent visitor, turning up on whim and often without an advance telephone call to say she was on her way.

The Queen subscribed to Louis XIV's maxim that punctuality is the politeness of princes, and followed it rigidly. When her private secretary Martin Charteris came for his prospective job interview in 1950 while she was still Princess Elizabeth, he arrived ten minutes early. At 11.20 a.m. her Treasurer, General 'Boy' Browning, said: 'The Princess is not very busy this morning and I am sure she will see you now.' He rang through on the internal telephone to announce Charteris. The Princess replied: 'I said 11.30'—and hung up. The rules had been established from the outset.

The mercurial Diana lacked her mother-in-law's sense of timing and would turn up at whim at the study door. If the Queen was in a meeting, she would be made to wait outside in the Page's Vestibule for up to half an hour, often in floods of tears.

Once she was ushered in, Diana would run through her stock list of grievances. A member of the Palace staff ticked them off: 'That no one understood her, that everyone else was to blame, that she was being victimized'.

The Queen kept careful note of these encounters. She prides herself on her excellent memory and can usually recall a date or event precisely. But if unsure, she has her diary to refer to which she keeps locked in her desk. She once admitted to a group of American students: 'My husband reads in bed and so does Prince Charles. But I write in my diary—and it's far more truthful than anything you'll ever read in the newspapers.'

In it she noted that the pleadings which had marked Diana's earlier meetings had come to be replaced by more strident protests. Her brother-in-law, Sir Robert Fellowes, was a particular target. Diana had demonized him in her imagination and she described him to me thus:—'He's absolutely dreadful, he's so pompous, he's a bully and he's insecure.' She told a member of the royal staff: 'He's a traitor.'

Fellowes had shown the ruthless side of his character in his dealings with Fergie. Diana was different. She was the wife of the Prince of Wales and the mother of a future king, and in ministering to his sister-in-law he was required by Court protocol to take his lead from the Queen—and the Queen was not giving one.

'She just procrastinated,' said a member of the household. 'She listened to what Diana had to say but no solution was ever put forward.'

The Queen came to dread these meetings with her daughter-inlaw. They left her feeling drained and despondent and confused—an uncommon state for a woman accustomed to the certainties of her position. After one especially upsetting session one of her footmen said, 'The Princess seemed very upset and cried three times in half an hour while she was waiting to see you.' With weary resignation the Queen replied: 'I had her for an hour— and she cried non-stop.'

Faced with a situation that was slipping out of her control, the Queen retreated from the problem and started seeing less of Diana. Diana chose to interpret this as jealousy. 'I was a threat, wasn't I,' she said. It wasn't a question, more an indication of how she was coming to view her importance to the royal family—and of the power that gave her.

In fact, the Queen rather admired Diana's ability to cut through the red-tape and communicate with ordinary people in a direct and intimate way. What she did not appreciate was the way the Princess used her gift as a ploy in the increasingly hostile press war she was conducting against her husband. She also objected to her vehement criticism of Charles's talents and abilities. And with good reason— no mother likes to hear her son disparaged, and most certainly not by a wife who, according to the Queen's way of thinking, should have made it her duty to provide Charles with support and encouragement.

Diana had promised to do just that, in an interview with Sir Alastair Burnett broadcast on ITV in 1985. Her most important role, she told an audience of 20 million people, is 'supporting my husband whenever I can and always being behind him and also, most important, being a mother and a wife'.

That was not what she was telling the Queen in their private meetings. Charles, Diana kept saying, was letting down the Monarchy.

Another thing she said on television which ran contrary to the darker reality was that she never quarrelled with her husband. Asked if they had disagreements, Charles had replied, 'I suspect that most husbands and wives find they often have arguments.'

'But we don't,' Diana interjected.

'Occasionally we do,' Charles insisted.

'No, we don't,' Diana contradicted.

But they did, and as the Eighties progressed, those rows became ever-more vicious, as the Queen well knew. Charles had tried to involve Diana in his interests and the year after his marriage, had brought in Eric Anderson to give Diana a weekly lesson in Shakespeare and English poetry. For once Anderson's didactic skills failed to enthuse his pupil and the sessions ended after less than six months.

Diana was never embarrassed by her lack of knowledge, and on the contrary, turned it into a weapon. At one dinner party Charles had started talking about Rudyard Kipling's *Just So* stories. Growing bored, Diana interrupted: 'Just so what, Charles?'

When he invited people to Kensington Palace to discuss architecture or whatever else had taken his often flighty interest, Diana would refuse to join in. 'She couldn't understand the requirement of duty, that you had to be sitting next to an architect or a don, and that you had to prepare yourself for it,' observed Michael Colborne. Instead, she would leave and go and have dinner with a girlfriend.

The traffic of put-downs, insults and growing indifference was not one way. Charles's insistence on following his own routine took no account of his young wife's interests. He disliked nightclubs and restaurants and dancing and popular music, and refused to participate in the kind of social whirl she was so keen to be a part of. Charles had described himself to Alastair Burnett as an 'ancient old thing'. When her temper was up, which it frequently was, Diana called him 'an old fart'. Each in their own way failed to come to terms with the other, and their incompatibility became a cancer. Their relationship soon slid into a sterile void of long, stony silences punctuated by sudden flares of temper and accusation.

The main battleground was Highgrove. In public, they still just about managed to keep up appearances. The pretence could be quite disconcerting. In 1991, I helped organize a polo match to raise money for the Gulf Trust and the Kuwaiti and British Women's Support group which was staged at the Royal Berkshire Polo Club where Major Ronald Ferguson was then based. The game was between two teams of Desert Rats. Prince Charles was on one side, Major Hewitt on the other. It was fiercely contested and the headlines were predictable. One read: 'Charles and rival in a polo ding-dong.' Unlucky in love, the Prince was equally unfortunate on the playing field—his side lost 4–1. But Charles gave his best and kept his cool.

Diana was equally phlegmatic. If, in the middle of a row, a secretary or an equerry would come and tell them it was time to leave for an official engagegment, Diana would say, 'Come along, Charles, people are waiting for us,' and out they would go, smiling for the cameras, occasionally bracing themselves to exchange a kiss. Once back in their Gloucestershire home, however, they could barely bring themselves to exchange a civil word.

Diana had never liked the house. 'It's always raining there,' she griped. She quickly decided that she didn't much like her husband, either, much to the horror of the staff who could not help but overhear their fights. When Charles went out to tend the plants in the garden on which he heaped so much attention (and to which he had once admitted he liked to talk), Diana would say: 'Who is getting the benefit of your wisdom today? The sheep, or the raspberry bushes?' If some new photograph of Diana appeared on the front pages of the morning papers, Charles would sarcastically observe: 'Quite the fashion model, aren't you?'

On one occasion, Diana started throwing crockery. On another, Charles jumped up and down as he stamped his feet in childlike rage. A member of staff said: 'His outbursts were utter fury and hopeless. Hers were hysterical and tearful.'

The cups weren't the only things that got damaged. In imitation of Lady Moon, who cut off the arms of the Savile Row suits belonging to her errant husband, Diana slashed the sleeve of one of Prince Charles's military uniforms. When Diana's sweet revenge was discovered the incident was swiftly hushed up and the uniform dispatched for repair.

Sometimes the rows were conducted by telephone. One member of staff recalled hearing the Prince 'screaming like crazy. You could hear him in his bedroom. It was a huge, high-pitched scream. It was scary to hear.'

As doors started banging and voices began to rise, the whisper would run though the servants' quarters: 'Action stations'.

Not even death could bring respite to this warring couple. In March 1992, Diana's father succumbed to a heart attack. The Waleses were skiing in Lech when the news came through. Diana tried to dissuade Charles from flying back with her. She demanded the right to grieve for her father without having to go through a 'masquerade'. A member of the household recalled: 'There was a huge quarrel as she didn't want Charles with her. We told her, "You have to go home with him as this is the royal family and you have to do what is considered correct, not what you want to do."' A telephone call was made to the Queen at Windsor who insisted that the couple put on a united front.

Diana reluctantly gave way. Once back in England, however, the rows started up again and the couple travelled separately to the funeral at Althorp; she by car, he by helicopter. Afterwards, Charles returned to London for a meeting with the Crown Prince of Bahrain, leaving Diana to attend her father's cremation without him.

Within a few days they were back in the emotional wasteland of Highgrove. It was a strange, almost surrealistic world the couple inhabited. They would arrive in separate cars on Friday night from Kensington Palace, and later drive back to London at different times, she on Sunday afternoon, he on Monday morning. In between, they would rarely eat together, even with their children.

They did not share a bedroom and therein lay, if not the pith then certainly the expression, of their problem. Diana insisted that this was Prince Charles's fault, that he was the one who physically rejected her in favour of Camilla Parker Bowies. The Prince's staff state otherwise. They maintain that it was

Diana who resolutely refused to sleep with her husband after Prince Harry was born—and that it was this that eventually led Charles to seek the companionship of Mrs Parker Bowles again.

The Princess was far more effective in getting her version across. But regardless of where fault truly resided, the result was a bolster of recrimination which became ever harder to circumvent the longer it was in place. By the mid-Eighties it was set in concrete.

Instead of lying with his wife, the Prince slept with his old, heavily patched Teddy, his comfort since childhood.

Diana's room, with its en suite bathroom, was along the corridor. She had a sofa at one end filled with a collection of large stuffed animals including a giant penguin, a felt frog, several teddies and, souvenirs from her Australia visits, a wombat and a large koala. The white linen sheets on her large double bed were washed every day to remove cakings of the body make-up she wore. Their housekeeper, Wendy Berry, recalled: 'She kept her contraceptive pills in a mug by the sink. Diana took them religiously every day, even though there was never any sign that she and the Prince spent the night together.'

Only when Diana was away would Charles move into his wife's bed—taking Teddy with him.

There were intermittent attempts at

reconciliation. Charles would creep up behind his wife and try and kiss her on the neck, only for Diana to pull away. When she tried to be affectionate towards him, he would be equally standoffish and she would turn and run crying back into the house. Charles would call out, 'Darling, come back, of course I want to hug you,' but she never did. She would lock herself in her bedroom where she spent hours watching television or listening to tapes of ballet music on the ghetto-blaster she brought down with her from London. The weekends often ended with Diana leaving by the back door, eyes sunken and lustreless.

One night, after a particularly venomous exchange when she had shouted 'I hate you' several times at her husband, she had run out of the house, got into her car and driven off into the night, slewing her car from one side of the road to the other in her rage. The police gave chase but she made it halfway across Gloucestershire before they caught up with her.

When they were at home they seldom had people to stay because they had so few friends in common, and they were not interested in socializing with their neighbours, as Princess Anne had discovered to her embarrassment when she had organized her welcome party for them at Gatcombe.

Even the Queen stayed away. She found the atmosphere at Highgrove too tense and the lifestyle there too grand for her comfort. She much preferred to visit Gatcombe Park where she was able to relax and let her hair down, in an almost literal sense. Highgrove and Gatcombe were separated by only a few miles, but the ambience of each was a world apart.

Princess Anne had been taught to curtsey to her mother when she entered a room, and in adulthood would unconsciously get to her feet if she happened to be speaking to the Queen on the telephone. Her own children, however, were allowed a greater liberty: Peter and Zara were expected to be polite, but that was about the extent of it. To them the Queen was simply 'Granny' and they climbed up on to her lap, got her to play with their toys and insisted she sit and watch their videos with them. They had a large collection of tapes which they kept in the drawing room, and many was the afternoon that the Queen, dressed in twin set and pearls, spent with her grandchildren watching cartoons. Donald Duck was a special favourite. It made an engaging picture, the sight of the Queen taking time off from her dispatch boxes to join two little children in laughter at the animated antics of a squawking, bad-tempered duck.

One day, Zara grabbed hold of the Queen's pearls, broke the string and sent the precious beads cascading on to the floor. Without complaint, the Queen got down on to her hands and knees with her grandchildren and carefully collected them up again.

*   *   *

The Queen lives in unrivalled splendour with upwards of two hundred servants on call. However, most are there to help her fulfil her role as Head of State (the President of the United States employs that same number in his press office alone). Left to her own devices, she would have much preferred the homely comfort of a small household. She would rather stay at Wood Farm on the Sandringham estate than in Sandringham House itself, and favours self-catered barbecues over formal banquets. 'She does not enjoy "society",' Harold Macmillan had observed.

It was very much in line with her own thinking, therefore, and not just because of mounting political pressure, that the Queen started making swingeing cuts in the royal budget. The Earl of Airlie was appointed Lord Chamberlain in 1984. A banker by profession, he had brought in the auditing firm of Peat Marwick McLintock, which by 1986, had completed a 1,500-page report suggesting a number of ways costs could be brought under accountable control. Some of the economies smacked of petty-mindedness. The staff in the Royal Mews who look after the state coaches and the horses that draw them were made to buy their own soap and pay for their own petrol when they drove to Sandringham.

On occasion the Queen turned it into a joke. Ever cost-conscious, she insists on keeping the central heating down low and has been known to sit at her desk wearing a mink coat. She once asked her then private secretary Sir Philip Moore for the Buckingham Palace accounts. Sir Philip, who took everything very seriously, waited some time before asking the Queen if she had come across any way of saving a few extra pennies. The Queen turned and looked at him for a moment, and then, with a completely straight face, said, yes, she thought the household could economize if, when writing letters they stopped dotting the 'I's and crossing the 'T's, in order to save on ink.

Slowly but surely, the household budget was reined in and brought under more effective management. The Queen made her own input. 'Why have I got so many footmen?' she asked. Several were let go.

Trying to get the Queen Mother to follow suit proved an impossible task, however. Britain's last Queen-Empress, she continued to live in grand imperial style. She maintained one country house, one castle and two homes, Clarence House and Royal Lodge, which are palaces in all but name. She kept a string of racehorses and late into her nineties, insisted on ordering dozens of new frocks and hats every season. 'I'll never know why she wants all those clothes, as they are all the same,' the Queen protested.

Complaining made not the slightest difference, however. When the Queen, in a moment of irritation, asked her mother to show a little financial moderation, the Queen Mother replied that she had just had her tablecloths patched instead of replaced. With a resigned shake of the head, the Queen observed: 'You won't change her.'

The Queen felt she had no choice but to put up (and fork out, to the tune of over £2 million a year) with a mother from under whose shadow she never quite managed to escape. She was, though, decidedly disapproving of the lavish ways of her heir and his wife.

There were never less than ten staff at Highgrove. They included housekeepers, maids, valets, nannies, dressers, butlers, footmen, chauffeurs, and sometimes two cooks, all of whom often had to work up to fifteen hours a day. The Queen thought this an unwarranted number to attend to the needs of two people who entertained infrequently and whose two little boys were soon away at school for most of the year.

The wastage was at times unconscionable. Upon returning from hunting, Charles liked to have an egg soft boiled for exactly three minutes. To ensure one was always ready, batteries of eggs had to be kept on the go, to be thrown away if the call did not come through in time.

Diana was just as thoughtless. She would order chicken or some more elaborate dish, then at the last minute change her mind and decide on a salad. Charles's Jack Russell terriers, Tigger and Roo, dined off Diana's rejects.

Even more disturbing was their attitude towards the gifts which were showered their way. According to Wendy Berry, who was employed as the Highgrove housekeeper for seven years from 1985 until 1992, they arrived 'by the lorry-load. When that happened there was a general free-for-all after the Prince and Princess had had first choice. The rest were burnt in big incinerators at the back of the house. It never ceased to amaze me how many gifts and clothes were thrown away . . . The clothes and ornaments were systematically put into black plastic bin-liners every month and stuffed by Paddy, [Paddy Whiteland, Charles's groom and general factotum] or his workmen into an incincerator.' Among the presents committed to the flames were teddy bears, designer clothes, furniture and 'a finely carved wooden rocking horse'. Mrs Berry wrote: 'It would make me feel quite sick with anger at such waste.'

When she objected, she was told that the gifts had to be burnt in case 'someone' got hold of them and tried to sell them for their royal association. Who that 'someone' might be, was never explained. But in Highgrove's forlorn atmosphere, distrust was only a step away from paranoia and, as the decade wore on, the newspapers denoted ever-more space to chronicling the marital woes of the Waleses.

Prince Charles affected not to notice and told me that he never read the papers. When I mentioned this to Diana, she burst out laughing.

'Of course he did,' she said. 'He would get up early every morning, go downstairs, look through them, carefully fold them up again and put them back on the table. But I knew what he'd done; you could see by the way the papers were folded that he had been reading them.'

When Diana came down for breakfast she would similarly ignore them. As soon as Charles left the room, however, it would be her turn to flick through the pages to see what was being written about them that day.

It was an eccentric and unhealthy way for a couple to conduct themselves, but in the absence of conversation it was the only way they had of keeping track of each other's doings. But then, of course, they both had a great deal to hide. In 1986 Charles had again taken up with Camilla Parker Bowles, while Diana was spending as much time as she possibly could with Major James Hewitt.

She had first met her 'riding instructor', as she called him, at Buckingham Palace, where he had been attending a meeting with the Queen's equerry and future son-in-law Tim Laurence, to discuss the arrangements for Prince Andrew's wedding to Sarah Ferguson. Hewitt recalls seeing Diana standing barefoot at the bottom of the stairs and feeling 'completely bowled over by someone so feminine and friendly and captivatingly beautiful'. They met again at a drinks party arranged, at Diana's instigation, by Hazel, the wife of Lieutenant-Colonel George West, Assistant-Comptroller in the Lord Chamberlain's office. Their affair began in the autumn, in her bedroom at Kensington Palace after a dinner of smoked salmon, chicken in a lemon and cream sauce accompanied by mashed potatoes, mangetout and French beans. She drank still mineral water, he several glasses of Chablis from Prince Charles's cellar. Hewitt's abiding memory of the night was the smell of Lily of the Valley, Diana's favourite scent.

Camilla, too, would come to associate her lover with a distinctive aroma. On Sunday nights, now that Diana had a real reason to hurry back to London, Charles would bathe in his large bath scented with Floris's Rose Geranium. Then, shortly before 8.30 p.m., and dressed in a blazer and open-necked shirt, he would set off in a nondescript Ford to Camilla's home, Middlewick House at Allington, near Chippenham, seventeen miles away.

When Hewitt visited Diana he took with him boxes of Bendicks Bitter Mints. When Charles went to see Camilla he took with him either chocolates or flowers he had picked from his greenhouse.

A detective always accompanied the Prince to Middlewick House. One of Diana's Personal Protection Officers was always on duty when Hewitt called at Kensington Palace. There is no record of Camilla ever staying overnight at Highgrove while Diana was still its official mistress.

The Princess adopted a more casual approach. One weekend in the spring of 1987 when Charles was away, Hewitt was invited to Highgrove. Diana also invited Hazel West and her old flatmate Carolyn Bartholomew 'so that it seemed just a normal weekend house party with a few friends,' as Hewitt recalled.

Hewitt slept with Diana in the bedroom Prince Charles so rarely visited. 'Diana even came into my room one morning to make sure I'd ruffled my bed sufficiently so that it looked slept in. She was careful and even calculating in the ways of deception,' Hewitt would later recount, with the bitterness of hindsight.

A pattern was soon established, and when the Prince was not in residence, Hewitt frequently was. He made friends with William and Harry and engaged in fierce pillow fights with the boys at bedtime.

In the effort to maintain a semblance of

decorum, Diana and her paramour did not embrace in front of the servants or when they were walking in the gardens which are under constant closed-circuit television surveillance. The staff knew very well what both Charles and Diana were up to, however, and the information was passed along the servants' grapevine to Buckingham Palace, where it was eventually brought to the attention of the Queen.

On the days the Queen and Prince Philip breakfasted or dined together in her private dining room lined with pale pink silk wallpaper, the state of their son's marriage would inevitably crop up in conversation. The room is light and airy but the mood frequently wasn't. Philip, leaning back on the Chippendale-style chairs and adamant as always, would urge his wife to 'do something about it'.

Philip himself had tried to do what he could and had written Diana long and surprisingly sympathetic letters outlining the problems which he had encountered when he had married into the British royal family. He also sent her a formal missive outlining the duties of the Princess of Wales saying there 'was much more to it than being popular'. And when Diana's nerve failed her, which it frequently did in the early days, it was Philip who had urged her on by putting an arm around her waist and virtually dancing her out to her public engagement. As her self-assurance in her position increased, however, Diana came to resent what she saw as her father-in-law's uncalled for interference, and signed off her last letter to him with 'It's been nice getting to know you like this.'

Philip had also tried to talk to his son about his difficulties and the effect they were having on the institution he was born to head. It was meant as fatherly advice, but because of the distant nature of their relationship, the two found it uncomfortable to exchange confidences and their conversations usually ended with Charles looking at his watch and making an excuse to leave the room.

Thwarted in his own efforts to introduce some sense into an increasingly senseless situation, Philip asked his wife to bring her authority to bear. This the Queen consistently refused to do—much to Philip's exasperation. So intimidating to those outside her own family who overstepped the mark, she was unwilling to confront those within it when they failed to reach it.

That is not to suggest that she was blind to her offspring's difficulties or to his own culpability in bringing them about. She quietly let it be known to Charles that she was concerned about the grandeur of his lifestyle, and several times urged him to show more tolerance and tact in his dealings with Diana. But that was the closest she ever came to

298

getting 'off the fence', as her staff called it, to read the regal equivalent of the Riot Act.

It was going to take more than the patience and goodwill she kept advocating to hold the Waleses' marriage together, however, and as the Eighties progressed, so did the rows.

*   *   *

The Queen tried to maintain the much-vaunted 'continuity' which is the Monarchy's greatest strength and justification. At the same time, Prince Philip kept to his old habit of saying whatever came into his mind, most memorably in China in 1986, when he cheerily remarked to a group of British students in X'ian that if they stayed there long enough they would get 'slitty eyes'. The Queen, with forty years experience of Philip's 'gaffs' to look back on, regarded the incident with amusement. So it seems did the Chinese, who remained remarkably uninsulted, despite the furore the comment aroused in Britain and the United States. It was no longer the good works of the Sovereign or the faux pas of her consort which now characterized the royal family, however, but the antics of the next generation.

Charles had tried to bring gravitas to his role, and much of what he said struck a receptive chord, particularly among younger people. As Prince of Wales, he was not subject to the same restrictions as his mother who constitutionally was required to stay out of controversy's way, and he had launched a series of stinging attacks against established interests ('I detest privilege,' he had once remarked, with no sense of the ironic).

Prince Charles had addressed global warming. 'We thought the world belonged to us,' he declared. 'Now we are beginning to realize that we belong to the world. We are responsible to it *and* to each other. Our creativity is a blessing but unless we control it, it will be our destruction.' The environment, he argued, had to be protected. 'Like the sorceror's apprentice causing havoc in his master's home when he couldn't control the spell which he had released, mankind runs a similar risk of laying waste his earthly home by thinking he is in control when he is not.'

He had taken on the architectural fraternity responsible for the soulless concrete developments which had replaced Britain's ancient townscapes in the Fifties and Sixties. Addressing the Royal Institute of British Architects at their 150th anniversary dinner at the appropriately ancient Hampton Court, he said: 'A large number of us have developed a feeling that architects tend to design houses for the approval of fellow architects and critics, not for the tenants.' A good architect, he insisted, must be 'concerned about the way people live, about the environment they inhabit and the kind of community that is created by that environment'.

Putting his money where his mouth was, he turned 650 acres of the Highgrove estate over to organic farming and marketed the produce under his own Duchy of Cornwall brand label.

It wasn't what was taking place out in his fields which interested his future subjects, however, but what was going on inside the house. The reports that came dribbling out were dire in the extreme. A picture started to emerge of a prince who lacked organizational skills, whose office as well as his marriage was in chaos, and whose enthusiasms bore the imprint of the last person he had spoken to (Prince Philip went so far as to call him an 'intellectual pillow').

He also had a habit of shying away when those he had criticized struck back. When, for the third time, he cancelled his appointment to meet Richard Rogers for a clear-the-air meeting, Britain's leading architect angrily exclaimed: 'This is the reason that in the past some countries beheaded their kings.'

The Queen did not approve of the course her son was steering and a frostiness soon developed between the Prince's advisers and the Queen's courtiers. The old guard wanted Charles to be more circumspect, the Prince insisted on his right to pursue his own interests as he best saw fit and by the end of the decade the two sides were at loggerheads in a public squabble between sovereign and heir as old as the Monarchy itself.

The laurels usually went to Charles. Only once did the Queen succeed in putting a block on her son's activities. This was when, in 1985, she called Charles to Buckingham Palace and ordered him to cancel his plans to attend mass with the Pope in the Vatican. This was one breach of protocol the Queen, as Supreme Governor of the Church of England which had broken from Rome over four centuries earlier, was not prepared to countenance. However, on such matters as inner-city rejuvenation, youth unemployment and the environment, Charles was normally able to side-step the reproach of Buckingham Palace and get his own way.

But this did not give him the sense of personal achievement he was seeking. It upset his mother, who had been a remarkably compliant and obedient daughter and was saddened by her son's wilfulness. Nor did it earn him any plaudits from Diana, who regarded her husband's preoccupations with barely disguised indifference. Only in Camilla did he find reassurance. She told him how much she loved him and how she admired him but that, given the circumstances, was hardly the best solution to a royal plot which was going seriously astray. The closer Charles drew to Camilla the more vitriolic Diana became, and the more helpless the Queen felt herself to be. She continued to urge forbearance but that only seemed to exacerbate the difficulties.

In the late winter of 1989, Diana plucked up the courage to confront her rival. The meeting took place at the fortieth birthday of Camilla's sister, Annabel Elliot, held at the Richmond home of financier Sir James Goldsmith and his wife, Lady Annabel. It was an appropriate setting for a wife to come face-to-face with a mistress. The buccaneering Sir James had never made any secret of his own philandering, and lived openly in Paris with another woman who had born him two children and who in turn was installed in a house next door to his former wife. It was the kind of sophisticated arrangement Camilla's great-grandmother, Alice Keppel, would have understood. The mistress of Edward VII, Charles's great-great-grandfather (the British upper classes frolic in a small circle), she had remarked when surveying the shambles of Edward VIII's affair with Wallis Simpson, 'We did things better in my day.'

She might have said the same about Charles's liaison with Camilla, although Diana did manage to keep her temper under control and the showdown was not the screaming match that might have been expected. The Princess had joined Camilla as she stood with Charles chatting to a friend. She asked if she could speak to Camilla alone. Charles retreated upstairs and Camilla and Diana exchanged a few polite pleasantries.

In one account Diana gave of the meeting, she recalled ordering Camilla to sit down, and telling her, 'Don't treat me like an idiot.' The reality appears to have been rather more prosaic. According to one of the guests, Diana asked, 'What makes him want to be with you and not me?' Camilla, wrong-footed, gave a non-committal reply. And that, as far as everyone at the party was concerned, was that. The next day Diana recounted what had happened to her lover, James Hewitt. He congratulated her on her bravery.

Diana looked back on the meeting as a 'tremendous shift . . . That was it, it was a big step for me.' But not for the Prince. Estranged from his mother, alienated from his father, under attack by the architectural community, at odds with a number of senior Cabinet ministers who considered him a meddlesome irritant, only able to fleetingly see the woman he had grown so dependent upon emotionally, and increasingly isolated from his children, Charles was caught in a situation which he likened to 'a Greek tragedy'. In June the following year he sustained a badly broken arm in a polo accident. The pain was excruciating (the arm had to be rebroken and set with a metal pin and bone grafted from his hip to help the mending process). However, it was not the physical damage, as severe as that was, which caused his friends concern, but his mental state.

Diana seemed able to take her own infidelity in her stride. Charles could not. Brought up to believe in the sanctity of marriage and acutely conscious of where his duty lay, he was confused and frightened by the way his life had gone 'so horribly wrong'.

Confidants like Nicholas Soames and Norton Knatchbull tried to make light of the situation and jovially dismissed it as 'a mid-life crisis'. Privately, however, they were convinced that he was suffering from 'clinical depression'.

The Queen had grown accustomed to dealing with the mental vagaries of her family. She had witnessed her father's rages and incapacitating attacks of nerves. She had seen her mother deal with crises by making herself ill and retiring to bed. She had also witnessed her sister Margaret's nervous breakdown. This occurred in 1974 when her marriage to the Earl of Snowdon was falling apart and her love affair with Roddy Llewellyn was breaking up.

Margaret's final years with Snowdon were marked by fights and long silences which mirrored with uncanny accuracy the problems to come in the Waleses' union. Tired of royal life and the constraints it placed on him, and bored with Margaret, Snowdon took to leaving his wife insulting notes (one missive read: 'You look like a Jewish manicurist and I hate you').

Margaret's extramarital love affairs had contributed in no small measure to the unhappy situation she found herself in, but she was nonetheless deeply wounded by her husband's vitriol. She became by turns morose, weepy and irrational. This so concerned Lord Rupert Neville, whose Gothic house near Uckfield, Sussex, had been the setting for her final meeting with Peter Townsend, that he secretly arranged to record a row between the Snowdons and then sent the tape to a Harley Street psychiatrist. Without knowing who the people were, the doctor said: 'This lady needs help—and she needs help soon.'

The Queen took a more relaxed view of her sister's difficulties. When a relation telephoned her and told her that Margaret had just called to say that if he did not come over immediately she would throw herself out of her bedroom window, the Queen coolly replied: 'Carry on with your house party—her bedroom is on the ground floor.'

Depending on the point of view, the Queen's remark was either humorous or appallingly callous. In fact it was a perfectly natural response, which reflected both her wit and her practical approach to life's tribulations, and she later adopted the same attitude in her dealings with Diana. She recognized that her daughter-in-law was ill, and gave her what support and comfort she could. There was only so far the Queen was prepared to go, however. A firm believer in self-control, she regarded any undue show of emotion as 'phoney'. And she had noted (how could she not?) that for all her troubles, Diana was still out there batting her corner—and pummelling the royal family as she did so.

Charles's case was slightly different. He was not like his wife, noisily demanding attention or some ill-defined form of communal 'help'. Instead, he withdrew ever deeper into himself in a way that suggested his friends might well be right when they warned that he was edging towards a serious breakdown. He was, he told one, a 'prisoner' in his own life.

It was a thought the Queen was beginning to share. Slowly but surely, she was losing command of her family in a way which would have been incomprehensible to her predecessors, who for over a century had maintained an autocratic grip on the lives of their offspring and their spouses. Even the irresponsible Duke of Windsor had been too frightened to directly challenge the will of his father, George V, in matters of state conduct. But the old rules no longer applied and the Queen was unable to come to terms with the new. Indifferent to the normal canons of good manners, Charles and Diana continued their bickering when they came to stay at Sandringham and Balmoral, while Fergie made no attempt to disguise her growing indifference towards Prince Andrew.

Charles's cousin, George, the fourth Marquis of Milford Haven, was often a guest at Balmoral and recalled the embarrassment he felt at the contemptuous way the two treated their husbands in front of the Queen—and at the way the Queen, unwilling to interfere, pretended not to notice.

To compound matters, Fergie and Diana were at each other's throats. Once friends, they were now competitors in the royal firmament. Initially, it was Diana who had tried to keep up with Sarah, aping her style of dress, envying her *joie de vivre*, irritated at the way members of the royal family would say, 'Why can't you be fun—like Fergie?'

The balance changed when 'red carpet fever' took a hold on Sarah. When her star went into the descendency, Diana started to distance herself from her rowdy sister-in-law. As unhappy as she was, Diana was far too canny to allow herself to be compromised by Fergie's excesses—or to involve herself in foolish plans for the two of them to stage a joint royal walkout.

In November 1989 the Duchess, five months pregnant with her second daughter, Eugenie, had flown to Texas 'to pay' as she put it, 'tribute to that city's Grand Opera'. It was another of the 'freebie', all-expenses-paid trips of the kind for which she was being roundly criticized. Never one to resist temptation, she went ahead anyway. In Houston she stayed at the home of Lynn Wyatt, wife of an oil millionaire, whose previous husband had been sentenced at the Old Bailey to six years imprisonment for killing his girlfriend while on an acid trip. Without thought for the consequences, she embarked on an affair with Lynn's son, Steve.

Diana had tried to keep her liaisons a secret from everyone but her closest friends. Fergie could not be bothered with such subterfuge and continued her fling when Steve Wyatt moved to England to work for his stepfather. After the birth of Eugenie, Wyatt arranged for her to spend five days at the Gazelle d'Or, an expensive hotel on the edge of the Sahara in Morocco. As she was walking out of a Turkish bath she unexpectedly bumped into 'Cappy' Hesketh, the rotund, jocular brother of Lord Hesketh, a junior minister in the Department of the Environment who had once bankrolled his own Formula 1 Grand Prix racing team. Cappy waggishly enquired: 'How did you enjoy the hammam, ma'am?' Fergie fled. With good reason: in the closed circuit of London society people make it their business to know what everyone else is doing—and with whom.

The Palace certainly knew. Sarah had used one of the Queen's luggage cars to help Wyatt move into his apartment in Cadogan Square which was duly logged in the Palace records.

She had also made a spectacle of herself over Wyatt at the Palace's Privy Purse's door. It was Christmas Eve, and Wyatt was leaving for America. Fergie came rushing down shouting, 'I have a parcel to deliver—has it arrived yet?' The parcel contained a gift for Wyatt. One senior member of the household recalled: 'She stood there in full view of the staff, hopping from one foot to another, waiting for the parcel to arrive from the shop.'

When it came, it was too late to be delivered with any certainty to the Gatwick Express which Wyatt was catching to the airport. In a panic, Fergie went to Victoria station herself, found Wyatt and took the train with him to the airport. 'You didn't have to be Solomon to work out what was going on,' the courtier observed. Sarah, however, was infatuated by Wyatt who, she insisted, 'cared nothing about my title'.

Contrary to public perception and expectation, the royal family is not a closed institution, its inmates bound by a monastic code of conduct. But the freedom members enjoy to make a mess of their lives as they see fit does not include the right to ignore the regulations and policies of the state they are pledged to serve. Fergie succeeded in doing just that when, on Wyatt's prompting, she invited an Iraqi oil dealer to the Palace a few weeks after his country had invaded Kuwait.

The Duchess would later claim that she had discussed with a senior courtier the visit of Dr Ramzi Salman, the head of marketing for Iraq's state oil, and that he had given official approval. Either she was set up, or she was not telling the truth, because no one at the Palace recalled any such conversation ever taking place with any of the Queen's advisers. Even if it had, which is highly unlikely, common sense should have warned her of the diplomatic dangers of entertaining a senior representative of the regime Britain was about to go to war with.

Sarah arranged for Salman to come into the Palace through the Sovereign's Entrance which is reserved for the Queen, and then serve him drinks in the White Drawing Room.

The repercussions were as fierce as they were inevitable. The Duchess was called before Sir Robert Fellowes and two of his colleagues for an hour-long dressing down. She was told that her behaviour was inexcusable and that 'You have abused Her Majesty and her kindness.'

The Duchess asked on whose authority they were acting. She was told: 'We have Her Majesty's full authority to tell you this.'

The following Sunday the Duchess cornered the Queen at Windsor and asked why she had authorized those she called 'the men in grey' to give her such a 'pummelling'. In order to avoid an unpleasant scene the Queen feigned ignorance. Once again, she had left it to her advisers to do her bidding—and shoulder the blame for any ensuing fall-out.

*   *   *

The Queen's forbearance at the time was nothing short of remarkable. On Diana's insistence, James Hewitt had been invited to Prince Charles's fortieth birthday party at Buckingham Palace. Two years later, Fergie wheedled an invitation for Wyatt to attend the even-more lavish ball held to celebrate the ninetieth birthday of the Queen Mother, the fortieth birthday of Princess Anne—and the thirtieth birthday of her own husband, Prince Andrew. Whatever their objections may have been to royal life, both women enjoyed the perks that went with it and were keen for their paramours to share in the jollity and to slosh back the royal champagne.

'You take in two girls from broken homes and look how they repay you,' the Queen remarked caustically to one of her staff.

There was only so much even the Queen was prepared to tolerate, however, and she finally felt moved to suggest to her daughter-in-law that Wyatt was not 'quite the sort of person you should be encouraging'. It was the end of the affair. It was also the beginning of the end for Fergie.

Her father had already taken himself beyond the pale by being caught leaving a West End massage parlour, and the ensuing unpleasant publicity eventually forced him to resign as Prince Charles's polo manager. Then, while Wyatt was embarking on an affair with Major Ronald's mistress, a middle-class adventuress named Lesley Player, Sarah was taking up with Wyatt's old friend, the financial adviser John Bryan.

In the late summer of 1991, Fergie and Diana were again at Balmoral and behaving like spoilt schoolgirls. They drove a quad bike over the golf course and churned up the greens. They roused Fergie's cousin and Diana's brother-in-law from his slumbers by beating on his lodge door shortly before midnight. And they 'liberated' the Queen Mother's Daimler from its garage and did gravel-spins around the castle courtyard with Diana at the wheel and wearing a chauffeur's hat.

'We had no idea where we were heading but we knew we could not sit tight,' Fergie recalled. The idea they came up with was that they should both leave their husbands at the same time.

Fergie was the first to jump. Prince Andrew had spent weeks trying to find the right moment to discuss with his mother the problems in his marriage, but every time he tried to raise the matter, she would deliberately change the subject. Not until the following January, and then only on his wife's promptings and with Fergie at his side, did they finally manage to get the Queen to listen.

The meeting was brief and painful. Andrew muttered words like 'mutual incompatibility'. Sarah apologized for her behaviour which she agreed had been a long way short of what was both expected and required. The floodgates were bursting, yet the Queen still clung to the delusion that time would heal the breach.

Fergie wrote: 'She asked me to reconsider, to be strong and go forward.' According to the Duchess, 'The Queen looked sadder than I had ever seen her.'

To placate the Queen, the Yorks agreed to delay any final decision for six months. This patchwork solution did not survive three months. Later in January, compromising photographs of the Duchess and her former lover on holiday with her children in the south of France were found in the Cadogan Square flat Wyatt had vacated when he returned to the United States. In March, the lawyers were called in and the divorce was set in motion.

Fergie genuinely expected this to be a double-header. She had spent months whispering and plotting with Diana. The plan had been for Fergie to make her announcement, then for Diana to follow suit.

Fergie kept her side of this asinine bargain and leapt into the chasm. When she looked round Diana was still *in situ* and Sarah suddenly realized that she was on her own. 'Madame' Vasso Kortesis, the Duchess's 'personal spiritual adviser', recorded: 'Sarah felt let down by the woman she had come to rely on as her closest friend. She was particularly angered that Diana had

314

encouraged her to leave Andrew when she obviously had no immediate plans for leaving Charles. For Sarah, it meant that overnight she was stopped from taking part in all official royal engagements and tours, while Diana was allowed to carry on as usual.'

The Queen was unaware of her daughters-in-laws' conspiracy until much later, but the Palace did indeed move quickly to isolate Fergie. She was still an HRH but in name only: staff, who only a few weeks before would have bowed and curtseyed to her, now walked past her as if she didn't exist. In royal terms she had become a *persona non grata*.

'The men in grey are out to get me,' Fergie told me shortly afterwards, and so they were. The Queen's press officer, Charles Anson, briefed the BBC's court correspondent Paul Reynolds, and told him that Fergie was 'unsuitable for royal and public life'. Reynolds, a seasoned journalist who had reported the civil war in El Salvador and covered the Falklands War from the Argentinian capital, Buenos Aires, went on the air to declare, 'The knives are out for Fergie.'

Anson offered his resignation which the Queen refused to accept for the very good reason that he had been acting on her authority.

The Queen's reaction had been partly shaped by the attitude of her husband. Philip, recalled a member of the household, was 'incandescent' with anger. There was an element of personal animosity in this. There had been several occasions when Fergie had come to Andrew's defence when he was being berated by his father for some perceived weakness or other, and as the Queen had noted, Philip was not a man 'who likes to be contradicted'. It was her public deportment rather than any private disagreements, however, which so annoyed the Prince. An outsider himself who had had to learn to adapt to the exigencies of royal life, he was able to take an objective view of its requirements, and regarded his daughter-in-law's behaviour as selfish and reprehensible. He declared: 'If she wants out, she can get out.'

The Duchess hit the telephone desperately looking for support. She telephoned me and said that Andrew 'is still my best friend' and that she had been driven to take this drastic action because of the hard and uncompromising attitude of the Palace officials who, she said, had made her life 'a misery'.

Diana watched and took note and refused to take Fergie's calls. Too cognisant of her own status to be led into climbing over the Palace wall with the bad girl of the class, she decided on her own course of action. The one she chose was dramatic and destructive to the extreme.

In the summer of 1991, she was approached

by one-time tabloid journalist Andrew Morton, who was working on a biography of the Princess. He asked her for her consent to approach her friends and ask them about various aspects of her life. It is a standard request by royal writers which is usually refused. Diana, however, liked Morton. He was good-looking in an owlish way (Diana called him Clark Kent, after Superman's alter ego), and he had also written with consistent sympathy about her over the years. The timing also was right. Diana was still ill, still unhappy, still unable to cope with the pressures of royal life and the attitude of a family she was convinced (by then with some reason) was ganging up against her, and was fired by resentment towards her husband. She not only gave her consent, but went one enormous step further and agreed to put her thoughts on tape and have them delivered to Morton through an intermediary, on condition that her comments and observations be attributed to 'friends'. Morton had hit commercial mother lode.

Diana, Her True Story was serialized in the *Sunday Times* in June, 1992. It was a savage portrait which painted Charles as an uncaring father and an adulterous villain of Gothic proportions, who had dumped his young bride for an old mistress, and in so doing had driven his pregnant wife to the point of suicide.

The Waleses were at Highgrove when the

first instalment was published. Because of the late delivery of the papers on Sunday morning in Gloucestershire, the Prince had arranged for his office to fax him the relevant pages as soon as the *Sunday Times* 'dropped' in the early hours of 7 June. They were laid on the dining table when the Prince came down for breakfast. Diana appeared shortly afterwards, took one look at the crumpled face of her husband reading through what she had helped write and went back upstairs to her bedroom.

The interior designer Robert Kime and his wife Helen were staying that weekend, and after a breakfast eaten in the silence of a morgue, Charles asked them to walk with him through his garden before seeing them off. He then went upstairs to Diana's room, taking the faxed copies of the *Sunday Times* with him. A few minutes later Diana left the house and fled back to London.

The Queen was at Windsor that weekend. She was stunned by what she read. She was well aware how unhappy her daughter-in-law was but she had never imagined that Diana would resort to airing dirty linen in such a public way.

Intriguingly, though, her mask of composure never cracked. She calmly went about her business as if nothing out of the ordinary had taken place that weekend. Only later did she reveal just how startled she had been by Diana's disclosures, and then only in the most elliptic way.

Even the Queen's extraordinary ability to compartmentalize her difficulties could not completely protect her from Diana's broadside. No ship of state, however well-constructed, is entirely waterproof, and Morton's disclosures had blown a ragged gash in the Monarchy's plating. It wasn't so much what was said—the royal family's good name and the state of the Waleses' marriage in particular had been taking a battering for the better part of five years—but the manner in which it was said that caused such damage. *Diana, Her True Story* was one-sided and subjective. Incidents had been exaggerated and dates had been moved to fit Diana's interpretation of events. But the overall picture—of a family so cold and self-absorbed that it was incapable of responding to the plight of a young woman who should have been at its very heart—carried a ring of truth which was so persuasive as to be almost incontrovertible. No woman had ever taken such devastating revenge for slights real or perceived.

The royal family's first reaction was to deny Diana's complicity. Sir Robert Fellowes asked Diana several times if she had cooperated with Morton. She assured him that she had not. Fellowes believed her and passed on her denials to Lord McGregor, the chairman of the Press Complaints Commission who was preparing a blistering attack on the *Sunday Times.*

By midweek, however, Diana herself had blown apart her own defence. The Fleet Street newspapers received a telephone call from a well-spoken woman who sounded remarkably like the Princess herself, telling them that Diana would be going to the home of Carolyn Bartholomew, one of the people quoted in the Morton book. Next day the photograph made the front pages. It was interpreted for what it was—a public show of support for a friend which gave the lie to the Palace's statement that Diana had had no hand in Morton's book.

Fellowes had been made to look a fool which, given Diana's opinion of her brother-in-law, was probably one of her intentions. He apologized to Lord McGregor for misleading him. He then did the honorable thing and offered the Queen his resignation. She refused it on the grounds that it was her daughter-in-law, and not her private secretary, who was guilty of misleading her.

In most families this would have sparked a bitter and explosive bout of rows and recriminations and, more than likely, an immediate end to the marriage. But the royal family is governed by its own needs and even at this juncture the Queen clung to the vain hope that given time the situation could be resolved.

The Saturday after the first *Sunday Times* serialization was the Queen's official birthday and Diana had stood beside her mother-in-law on the balcony of Buckingham Palace, looking as if absolutely nothing was amiss.

The following week, she was at Royal Ascot with the rest of the family, as the second instalment of Morton's revelations was rolling off the press.

Charles and Diana had a meeting with Prince Philip and the Queen which the Princess said left her 'shaken rigid'. When the question of a separation was raised, however, the Queen insisted that the couple make yet another attempt to resolve their differences.

It was the Monarch talking, not the mother. But it only made the situation even more unpalatable. Instinct suggested that the couple had long passed the point of reconciliation and should be allowed to go their separate ways. Yet even at such a late stage, this remained in the realms of the unthinkable for a sovereign whose throne rested on the foundation of a dutiful, and above all united family. Unwilling to face up to the constitutional implications of a separation, the Queen instead ordered a six-month cooling off period.

Charles, who even in his forties remained in awe of his mother, meekly agreed. So did Diana. For all her grievances, she was astute enough to realize the difficulties that would face her once she was on the outside. She had seen what had happened to Fergie which is why she had refused to honour her side of the pact. In the effort to protect her own increasingly volatile position, she agreed that the charade should continue.

The tension was there for all to see at Ascot, however. Prince Philip snubbed Diana in full view of all the other top-hatted people in the Royal Enclosure. But at least she was there. Fergie wasn't: she had been banished to social Siberia. Instead of sipping champagne dressed in her expensive finery, she was reduced to standing with her daughters Beatrice and Eugenie in Windsor Great Park watching with the hoi polloi as the Ascot landaus drove past.

The head coachman, Steve Matthews, who was leading the royal procession, was the first to notice the Duchess. He gave them a neat salute. The Queen, nonplussed, gave them an automatic wave. The household was not so obliging. Later that day, the Queen's lady-in-waiting, Lady Susan Hussey, gave Fergie what she described to me as 'a severe bollocking' for this violation of royal protocol.

The next day she persuaded Andrew to accompany her in a show of 'solidarity'. There was nothing her estranged husband could do to shield her that August, however, when photographs appeared of her topless in the south of France having her toes sucked by John Bryan. She was at Balmoral with the family when that fatal nail was driven into the coffin of what was left of her reputation.

The Queen, Philip, Charles, Diana, Anne, Andrew, Edward, Princess Margaret and her daughter Lady Sarah Armstrong-Jones, were all staying at the castle. When Fergie came down to face her in-laws, she told me, 'I looked at the assembled company and thought to myself, "There but for the grace of God go the lot of you." '

But they hadn't. Once again it was Fergie, the bouncy, too-eager-to-please labrador of a woman whose tail is forever knocking cups off the coffee table, who had slipped up yet again.

Prince Philip likened her to Edwina Mountbatten, whose morals had long been a source of embarrassment to the royal family. He said to her: 'You belong in a nunnery—or a madhouse.' The photographs suggested that a convent would be the less appropriate option.

The Queen, Sarah recalled, was 'furious'. She did not scream or shout. That is not the Queen's way. Rather, she was cold and abrupt as she berated her semi-detached daughter-in-law for exposing the Monarchy to ridicule. 'Her anger wounded me to the core,' Fergie said.

With nowhere to run to and absolutely nowhere to hide, Fergie stayed at Balmoral for a further three days, enduring the prurient looks of staff and family alike, taking the perverse pleasure of a flagellant in the disdain of those around her, deriving, she said, 'some satisfaction in that unmitigated hell'.

By the week's end it was Diana's turn to come under the lash—with far greater consequence to the royal family. The toe-sucking pictures had appeared in the *Daily Mirror*. On the basis that one scandalous scoop deserved another, its rival the *Sun* countered by publishing the transcript of a three-year-old tape recording of an intimate conversation between the Princess and James Gilbey, who worked in the car business.

In 1989 Hewitt had been posted to Germany. Diana had begged him not to go and offered to pull strings to allow him to stay in England. When Hewitt insisted on following his regiment, Diana stopped taking his calls and took up with Gilbey, a relation of the gin family. During their 23-minute conversation, recorded on New Year's Eve, 1989, Gilbey called her Squidgy, which led to the tapes being dubbed Squidgy-gate. As well as disparaging the royal family, Diana exchanged some mildly salacious sexual innuendoes with Gilbey, thereby confirming the entries in her Protection Officers' private logs.

Just as Fergie had done, Diana tried to persuade the Queen that she was being set up and hinted darkly that she believed that certain of her courtiers were conspiring to discredit her. The Queen dismissed this for the arrant nonsense it was—the Palace had no reason to mount a dirty tricks campaign which would only cause further damage to the

Monarchy it was pledged to protect. And if they had, it certainly did not have the expertise, as its lamentable efforts to safeguard the good name of the royal family so graphically illustrated. It was the young women's own actions which had brought them to this impasse. Both had assiduously courted their journalistic contacts (indeed, the Prime Minister John Major had taken the highly unusual step after the Morton book was published of warning Diana who was still officially his future queen that he could offer her no help 'if she tried to manipulate the press'). They had set the agenda. Now they were facing the consequences.

As for the Palace, rather than the cunning strategy Diana and Fergie suspected, there was only the chaos of indecision and confusion as Queen and courtiers watched aghast while the younger generation pressed the self-destruct button.

The Prince of Wales was more bewildered than most. On his wife's urging, he had once given up shooting pheasant and given his shotguns to Prince Andrew. Now he was being blasted with both barrels—first the Morton book, then the 'Squidgy' tape. To add extra insult, it was Gilbey who had been quoted by Morton as saying of Diana and Charles: 'She thinks he is a bad father, a selfish father; the children have to tie in with whatever he is doing.' In the face of this twin assault, Charles became listless and apathetic and his depression became ever-more pronounced.

Diana, a great believer in New Age treatments, suggested they both seek therapy. Charles refused. He had been born and raised to be king. He had talked with friends like Eric Anderson and Laurens van der Post, but he was not psychologically capable of coming down off his pedestal to discuss his marital problems with total strangers. By the autumn he was quietly consulting lawyers, as was Diana. But like his mother, he still clung forlornly to the hope that his marriage could somehow be saved.

It was for this reason that, against his better judgement, he agreed to go ahead with his scheduled tour of Korea. This was one pretence too far for Diana, however, and she stoutly announced that she was not going. Only when Charles, at the end of his emotional tether, told her that she would have to make her own excuses, did Diana agree to accompany her husband.

It might have been better if she hadn't. Diana had become the mistress of gesture, as she had proved earlier in the year on the trip to India when she had seated herself in front of the Taj Mahal, the world's most famous monument to marital devotion, and encouraged the photographers to picture her as the rejected wife. In Korea there was no need to stage-manage the shots. There for all to see, was a couple who could not stand the sight of each other.

It was yet another row over the sons who should have brought them together which finally brought down the curtain on Charles and Diana's marriage. Back from Korea, Charles arranged a shooting weekend at Sandringham to coincide with William and Harry's exeat from Ludgrove. Diana refused to go, and informed Charles that she was taking the boys to Windsor instead.

Charles snapped. He telephoned his mother. When she again pleaded patience, he abandoned the training of a lifetime and shouted down the line at the Queen, 'Don't you realize she's mad, mad, mad!' and slammed the receiver down.

The royal family was going up in smoke—quite literally. On 20 November, Windsor Castle was engulfed by flames.

The fire was started by a restorer's lamp which set a curtain alight. It quickly spread through the Queen's private chapel and devoured St George's Hall. Prince Andrew organized the rescue of many of the ancient works of art but great parts of the building itself were consumed in the blaze.

Windsor Castle, the symbol of the Monarchy for almost a thousand years, had been nearly reduced to a smouldering rubble. It was the Queen's forty-fifth wedding anniversary. Prince Philip was in Argentina.

Two days later, the Queen addressed the Guildhall. With Philip back at her side, she said in a voice hoarse with flu and emotion: '1992 is not a year on which I shall look back with undiluted pleasure. In the words of one of my more sympathetic correspondents, it has turned out to be an *annus horribilis.*'

There was yet worse to come, as the Queen now knew. On 9 December Prime Minister John Major stood up in the House of Commons and said: 'It is announced from Buckingham Palace that, with regret, the Prince and Princess of Wales have decided to separate . . . this decision has been reached amicably, and they will continue to participate fully in the upbringing of their children . . . The Queen and the Duke of Edinburgh, though saddened, understand and sympathize with the difficulties that have led to this decision . . .'

The Queen was at Wood Farm with only a handful of staff in attendance when the announcement was made. It was a poignant setting, for it was here in 1919, in this red brick house hidden from view at the end of a long tree-lined drive, that the Queen's thirteen-year-old uncle, the pathetic Prince John, had died of an epileptic fit, alone and all but forgotten.

She did not watch the Prime Minister on television. Instead, she did what she always did when she was agitated, and took her corgis for a walk through the wintry woods and ploughed Norfolk fields. When she got back she dried the dogs off and then almost immediately took them out again, a displacement activity Prince Philip called her 'dog mechanism'.

When she returned to the back door a member of staff approached the solitary figure of his Sovereign who was dressed in wellington boots, loden coat and a head scarf. He said how very sorry he was to hear the news. The Queen replied: 'I think you'll find it's all for the best.' She then walked out again into the drizzle.

CHAPTER TEN

SEPARATION

On the day their separation was announced Charles and Diana met in the first-floor drawing room Diana called the salon of her apartment at Kensington Palace. They sat together on the yellow brocade-covered sofa.

'We asked each other, "Why did this have to happen?"' Diana recalled, when we met in the same room. Half a decade had passed since that day when the curtain had come down on her marriage. The Princess was now more content, more at ease with herself, than I had ever seen. Looking around the room, it was hard to imagine the scenes that had taken place there, or to visualize that anguish and anger that had once blighted its elegant atmosphere.

A tapestry hung on one of the pastel yellow walls. There was a grand piano in a corner, its top crowded with leather-framed photographs of her children. There was a second sofa and a pair of well-worked antique chairs. It is a large room, but it was too small for them both. One evening when Charles had walked in and seen his wife sitting in the very place where I was sitting now, he had turned on his heels and walked straight out again. There had been occasions when Diana had fled the room in tears, slamming the ornate double wooden doors behind her, opening them, and then banging them shut again, shouting all the while, 'I hate you, Charles.'

On that morning, however, the couple whose marital problems had become the world's most publicized soap opera had turned to each other for comfort.

'We told each other that we loved each other,' Diana said, and when she saw the look of disbelief on my face, she insisted: 'But we did—we really did.'

Charles, an emotional man underneath his royal veneer, was overcome by a sense of his own failure. He had wanted a home and a family, not just for dynastic reasons, but out of a deep-rooted personal need, and in the

330

turmoil of that morning he blamed himself for the failure of his marriage. Diana, still ill, still unsure of herself, was looking into a void and was petrified by the prospect of what lay ahead. Overwrought, the pair embraced in a way they had not done for years, and sought solace in each other's tears.

Diana dropped her head to one side and wrung her hands at the memory. There were no tears in her eyes that morning, just the plaintive gaze of what I took to be regret.

It was then that she delivered her bombshell. She suddenly looked up and said: 'It wasn't Camilla who really destroyed our marriage.'

'It wasn't Camilla . . .' The words hung suspended uncomfortably in my disbelief. For the better part of ten years all we had heard about, via leak and the testimony of friends, and through the evidence in her own televised confession, was Camilla and the part she had played in turning one young woman's fairytale into a brutal nightmare. If not Camilla, then who in heaven's name had been responsible for destroying the royal marriage and bringing the entire Monarchy into such disrepute in the process?

The Princess appeared embarrassed by what she had said. But this was not the blushing 'Shy Di' of old, hiding her thoughts in monosyllables and then lashing out with a torrent of accusation. She was now thirty-six years old, and age had afforded her a perspective which had been absent during those traumatic, enervating years she had spent cooped up in the royal family (she used the word 'imprisoned'). She was at last able to see herself and the situation she had found herself in with new-found clarity. She said: 'It was the people around us.' By that she meant the Palace system and the demands of a job she was untrained to cope with and, above all, the army of courtiers who had tried to keep her in check rather than offering her the hand of encouragement. 'They didn't give us a chance,' she said.

She was certainly not offering the hand of forgiveness to Mrs Parker Bowles when she said that. She was too passionate ever to do so, and at the mention of her name Diana had rolled her eyes towards the ceiling in a way which signified nothing but scorn. It was as close to a tacit admission as the Princess ever came, though, to admitting that there were factors other than the intrusion of another woman—however hurtful that may have been—which contributed to the breakdown of her marriage.

The fact that she could make it was an indication that the mental malady which had caused her such suffering was at last, if not cured, then at least in remission. 'I still feel lonely,' she said, and admitted to me that she was still in need of love. But her needs that summer morning when we met no longer appeared to be driven by an unmanageable, near-hysterical force. A calmness which had been so notable in its absence before, had settled on her. The cost, however, had been enormous.

The turbulence generated by the Waleses' separation had induced a state akin to panic in the normally drowsy corridors of Buckingham Palace. The official line, as stated by John Major, was that the parting had been 'amicable' and that 'Their Royal Highnesses will continue to carry out full and separate programmes of public engagements and will, from time to time, attend family occasions and national events together.'

That simply was not true. The parting had been anything other than friendly, the couple had no intention of appearing in public together, and it was made quite clear to the Princess that she would no longer be allowed to represent the Queen at any official engagement.

In a further misleading interpretation of the facts, the Prime Minister had also stated that 'the decision to separate has no constitutional implications. The succession to the Throne is unaffected by it . . . there is no reason why the Princess of Wales should not be crowned Queen in due course.' The Prime Minister knew he was playing with the truth when he uttered those lines. The Monarchy would not have survived the spectacle of Charles and Diana sitting side by side in Westminster Abbey, united only by mutual loathing as the crowns were solemnly placed on their heads. But this clearly was not the moment for a destructive debate on the constitutional implications of the separation: John Major had not become first minister of the Crown to preside over its dissolution. The unthinkable had caught both the government and the Palace unprepared. It was a case of all hands to the pumps and if truth got jettisoned in the process, it might at least buy a little time.

The Queen was badly shaken. She was too well trained to allow her feelings to show in public. It was at home that the cracks appeared in the regal façade. Always partial to a well-mixed cocktail, she started taking one or two more than was her custom, and one member of her staff recalled seeing her walking unsteadily along the corridor at Sandringham that Christmas. She belonged to a generation which did not believe in pills or personal confessions. Instead she had turned to more traditional remedies.

'The previous year she would complain that the drinks were too strong,' a member of the household recalled. 'After the separation she never complained.'

Another member of staff observed: 'It was Martinis and Princess Anne that kept her going.'

Charles, rather than being a comfort, had become yet another cause for concern. Once the separation was announced, his mood noticeably revived. Shortly afterwards, he had returned to Highgrove and hauled everything belonging to his wife into one room. Every photograph of Diana was removed from sight. Staff who had been loyal to the Princess, including their butler Paul Burrell, were told that their services would no longer be required. The tears he had shared with his wife on the sofa had dried quickly. He was, he told friends, going to make a clean break.

It was a false dawn. In January 1993, another illegal telephone conversation was published in what inevitably became known as Camilla-gate. It had been recorded four years earlier, and it featured Charles and Camilla Parker Bowles, who by then were both in their forties, cooing like lustful teenagers. Not only did the conversation confirm Diana's charge of adultery against her husband, thereby invoking the wrath of hardline clerics in the Church of England he was born to lead; it also exposed him to ridicule. The most damaging passage was where the Prince told Mrs Parker Bowles that he would like to be her tampon which was hardly the comment expected of a future king. 'He will never recover from that,' remarked the former Labour Cabinet minister Denis Healey.

The Prince's reputation, already severely

battered, had taken another nosedive, and strident questions as to his fitness to inherit the throne began to be asked. The call went up for Charles to be bypassed and the Crown to skip a generation to Prince William. The Queen viewed all talk of such kind as a threat to the Monarchy, as indeed it was—to suggest a change in the rules of succession invited doubts about the need for a monarchy at all.

It wasn't just Diana who was jumping at shadows now. A feeling that there was a conspiracy to 'get' the royal family began to pervade the Palace itself. How was it, they asked, that these recordings had come to be made? One suggestion was that GCHQ, the government's top-secret listening station was in some way responsible, but spokesmen for MI5, which handles counter-espionage, and MI6, the James Bond organization which does the foreign spying, strenuously denied any involvement.

The likely explanation is that Charles and Diana had fallen victim to amateur ham radio enthusiasts. Both had been warned by their Personal Protection Officers that mobile telephones were not secure but had carried on using them regardless (Diana had gone so far as to give James Hewitt a cell phone so that they could keep in close touch at all hours). The royal family were being caught with their conversational pants down by a technology whose limitations and defects they did not fully understand.

Trying to convince them that they were to an extent responsible for their own troubles was not easy in the climate of suspicion washing through the royal family. Unused to having to justify their behaviour, they sought fault in others and the person who took most of the blame for the perturbing situation they found themselves in was Diana.

*　　*　　*

The Princess had not found life outside the royal cocoon as liberating as she had imagined and her behaviour, always erratic, acquired an air of desperation. In search of a solution to her emotional problems, she became an alternative therapy junkie. As well as consulting the crystals—a habit she had picked up from Fergie who had been introduced to them by Wyatt—she experimented with acupuncture, colonic irrigation, shiatsu, aromatherapy, astrology, Prozac, chiropractic and osteopathy. She also sought the help of 'energy healers' like Simone Simmons, who became a friend and confidant. The treatments often contradicted each other and left her feeling even more exhausted and on edge. But instead of cutting back on her charitable activities and public appearances, she insisted on keeping to a punishing schedule, even if she didn't have to—and, on occasion, where she wasn't wanted.

In April 1993, she attended a state banquet held at Buckingham Palace in honour of the president of Portugal, Mario Soares. She stood next to Prince Charles, ostentatiously displaying her wedding ring of Welsh gold. She was the uninvited guest.

When she joined the rest of the royal family for pre-dinner drinks in the Audience Room just off the Queen's sitting room, the Queen Mother, who had come to dislike her intensely, clutched at her diamond necklace and asked of the Queen in a loud whisper: 'What is *she* doing here? I can't understand it. Why *have* you allowed it?'

The answer lay in the complicated bond that existed between the Queen and her daughter-in-law. Prince Philip and the Queen Mother had found common ground in urging the Queen to banish Diana from the Court. This the Queen had steadfastly refused to do. She argued that Diana was still married to the Prince of Wales, and that with understanding and kindness (the Queen's perennial cry against the wind) she might be persuaded to reconcile her differences with her husband and settle down once again to married life. And even if she didn't, Diana was still the mother of a future king and as such was entitled to the courtesies that went with that position, if only for William's sake.

That was not how the Queen Mother or

Prince Philip viewed the situation. To their way of thinking, Diana was a danger who had to be isolated before she caused even more damage. The Queen appeared to go along with her mother and her husband's line of reasoning. Whenever Diana appealed to her personally, however, she usually gave way.

Diana had her own reasons for wishing to appear at the Soares banquet, a state occasion of the kind she had always professed to dislike. She telephoned the Queen and told her that she was anxious to attend. The Queen had said yes but, fearful of the anger this would provoke, had failed to inform the rest of the family. 'How *could* you?' the Queen Mother asked. 'I am so shocked.'

The Queen Mother was of the firm opinion that Diana should be banned, regardless of the bad publicity such an act would have prompted. Better to act now, the Queen Mother reasoned, than allow Diana to create more havoc. There were many in the Palace who shared the Queen Mother's conviction. One of the Queen's ladies-in-waiting was particularly incensed by the tolerant attitude adopted by the Sovereign towards both Sarah and Diana. She told the Queen: 'You cannot keep trying to say that they mean no harm— they have nearly brought down the royal family!'

The lady-in-waiting went further, bluntly stating to the Queen that the Monarchy was 'in a very bad situation', that things had to change, and that the first logical step would be to cut Sarah and Diana adrift. The Queen did not take kindly to being lectured to and relations between her and her lady-in-waiting went into frosty abeyance. It was, another member of the household remarked, 'a case of no speakies'.

The rift lasted no more than a few days but when conversation was resumed, the Queen chose to ignore her lady-in-waiting's well-intentioned advice and persevered in treating Diana with kindness. She continued to listen to her complaints, put up with her tears, and offered encouragement when Diana talked excitedly of her latest impulsive plans for the future.

Having caused her mother-in-law such distress, Diana now seemed determined to ingratiate herself back into the Queen's favour. For all her good intentions, however, Diana only succeeded in exacerbating an already unhappy situation. On 21 April the Queen turned sixty-seven. The Duke and Duchess of York and their daughters, Beatrice and Eugenie, were the first to arrive at Windsor Castle and were shown up to the Oak Drawing Room. Diana arrived a few minutes later. She asked, 'Who else is here?' On being told that Fergie had just gone up, Diana said, 'Ohh', and pulled a sarky face.

The Duchess and the Princess were not

talking to each other at the time, and started competing for the Queen's attention. First Sarah, then Diana, would lead their mother-in-law off into a corner for another of the 'chats' the Queen had come to dread. Diana then decorated the room with balloons and handed out paper crowns, much to the annoyance of the Queen who disliked such displays.

'The Queen put a brave face on it, but it left her in a really bad mood,' one of the staff remembered.

Afterwards, the Queen remarked: 'Of course, both my poor daughters-in-law are quite mad.'

Yet still the Queen remained firmly on the fence. It was proving to be a very wearying position. Normally so resilient, she started coming down with colds and bouts of flu, and rather than battling through, as she had always done before, took to her bed instead. Her staff noticed that she was moving more slowly and looking older. She started showing all the listlessness of depression. Even the fortieth anniversary of her coronation in June failed to stir her interest, and it was on her instructions that the event passed all but unremarked. There were no street parties of the kind which had united the country at the time of her Silver Jubilee, but that was hardly surprising—in 1993 the royal family had very little to celebrate. Recalled one member of the household, 'The Queen got herself into such a state that if they had brought her up the Abdication papers she would have signed them then and there.'

What so disturbed the Queen, one of her household recalled, 'was that the Duchess and the Princess were forever saying that they wanted privacy and a private life, that they wanted out, and then, before you knew what, they were doing almost a full round of engagements and appearing in public every five minutes, upstaging the Queen and not doing a jot to help the royal family.'

The contrast in their styles was illustrated by the way Diana upstaged the state visit of the Portuguese president. Soares arrived on 27 April. Diana arranged to address an international conference on eating disorders at Kensington New Town Hall that lunchtime. She prepared for her eight-minute speech with former *Coronation Street* actor Peter Settelen, who made her speak with marbles in her mouth while her back, shoulders and neck were massaged. In it she said, 'I have it on very good authority that the quest for perfection in society can leave the individual gasping for breath at every turn.' The authority was of course Diana herself. Those with bulimia, she said, were 'locked into a spiral of secret despair'. She continued, 'From early childhood many had felt they were expected to be perfect but didn't feel they had the right to express their true feelings to those around them—

feelings of guilt, of self-revulsion and of low personal esteem, creating in them a compulsion to dissolve like a disprin. The illness they developed became their shameful friend.' That night she gatecrashed the Soares banquet.

The result was a foregone conclusion; the following day it was Diana who was on every newspaper's front page. There was no coverage of the state visit other than a mention of the fact that Diana had attended the banquet.

The Palace was outraged. As one of the private secretaries pointed out: 'If any member of the royal family appeared on the front page it should have been the Queen with the President of Portugal. This was an insult to the Monarchy.'

Prince Philip, already seething, 'went ballistic'. There was nothing he could do, however, for it was the Queen herself who, in yet another moment of weakness, had given permission for Diana to attend the banquet.

This need to be noticed extended to her holidays. She had taken William and Harry to Thorpe Park and arranged to be photographed coming down the water chute, much to the exasperation of the Palace which recognized a well-orchestrated photo opportunity when they saw one.

On a trip to the Bahamas, again with her sons, Diana told her police bodyguards that she was determined to enjoy a break away from prying camera lenses. Taking the Princess's instruction at face value, the four accompanying police officers arranged for her to stay in one house and then stationed themselves half a mile away in another to draw off any journalists who might be prowling the area.

The plan worked too well for Diana's liking: William and Harry came by every day to splash in the sea and one photographer managed to get a picture; Diana was left completely alone to lie semi-naked on the sand. After a couple of days she stormed down the beach and demanded of the policemen, 'Who's paying for your villa? The taxpayer, that's who.'

The police were left in no doubt that Diana was angered by her lack of press attention. A row ensued during which Ken Wharfe, the Princess's most loyal Protection Officer, was moved to ask of her: 'I'll do what you tell me—but tell me what you really want.'

The Princess's attitude was duly reported back to Scotland Yard, and from there it was passed to the Palace where it added fuel to the anger that was being directed towards Diana. Princess Margaret had added her voice to the Queen Mother's and Prince Philip's protests. So, too, had Princess Anne, whose view of her sister-in-law was not improved by the way Diana was turning her official engagements into public therapy sessions (at a luncheon in

November for Wellbeing, a charity concerned with the health of mothers and their children, Diana had said in her speech: 'I was supposed to have my head down the loo for most of the day . . . I thought I might postpone my nervous breakdown for a more appropriate moment').

*   *   *

With her own family so firmly united against her, the Queen at last made a move to bring Diana under control. Fellowes was instructed by the Queen to tell Diana that if she continued to behave in such a manner, her services would no longer be 'needed, for the time being'. Diana took this to be a greater threat than the Queen had intended and reacted with savage fury.

On 3 December, at a charity luncheon in aid of the Headway National Head Injuries Association, she made the melodramatic announcement that she would be withdrawing from public life. Jeffrey Archer, the bestselling novelist and soon-to-be disgraced Tory politician, helped her draft the speech. The Queen, who had got wind of what was afoot, urged her to tone down her announcement. So did the Prime Minister. But Diana had no intention of going quietly. 'I owed it to the public to say "Thank you",' she later explained.

It was short announcement, full of

breathless pauses, during which she blamed the media she had herself encouraged, for hounding her to distraction. She was careful not to attack the Queen whom she thanked, along with Prince Philip, for showing her 'kindness and support'. She made no mention of Charles. Once again Diana had stolen the high ground and, by omission, had portrayed her estranged husband as the villain of the piece.

The trouble from the royal family's point of view was that their own stiff upper lip did not fare well against a trembling Diana with tears in her eyes. Her cacophonous cries for help and her hints at a plot of persecution had struck a popular chord in a nation which was re-examining itself and its governing institutions. Diana had turned herself into the icon of the victim society. Compared to her, the royal family looked like dull, emotionally retarded representatives of an increasingly distrusted Establishment.

Even her transgressions were being forgiven. While Charles was being pilloried for his adulterous liaison with Mrs Parker Bowles, the Princess was able to form a string of extramarital attachments with other men without any undue criticism. It was no more than she deserved, so the general feeling had it, after the mistreatment she had suffered at the hands of her husband.

In 1992, before her separation was officially

announced, Diana had taken a shine to Oliver Hoare, a good-looking Old Etonian dealer in Islamic art who was sixteen years her senior.

Hoare, the middle-class son of a Czech immigrant mother and a retired British civil servant, had made his way in society by a combination of having an artistic eye and the entrée afforded by his wife Diane, the heiress to a great French oil fortune. His mother-in-law was a friend of the Queen Mother, and through her he was invited to Windsor Castle during Ascot Week in 1984. There he struck up a friendship with Prince Charles whose interest in Eastern mysticism echoed his own devotion to Sufism, a mystic sect of Islam. The Hoares were soon entertaining the Prince and Camilla to dinner at their lavish £2 million home in Kensington.

Social ambition had never been allowed to deflect the good-looking Hoare's interest in pretty women and when Diana started showing an interest in him, he responded in kind. It turned out to be a fatal attraction.

The Queen at this juncture had no inkling of Diana's latest infatuation and still believed that a reconciliation with Charles was possible. She had always detested the idea of divorce. She would get depressed when the marriages of any of her friends broke up, and would say: 'Why do people do it? How can they break up a home when there are children to consider?' With this in mind, she insisted on inviting

Diana to spend Christmas with the family at Sandringham. Philip was vehemently opposed to the idea, but was overruled by his wife.

There were no tearful scenes of the kind which had marred previous Christmases, but that, as a member of the household recalled, 'was about all that could be said for it'.

Diana arrived at 5 p.m. on Christmas Eve and was given her own suite. The following morning she accompanied the sixteen-strong royal party to church, wearing an eye-catching red coat with a piratical black hat and veil tipped over one eye which drew the cameras. Once again she had stolen the show. Nonetheless, it was a show of family unity which delighted the Queen.

No sooner was the service over, however, than Diana left for London. She told the staff: 'I haven't been invited to lunch.'

In fact Diana had been invited, not only to lunch but to stay as long as she wished. Indeed, it was Diana herself who had first suggested to the Queen that she spend at least three days at Sandringham. The Queen, so keen to reunite her family, had readily agreed. As Diana drove away, Prince Philip turned to the Queen and said, 'I told you so.'

Princess Margaret threw in the acid aside: 'She'd better put her foot down and get through the gates before the press leave or they won't see her go.'

In total, the so-called reconciliation had

lasted nineteen hours and fifty minutes. As far as the family were concerned, Diana was dealing in gestures.

It brought her no cheer, however. Diana spent an utterly miserable Christmas locked in her own unhappiness. One by one the royal family had turned against her. The Queen Mother looked at her with pity, Prince Philip with animosity, Prince Charles with dislike tempered by guilt. Princess Anne made no secret of her feelings towards her, and never had. Princess Margaret, who had once been her most ardent fan, had rounded on her as her behaviour became ever-more eccentric. Their attitude was one of self-preservation. They held her personally responsible for many, indeed most of the problems which had come to beset them. It was a self-centred point of view but hardly an unexpected one: royalty, insulated by the cotton wool of veneration, does not make a habit of criticizing itself.

Only the Queen had the perception to appreciate her daughter-in-law's anguish, but even she was having her patience sorely tried by the temperamental way Diana kept throwing her sympathy and advice back in her face.

The tragedy (and tragedy was what her life was heading towards) was that the Princess could not help herself. She was unwell and neither highly qualified psychiatrist nor New Age therapist had been able to cure her. Its cause, as she acknowledged in her address at Kensington New Town Hall, lay buried in her own childhood. Becoming a member of the royal family had not helped. But nor had Diana been able to help herself. She had struggled to control herself and from time to time bravely declared that her eating disorder had been conquered, that she was on the road to recovery, that she had at last taken charge of her life; but then some small and seemingly insignificant incident would reopen the psychological wounds and the tears would start flowing again. She had, as she said, the ability to 'put on the most amazing show of happiness' however bloody she was feeling, and in a perverse way this only added to her appeal. It was the same combination—of glamour and vulnerability—which had made Marilyn Monroe such a star.

Diana resented the comparison. 'I'm not like her at all,' she insisted. The woman she did identity with, she told me, was Jackie Kennedy Onassis. *Vanity Fair* magazine had published a profile of the president's widow, recounting how badly she had been treated by his family after his death. After reading it Diana declared, 'I know all about being treated like that.' When we were talking about the future and what kind of man she would like to share it with, Diana told me: 'I need someone like Aristotle Onassis.' She then gave a tinkly giggle and said: 'No, perhaps Fergie needs him more.' Yet despite the attempt to dilute what she had said with wit, Diana had left a clear impression that she was the one who was on the look-out for a rich Greek shipowner or his equivalent.

It seemed a lowly, trite ambition for a woman who could have been Queen. But being Queen was something Diana had dreaded. Racked by what she called 'low personal esteem', the responsibility of the job evaded her. In her young mind she had married into what she thought would be a fairytale, only to be overwhelmed by the spirit-sapping restrictions that lay behind the glitz.

The Queen, on coming to the throne, had been equally daunted by the demands of the position and only by sublimating her feelings had she been able to carry out her treadmill of duties. Diana was psychologically incapable of following suit. 'From day one I always knew I would never be the next Queen,' she admitted. The difference here was that while the Queen had been born to the job, Diana had to learn the steps from scratch. It had proved impossible, which added to Diana's insecurity and opened up a gulf between the Queen and daughter-in-law.

This was not the Queen's doing. Without taking sides, and blessed with more compassion than many in her family, her own mother included, she had gone out of her way to assist Diana as best she could. The Princess, however, stood in awe of her mother-in-law's majesty. Even over tea and tears the Queen was still the Queen—and not the mother figure Diana had spent most of her life searching for.

*   *   *

Mrs Shand Kydd had failed to measure up to the role. Indeed, it was her departure from the family home and the unpleasant manner of her leaving which had laid the foundation for so much of her daughter's future unhappiness. Their relationship was at best fluid and there would be long periods when they did not talk, including, sadly, the months leading up to Diana's death. In her absence, Diana had turned to a succession of older women for counsel. They included, at various times, Arts Council chairman Lord Palumbo's wife Hayat, Lady Annabel Goldsmith, the Brazilian ambassador's wife, Lucia Flecha de Lima, Viscount Monckton's daughter Rosa who was just eight years older but much more worldly, and Elsa Bowker, the wealthy widow of a British diplomat who was almost the same age as the Queen Mother.

Mrs Bowker recalled how Diana would spend hours lambasting the Queen's staff, 'complaining that the Palace would have preferred anyone but her. Yet in the same breath she would say how the Queen didn't want her to divorce Prince Charles and how good the Queen was to her, how much Her Majesty had protected her in Buckingham Palace.'

As she did with the Queen, Diana would suddenly appear on Mrs Bowker's doorstep, craving sympathy. 'Once, she phoned me and asked me whether she could come round for a talk,' said the half-Egyptian, half-Lebanese grandame who had first met Diana as a little girl at Althorp. 'I said I had to go out and would be back later. She seemed distraught and, when I got back home, I heard sobbing in the hallway and it was her: she was waiting for me.'

It was part of a pattern born out of despair. 'I used to tell her that she was a woman with the world at her feet, but she simply ignored me, saying I simply didn't understand,' Mrs Bowker said.

The other surrogate mothers had similar experiences. Such was Diana's need for reassurance, however, that she would not accept any criticism from them. When Rosa Monckton, the daughter of Edward VIII's legal adviser and therefore well-versed in the ways of Court, upbraided her for her 'sulky public behaviour' on the Korean trip, Diana did not call her for four months.

On her good days, though, Diana could be as enchanting as her photographs suggested. 'When she was happy she was wonderful company,' recalled Mrs Bowker, referring to her 'sharp and occasionally wicked sense of humour. She wasn't stupid, or slow, as I first thought. People underestimated her intelligence.'

The one woman who really saw both the dark and the bright sides of Diana was her stepmother, Raine. An imposing, impressive lady with an iron hairstyle to rival Lady Thatcher's, she had married Earl Spencer in 1976—and run straight into the razor wire of her stepchildren's hostility. As children they used to chant, 'Raine, Raine, go away', with Diana taking the lead, and many was the lunch which ended with her and her sisters, Sarah and Jane, and their brother Charles being sent to their rooms as punishment for their impertinence. Relations did not improve and in adulthood they called her Acid Raine.

Diana's brother in particular developed a deep and trenchant dislike of her. He disparaged her chocolate-box style of refurbishments of Althorp, and when she tried to rationalize the house's finances he all but accused her of selling off the family heritage through the backdoor. Raine responded by remarking, 'My stepson thinks Botticelli is a pop group.'

The feud reached bizarre proportions on the night of Raine's sixtieth birthday when Diana and her siblings were to be seen climbing down a ladder out of the old nursery window with black plastic bags filled with linen. They were probably the sheets under which their cousin, Sir Winston Churchill nestled as he wrote *Marlborough: My Life and Times*, and over which he spilt ink. They were, they explained, trying to save something from what they saw as Raine's Philistine grasp.

Spencer defended his wife and stated that Raine was acting on his authority. His children refused to listen and the row rumbled on. It was Diana, however, who turned unkind words into harsh deeds. Prince Charles quite liked Raine and her wit. (On the night before Diana's engagement was announced, Johnnie and Raine Spencer had come to Buckingham Palace for a drink. As he was helping her on with her floor-length mink he remarked, 'This is a very nice fur coat', to which Raine replied, 'Yes, it's a little present—from me to me.')

Diana's simmering dislike of Raine came to its distasteful head on the eve of her brother's wedding at Althorp in 1989. Mrs Shand Kydd was there, and the presence under the same roof of the mother she believed had deserted her and the step-mother she so resented was more than she could handle.

As Raine started to come down the grand staircase, Diana, her face flushed with anger, came rushing up behind her and pushed her. Raise tumbled down the stairs and landed in a heap on the landing. Her personal assistant Sue Ingram watched the incident from below and said, 'Her ladyship looked frightened, shocked. Before she could struggle to her feet, Diana neatly sidestepped her bruised stepmother and marched off without a word or a backward glance.'

Another witness was her detective, Ken Wharfe. She told him: 'I have done something awful—I've pushed Raine down fifteen stairs because she was rude about my mother.' This seems unlikely; I have never heard Raine be rude about anyone other than her erstwhile stepson. But then Althorp was not a happy place that day. Her father was even more short-tempered as a result of the stroke he had suffered eleven years earlier; Mrs Shand Kydd was edgy at being back in the house where she had been so unhappy; the bride, Victoria Lockwood, who was suffering from anorexia and drug dependency, hated the way her hair had been put up for the ceremony and tore it down again. Althorp may be a big house but it was too small to contain such a snarl of emotions, and tempers quickly whipped loose.

Whether that could excuse pushing a middle-aged woman down the stairs is a moot point, however. And even if it did, there was no justification whatsoever for the treatment meted out to Raine on the death of her husband three years later.

Like his youngest daughter, Johnnie Spencer could be extremely difficult at times. On his way with his wife to lunch in the West End one day, an argument had broken out in the back seat of their car and Spencer was seen to pick up his copy of the *Financial Times*, screw it into a ball and use it to wipe the make-up off his wife's face. Extraordinarily, Raine maintained her dignity and when they arrived at the restaurant, let her husband out then ordered the chauffeur to drive her home. She had stood by him throughout his illness and never made a disloyal remark about him. Spencer came to depend on her and to ensure that her transition from mistress of Althorp to her inevitably less salubrious widowhood be a smooth one, he asked that she be allowed to stay on at the house for six months.

So low had relations sunk, however, that within hours of his death the staff at Althorp were called together and informed that the Countess was no longer welcome. At the funeral Diana had reached across and touched her stepmother's arm in what was seen as a mark of condolence. Once back at the house normal service was resumed. Raine was told she had to supply detailed receipts before she removed any of her possessions. When her maid was walking out with her mistress's clothes neatly packed in four Louis Vuitton suitcases, she was stopped by Diana and her brother and made to open the cases. Two of the Vuittons were engraved with the letter 'S' for Spencer. The Princess told the maid: 'Those are my father's suitcases. They do not belong to you.' On Diana's instructions the clothes were transferred into black plastic bin liners.

It was a humiliating exit from a house which had been her home for thirteen years, though Raine, whose ability to parcel her life into neatly separated compartments rivalled that of the Queen, professed to take the slights in her stride. She told me shortly afterwards: 'That part of my life is closed.'

And so it would have remained but for Diana's unpredictability. Having successfully demonized her stepmother ('People think I'm Dracula's mother,' Raine said), the Princess then took it upon herself to mend the fence she had so effectively broken. In the late spring of 1993, Raine became engaged to a Jean François de Chambrun, an impecunious French count seven years younger than her own sixty-three. Out of the blue, Raine received a bouquet of flowers at the Ritz hotel in Paris where she was staying with her fiancé.

The Princess was in the city on a shopping trip. It was an open-purse excursion during which she visited Chanel. She was spending so much that the couture house closed the doors of its boutique for her between 4 p.m. and 5 p.m. (when the story leaked to a British newspaper, Diana initially tried to deny that she had ever been near the shop, but to no avail, as the most respected fashion writer in Paris already had details of the clothes she had bought). Back in London, she followed up the flowers with a hand delivered letter of congratulation and an invitation to lunch at Kensington Palace.

Putting curiosity ahead of suspicion, Raine accepted. 'At first the atmosphere was difficult,' Raine recalled. Diana, however, was at her most charming. She said that she wanted to say something that was difficult but which came from her heart. She said: 'Raine, thank you for looking after my father. I know you loved him.' She then stood up, walked round to her stepmother, and embraced her.

'Sorry' was not a word in Diana's lexicon. This was her way of apologizing. Raine accepted the gesture at face value. 'Sometimes you don't have to say the word sorry to mean it,' Raine recalled. 'Thanking me for looking after Johnnie was her way of expressing it.'

Looking back on the years of animosity between Earl Spencer's wife and his daughter, Raine observed: 'It is very difficult to share a man.'

The ice of enmity broken, Diana and Raine forged a friendship which lasted until the Princess's death. They took to having regular lunches together and spoke on the telephone almost every day. Raine became Diana's closest and most trusted confidante. The Princess told me: 'I'd rather speak to Raine than to my mother. She is the mother I never had.'

As close as they were, there was one man

Diana was not prepared to share and that was Oliver Hoare. There is little doubt that she was totally besotted by him: according to Elsa Bowker she wanted him to divorce his wife and move abroad with her to either Italy or France.

This was not a romance Diana was prepared to publicize. Although separated, she was still the wife of the future king whom she had publicly branded as an adulterer. Another inconvenience was that Hoare was a married man for whom discretion was a compelling consideration, and on at least one occasion he was reduced to smuggling himself into Kensington Palace in the back of a car. Once inside, his high-handedness quickly irritated both her staff and, more especially, the policemen assigned to protect her. In the opinion of one, 'Oliver Hoare was the turning point.'

He was observed walking around the Princess's quarters as late as four o'clock in the morning, smoking a cigar, a habit which had led to so much friction with Edward Adeane. His proprietorial attitude extended beyond treating the royal palace as if he lived there. For motives that can only be guessed at, he urged the Princess to get rid of her Protection Officers. They were, he said, an inconvenience and a hindrance to her life.

It was advice which Diana heeded. She started trying to give them the slip, once running away from her bodyguard on a shopping trip to Kensington High Street. The policeman refused to follow. Diana returned two hours later and asked why he hadn't run after her, to be told that protection was a two-way business and that if she didn't want to fulfil her side, there was no point in her having a police bodyguard at all.

Diana had formed close attachments to her Personal Protection Officers (in the case of Mannakee extremely close indeed). They had been her friends and her companions, giving her encouragement as well as security. In her endeavour to disentangle herself from the royal family, however, she had come to see them as the eyes and ears of those officials at the Palace she called 'my enemies'. Convinced she was being bugged, and on Fergie's prompting (the two women were briefly talking again) she called in an independent security firm to 'sweep' Kensington Palace. The Scotland Yard officer regarded the efforts of the interlopers as 'risible'. It was time for a parting of the ways. It came shortly after Christmas in 1993.

The festivities at Sandringham were even more gloomy than they had been a year before. The Queen Mother had been forced to use a wheelchair because of an abscess on her leg, Prince Philip was cantankerous and Fergie had been banished to Wood Farm for the second year running. There was no talk from the Queen about a reconciliation this time.

361

This was a holding operation mounted in the cause of what ragged remnants were left of the family's 'unity'. At church the following morning the Queen Mother dispensed with the golf cart the Queen had bought for her and walked down the aisle to her pew, but her game performance could not save the show. No sooner was the service over than Diana was on her way back to London. 'I'm going to spend the afternoon with the homeless,' she declared.

As soon as she was gone, the atmosphere lightened and a holiday spirit which had been missing immediately took hold. The staff put a dish on the table. They lifted the lid to reveal a joke talking chicken made of rubber which reduced those who were left to helpless laughter. Four days later Diana announced that she was dispensing with her police bodyguards.

Getting rid of the Scotland Yard men brought her no closer to the Islamic art dealer, however. Hoare had engaged in a five-year affair with Ayesha, the Turkish wife of financier-cum-fraudster Asil Nadir, the head of Polly Peck who fled Britain for the sanctuary of northern Cyprus when his business misdealings were exposed. In 1989, when Ayesha's demands that he leave his wife, his two sons Tristan and Damien and daughter Olivia, became too insistent, Hoare ended their relationship.

Diana proved equally unrelenting in her demands. Their clandestine meetings began to end in tears. One night she leapt out of his car in Sloane Square and fled to Kensington Gardens where Hoare, who had been on his way to see his sick daughter Olivia, eventually found her weeping on a park bench, two hours later. According to Simone Simmons Diana started wounding herself, as she had done when she was with Charles, 'to call Hoare's attention to her'.

As Hoare tried to distance himself from her, Diana went in telephone pursuit and in a scene straight out of the Clint Eastwood film, *Play 'Misty' for Me*, started bombarding his home with silent telephone calls. His wife Diane insisted her husband report the matter to the police. He should have reported the matter to the Royal Protection squad who would have dealt with the matter quietly, but that was hardly possible, given his campaign against them. Instead he went to the local police who reported the matter to the Home Office. Hoare suffered the indignity of being brought in for questioning, and the story made its way into the newspapers. Diana tried to pass the blame, first on to her staff, then to a schoolfriend of one of the Hoare boys, but her excuses did not bear examination. The nuisance calls were traced irrefutably by the police to Diana.

The image of a woman possessed was not

one that Diana wished to present to a public increasingly confused, but still essentially on the side of the beleaguered princess. There were more tearful meetings with the Queen who, against the ever-sharper complaints of her family, continued to offer her sympathy.

In private, the Queen was becoming almost as aggravated with her daughter-in-law as the rest of the Court. Normally so reticent, she was now openly discussing the situation with her family and staff. With Bobo MacDonald gone (the old lady who had been at the Queen's side all her life had died in 1993), she sought the counsel of her mother. In a voice tinged with despair, she asked: 'What have I done with my children? It's all a disaster.'

The Queen Mother looked up from the card table where she was playing patience and said: 'Darling, I just don't know why you care any more. It's another generation. Let them get on with it.'

It was an approach the Queen Mother had followed all her royal life. The responsibility, however, was her daughter's and it was beginning to weigh heavily. She was caught in the middle with Philip, Anne and Margaret on one side and her daughters-in-law on the other. When Philip banned Fergie from Balmoral, the Queen waited until he had left and then invited the Duchess and her daughters to spend a few days at the castle. She was even more accommodating with

Diana. While Philip raged, the Queen stood by her guns and continued to insist that the Princess needed support, not condemnation. Her circumspection was to a large extent based on her fear of Diana's media power. She had become so concerned at the effect Diana was having on the Monarchy as a central force in British life that she even managed to convince herself that no one would turn up at Buckingham Palace for the fiftieth anniversary of VE Day commemorating the end of the Second World War in Europe. Throughout the early morning she kept looking out the window, anxiously checking to see if anyone was there. By the time she made her balcony appearance the Mall was full and St James's Park overflowing.

'Her Majesty was thrilled,' a member of her staff remembered. 'When she went on to the balcony she remained stony-faced for fear of showing too much emotion. She was actually close to tears.'

The response of the public on such a significant national occasion could not settle another looming fear, however. The Queen was becoming ever-more worried about the well-being of her grandson and eventual heir. As she explained, Diana *had* to be protected from the circling vultures—for Prince William's sake.

Another, although less well-articulated, reason for the Queen's tolerance of her daughter-in-law was that she was not getting on well with Prince Charles and was therefore more inclined to see the situation from Diana's viewpoint.

*   *   *

In the aftermath of the separation announcement the Prince had become evermore grand in ways that began to annoy the Queen. On his out of season trips to Scotland, for instance, he was no longer content with the modest comfort of the Craigowan lodge as the rest of the family were, and instead stayed at the Queen Mother's altogether more luxurious home, Birkhall. The Balmoral estate will one day be his. The Queen objected to the way he acted as if it already were. When she arrived at Craigowan for a short break, she found that the table lights were missing. She was told that Charles had personally ordered they be taken across to Birkhall. Angered by her son's presumption, the Queen immediately drove there, collected up the missing lamps and took them back to Craigowan. It was an inconsequential incident but indicative of the strains that were appearing in the Queen's relationship with her heir.

A further, and more serious, problem was the position of Mrs Parker Bowles. The Queen continued to look on her with favour. 'She is,' she said, 'a much maligned woman.' But well aware of the public's hostility towards her, she was keen for Charles to downplay his involvement with a woman who was still married to another man. The Prince, blinkered by self-interest, refused and insisted that the position of Camilla in his life was 'non-negotiable'. By so doing he played straight into the wrong hands, as the Queen warned him he would.

In June 1994, Charles gave a candid television interview to Jonathan Dimbleby to coincide with the authorized biography of his life and princely duties which the broadcaster was writing to mark the twenty-fifth anniversary of his investiture as Prince of Wales. It wasn't his good works that drew thirteen million people to their TV screens that summer night, however, but the leaked disclosure that Charles would come clean about his affair with Camilla.

The matter was actually handled with great tact. Dimbleby said: 'The most damaging charge that is made in relation to your marriage is that you were, because of your relationship with Camilla Parker Bowles, from the beginning, persistently unfaithful to your wife and thus caused the breakdown . . .' Charles responded by saying that 'Mrs Parker Bowles is a great friend of mine . . . I'm terribly lucky to have so many friends who I think are wonderful and make the whole difference to my life which would become intolerable otherwise.'

Ignoring the evasion, Dimbleby pressed further. He asked: 'Were you, did you try to be faithful and honorable to your wife when you took on the vow of marriage?' Charles replied, 'Yes, absolutely.' Dimbleby: 'And you were?' Charles: 'Yes. Until it became irretrievably broken down, us both having tried.'

The Prince then went on to say how 'deeply regrettable' that was and how it was 'the last possible thing I ever wanted to happen. I mean, I'm not a total idiot . . .' The date for the breakdown of the marriage, Dimbleby later clarified, was 1986.

The Palace, on learning what he intended to say, had followed the example of the Spanish court which consistently avoided personal questions, and strongly urged him not to discuss such intimate details of his life. The Prince refused to listen and had pushed ahead regardless, in the belief that by telling the truth he would put an end to the endless speculation. It was a naïve judgement. The interview was hardly a purple exposé of lust and licentious infidelity. But it was more than any British prince of the realm had ever confessed to and that was enough to brand him as a self-confessed adulterer—a label that would haunt him for years to come.

It was not a mistake his mother had ever made. She gave speeches, made addresses and passed comments. What she had never done is give an interview. The reason given, as her husband had explained, being 'I think, probably, the risks would be greater than the benefits.'

It was an opinion shared by the Queen Mother. On her engagement she had given an interview to a London evening paper, been severely reprimanded by George V for doing so, and never granted another one. The dangers were simply too great. By agreeing to discuss his private life, Charles had discarded royalty's protective mantle of silence.

Charles was not the only one, however, to underestimate the power of television to shape opinions in unwelcome ways. So, too, had Diana. The Hoare telephone calls had harmed her reputation, and her involvement with the England rugby captain, Will Carling, had further added to the unfavourable impression which was starting to form. Diana once again denied any impropriety but Carling's wife, Julia, made it quite clear what she thought of the Princess. She said: 'This has happened (to Diana) before and you hope she won't do these things again, but she obviously does.' Carling promised not to see Diana again. When he did, Julia demanded a separation in September 1995. In another pointed swipe at Diana, Mrs Carling declared: 'It hurts me very much to face losing my husband in a manner which has become outside my control.' The pitiable princess was starting to look more like what one newspaper called 'a homewrecker'.

To counter the bad publicity, she returned to public duties—much to the dismay of the Queen and her advisers who wanted her to keep her head down. But if the Palace wanted her off the stage, there were plenty of people willing to offer her a platform. Her glamour and her hands-on charity work for the broken and diseased had won her international approval, and on 11 December 1995, she received the Humanitarian of the Year award from former US Secretary of State Henry Kissinger in a ceremony in New York.

It was exactly the kind of appreciation Diana craved. She had found a role which had earned her praise and recognition. It could have been a glorious foundation on which to rebuild her life. By then, however, it was already too late. Three weeks earlier, on the night of her mother-in-law's wedding anniversary, Diana had taken a sledgehammer to her royal position and lost the support of the one person who had always had her best interests at heart—the Queen.

Her friends had implored her not to give the interview to *Panorama*. When she mentioned it to the Oscar-winning film-maker David Puttnam he warned: 'Don't even think about it.' The television presenter Clive James was equally adamant. He noted: 'I said if that happened, the two camps thing would go nuclear and continue until there was nothing left.' She deliberately did not mention it to either her press secretary, Geoff Crawford, or her private secretary, Patrick Jephson. As employees of the Crown they would have been duty bound to do everything possible to prevent her from committing an act of such folly. But Diana did not want to be dissuaded. She was determined to launch yet another broadside against the Palace and, most damningly, against her estranged husband.

Diana had been outraged by Charles's Dimbleby interview which she saw as a riposte to the Morton book and, as such, a deliberate attempt to discredit her. In fact, Charles had been very careful not to voice any direct criticism of his wife. The accompanying book, however, had made it quite clear that many in the Prince's entourage regarded her as mentally unstable. It was a charge she was determined to refute and to do that she chose the vehicle of television.

The interview, broadcast on 20 November 1995, was watched by an audience of fifteen million in Britain and many millions more worldwide. In it she declared: 'I do not want a divorce.'

That was no longer a matter for her to decide. In giving the *Panorama* interview, Diana had taken the future out of her own hands.

CHAPTER ELEVEN

WITHDRAWAL

Shortly after the *Panorama* interview, the Queen became irritated by a fly. She picked up a can of aerosol pest killer, squirted it, and watched the insect spiral to its fate.

In a voice as sharp as cut glass, she remarked: 'If only one could deal with all one's problems so efficiently.'

On the night of the broadcast the Queen had attended the Royal Variety Show, staged in her honour and starring Cliff Richard, Des O'Connor, Elaine Paige and a host of light entertainment artists. It was her forty-eighth wedding anniversary. But this was not an occasion when she could sit back and enjoy herself. Her mind was preoccupied, as well it might be. She had only heard of Diana's clandestine plan to go public with her complaints less than a week before, by which time the interview was recorded and in the can. She had been given no preview and it was not until the following day that the Queen had a chance to see and hear what her daughter-in-law was saying.

The programme had been recorded by a member of staff, and the Queen watched it on the video in her sitting room at Buckingham

Palace.

Her first reaction, oddly enough, was one of sympathy for Diana's plight. That, at least, was the impression the Queen gave, although members of the household later wondered if they had not misinterpreted the emotions behind the set of her face. Once the full impact of what was Diana had said sank in, however, there was no doubting what the Queen really thought. She was hurt, embarrassed and angry. The overriding emotion, though, was a sense of betrayal.

The Queen had given her unstinting support while others were baying for blood. She had shielded her from the wrath of Prince Philip and the rancour of the Palace courtiers. She had listened patiently to Diana's endless complaints, sat through her tears and believed her when she insisted, over and over again, that she had had no direct involvement in the Andrew Morton book. It was not surprising, therefore, that she felt so badly let down as she watched Diana pour out her heart and venom to the world.

Diana had gone to great lengths to conceal from the Palace what she was up to. Even her own family was unaware of what she was plotting. It was Diana herself who had opened her Kensington Palace door and shown the four-man television crew into her private apartment on 5 November, appropriately enough the 390th anniversary of the gunpowder plot when Guy Fawkes had attempted to blow up the Palace of Westminster and kill the Queen's predecessor, King James I.

She had also taken the trouble to prepare herself thoroughly for her assault on the Crown. All the questions had been submitted in advance and Diana carefully ran through the answers she was going to give. The Princess would later insist that the replies she gave to reporter Martin Bashir's questions were spontaneous. Not so, said Barbara Walters, the doyenne of American interviewers who discussed the interview with Diana after her network, ABC, paid $642,000 for the US rights. 'She rehearsed,' Ms Walters said.

Diana's responses confirmed this. Lines like 'three of us in this marriage' and 'Queen of hearts' came out too glibly from a woman whose most potent weapon had always been her tormented looks rather than what she said. And that arresting remark, 'There is no better way to dismantle a personality than to isolate it', was not off the cuff but a quote from former Beirut hostage Brian Keenan's book, *An Evil Cradling*. In other words, this was a carefully prepared onslaught on the integrity of the royal family.

That was certainly the way the Queen quickly came to regard it. It was not the cries of anguish that so upset the Queen. After all, she had been listening to those herself for the better part of three years. Nor was it her demand that she be allotted a more positive role within the royal family she had half removed herself from. The Queen had long been an admirer of Diana's ability to empathize with the sick and needy. And while she took exception to yet another admission of adultery in her family, she had come to agree with her mother's view that what her grown-up children and their spouses got up to was their own private affair, however contrary to her own moral beliefs that might be.

What was inexcusable and unforgivable was the way Diana, her eyes kohl-lined and haunted, accused the Palace of Machiavellian conspiracy and questioned the wisdom of allowing her estranged husband to ascend the throne. Both charges struck at the tap root of the Monarchy.

As Head of State the Queen relies on a secretariat of advisers whose integrity must be beyond question. Diana had portrayed them as conniving and underhand intriguers who were conducting a personal vendetta against her. Her foreign visits, she said, were being blocked, her letters intercepted. She called them 'the enemy'. The courtiers worked to the instructions of the Queen. By direct implication, therefore, Diana was attacking the Sovereign.

The slur against her husband was just as damaging. When Diana said 'because I know the character I would think that the top job, as I call it, would bring enormous limitations to him and I don't know whether he could adapt to that', she was effectively saying that Charles was unfit to be king.

This was more than any hereditary head of state could tolerate. In a desperate cry of defiance from the battlements, the Princess, reverting to the third person, declared: 'She won't go quietly. I'll fight to the end because I believe I have a role to fulfil and I've got two children to bring up.'

Diana did not go quietly. But go she had to and that was the Queen's decision. It was no longer possible, she reasoned, to allow a member of her family to carry on operating secretly behind her back in such a brutal and ruinous manner.

* * *

In the days immediately following *Panorama* Diana deluded herself that she had achieved her purpose (although quite what that was even she was at a loss to fully explain). She flew to Argentina on an official visit. It was precisely the kind of ambassadorial role she had claimed for herself in the interview. The reality of the situation she had placed herself in soon caught up with her, however.

Her press secretary, Geoff Crawford accompanied her—but only after tendering his resignation beforehand. Her private secretary, Patrick Jephson, followed suit a few weeks later. Princess Margaret, once her ally, wrote her a stinging letter in which she accused Diana of having let everyone down and being 'incapable of making even the smallest sacrifice'. Charles's friend Nicholas Soames, grandson of Sir Winston Churchill and a junior minister in the government, went on television and said she was showing 'the advanced stages of paranoia'. Her own friend, Rosa Monckton, wrote: 'It was Diana at her worst.'

Prime Minister John Major, concerned about the constitutional implication of the Princess's outburst, said that as the mother of a future king, she should have a 'worthwhile' public role, but former Prime Minister James Callaghan entered the fray to write sarcastically: 'I can only hope she was not being too literal when she said she wanted to be an ambassador for her country. The life of a real ambassador would bore her rigid.' The Foreign Secretary, Michael Rifkind specifically ruled out a formal job.

Lord Wakeham, the chairman of the Press Complaints Commission who had once been a supporter of Diana, and whom the Princess had been urging to introduce a privacy law, gave dire warning that those who voluntarily bring their private lives under scrutiny 'must bear the consequences of their action'.

One by one the forces of government were

lining up against her, as they were bound to. As Callaghan observed: 'The impact of the broadcast can only be to weaken the Monarchy, yet the constitution demands a Head of State firmly grounded in the people.'

It was as Head of State, rather than hitherto accommodating mother-in-law, that the Queen at last decided to take action. It was decisive in the extreme. Early in December she wrote two letters, one to Diana, hand-delivered to Kensington Palace, the other to Charles at Highgrove. In them she expressed her anger and frustration. And she spelled out her 'desire for an early divorce'.

This was more than a request. It was tantamount to an order. As the incident with the fly illustrated, she had reached the end of her tether.

Diana was stunned. She had convinced herself that she had scored a public relations coup and established herself as a 'strong' and 'independent' woman. Instead she found herself depicted as irresponsible and manipulative. Her 'energy healer' Simone Simmons noted: 'When she had to face the bitter truth from the Queen, Diana fell apart. She couldn't sleep at night and started taking very strong sleeping pills. She was constantly in tears, reflecting over and over on what might have been.'

The day after the contents of the Queen's letter were leaked to the press, Diana took

William and Harry with her to the Harbour Club in Chelsea where she worked out (and where she had enjoyed furtive trysts with Hoare and Carling). It was her way of spelling out her clear message that the future of her sons would be a vital factor in any divorce negotiations. In bringing the boys into play, however, Diana was confirming the Queen's worst fears. In the press statement which followed the letter, the Palace spokesman had emphasized that the Queen would continue to do all she could to help the Prince and Princess 'and most particularly their children in this difficult time'.

The Queen had been growing ever-more disturbed at the effect the Waleses' squabbling was having on her grandsons. Harry seemed to take it in his stride. William, on the other hand, was clearly wounded by the rows and by the way his mother insisted on involving him in her problems.

In the Morton book she had revealed how he would push tissues under the door as she sat crying in the lavatory. Now it was William who was locking himself away in the bathroom, sometimes for hours on end, and ignoring the entreaties of staff and mother alike to come out. When he eventually did, she would sit him beside her on her bed and pour out her woes.

It was an enormous burden to impose on a youngster confronted with the problems of adolescence. Any child would have been agitated and William was certainly no exception. As a youngster he had taken his mother's side, sometimes shouting at his father, 'Why do you make Mummy cry all the time?' As he grew older he began to take a more objective view of his parents' problems. Caught in the middle, more introverted and a lot more sensitive than his young brother, William responded by lapsing into long periods of silence.

He had watched *Panorama* at Eton. He had been called out of his bedsitting room during the quiet hour between 8 p.m. and 9 p.m. that evening and taken down to his housemaster's study. He was shocked. What perturbed him most was his mother's admission of her affair with Hewitt.

'I wish I had never mentioned Hewitt,' Diana told me. 'He was always so good to the boys—and to me.' Her regret was understandable: William refused to speak to her for several days afterwards. Slowly but steadily he was starting to distance himself from his mother.

This was partly to do with his age. He was entering a stage in life when he was determined to break loose from his mother's apron strings, no matter how tight she tied them. There were other factors at work, though, and one of them was Balmoral. As much as Diana disliked the place, William was happy there. In Scotland he was free to engage in the field sports of fishing and stalking and shooting which became his passion. He could drink wine and beer without being leapt on by the royal family's critics, drive quad bikes over the hills and old cars along the private roads without need of a licence. He also had a grandmother there to indulge him.

The Queen, so remote with her own children, was noticeably more benign with the next generation. She still believed in old-fashioned manners (when King Hassan of Morocco kept her waiting on an official visit, she remarked: 'That comes from not having a Scottish nanny'), and there was no place for elbows on tables or tongues poked out at any of her homes. High spirits, however, which had once been discouraged, were now looked on with amusement. At the Windsor Horse Show one year, Princess Beatrice, excited at seeing Prince Philip competing in the carriage driving, started shouting, in her shorthand for grandpa, 'Gamps, Gamps.' The Queen told me later: 'It quite put him off.'

She was increasingly easygoing in her Highland redoubt and thoroughly enjoyed having William and his brother to stay. When they were little, she had arranged for suitable ponies to be brought up from the Royal Mews in London for their pleasure, and taken them shopping for ice creams and sweets at the local shop in Ballater, just as she had Prince Edward when he was young. If the weather was too inclement for them to venture outside, she had made sure that there was always a stack of videos for them to watch. She often joined them in front of the screen and once remarked that she had sat through Steven Spielberg's *ET* more times 'than I care to recall'.

As they grew older both William and Harry became enthusiastic participants in the picnics and barbecues their mother so detested. They would travel up into the hills in the Land Rover driven by the Queen. After lunch they liked to go boating on the lochs or help the Queen prepare afternoon tea in one of the estate bothies like the one beside Loch Muick which Queen Victoria had described as 'our little wild place'. Consisting of two cottages linked by a connecting passage, it was where William's great-grandfather George VI had been sent to recover from whooping cough. Another cottage they used was the one in Ballochbuie Forest which the Queen had lent to another Beirut hostage, Terry Waite, and his family after he was freed in December 1991.

While the boys were up on the moor enjoying themselves, Diana was usually to be found, fuming and ill, back in the castle. She found the atmosphere at Balmoral debilitating and the weather atrocious. To protect herself from the cold she wore thick thermal underwear, which prompted the Queen to remark that her 'layers and layers of Damart' (a brand of thermals) meant she wouldn't need to spend any more money on overcoats. It was a lighthearted remark of the kind which was likely to bring on another bout of bulimia.

However much she objected, however, Diana had no choice but to bring her sons up to Balmoral every year. The Queen had made it clear that she saw it as Diana's responsibility to bring her children to Scotland so they could get to understand that part of their heritage and, more importantly, to get to know their grandmother. Diana was forever insisting that she wanted William and Harry to enjoy an 'ordinary' childhood. But the princes were not ordinary. William was born to be king, and although he was still too young to fully grasp the responsibilities that entailed, he was coming to enjoy the rhythms of the royal calendar. His mother took him to the Caribbean and down water slides at amusement parks, but it was Scotland and Sandringham where he was at his happiest, and in yet another poignant twist to the story, Diana came to feel that she was being slowly excluded from her son's life.

She was forcefully reminded of William's destiny when she threatened to move abroad, taking her sons with her. It was spelt out to her that William was second in line to the Throne and that under no circumstances would he be allowed to leave Britain to be brought up in America, Italy or anywhere else. The Queen was not trying to deny Diana reasonable maternal rights. She was simply protecting her dynasty.

What Diana dreaded most was that even if she stayed in Britain, attempts would be made to take her sons away from her on the grounds, as she herself put it, that she was 'a basket case'. Such an option was never considered. The Queen was of the strong opinion that William and Harry should see as much of their mother as possible. She was equally determined, however, that they should have a stable upbringing. She wanted no repeat of the Marina Ogilvy saga.

The daughter of Princess Alexandra and Angus Ogilvy, Marina, had rebelled against her royal background. She had accused her father of drinking too much and her mother of ordering her to have an abortion to protect the good name of the Monarchy. The Queen, who had always considered her young cousin to be such 'a lovely young girl', immediately excluded her from the royal presence and struck her off her Christmas card list. Marina was proof, if any were needed, that the strictures which once bound the royal family together no longer held fast. What was unfortunate in a distant relation would have been a disaster for the immediate family, already coming apart at the seams.

Prince Charles was aware of the problem. He had been a somewhat distant father when

William and Harry were in their infancy. He had bathed with them when they were babies but in their junior years it was with their detectives that they romped and wrestled. 'Please fight with us, too,' William had begged, but Charles was not comfortable stripping off his shirt and getting down on the floor for a rough-and-tumble. When they entered their teens, however, he started drawing closer to them. He took a growing interest in their development, and insisted that they be allowed to enjoy their youth in a way he had been denied.

Over afternoon tea at Highgrove one day, he had voiced to me his concerns about the pitfalls that might befall them on the way. One of his major concerns, as it is for all parents, was drugs. He asked me: 'But how do you warn them of the dangers?' His own experience of such matters, he explained, had been confined to the occasional cigarette, smoked surreptitiously behind the chicken coops at Sandringham. 'And I gave that up when I was eleven,' he said. The best thing he could do, he continued, was drum into his sons a sense of moral responsibility.

It was with that end in mind that Charles arranged for William to see his grandmother on Sunday afternoons. He would cross over the bridge from Eton and make his way the few hundred yards to Windsor Castle. The Sovereign and the sovereign-to-be met for tea in the Oak Drawing Room overlooking the quadrangle where Diana had danced by herself with such abandon on the night of Prince Andrew's twenty-first birthday party.

They talked over their week. William would tell his grandmother what he had been doing at school. She explained what she had been doing, ever-mindful that one day, God willing, William would be in her position.

The Queen enjoyed these sessions with her grandson which continued throughout his time at Eton, and her staff noted how pleased she always was to see him. Diana protested that no one had helped her adjust to being a princess. William was being taught from an early age what it meant to be a king.

As William started to assume his rightful position within the royal family, so Diana began to withdraw to its outer edges. For the sake of form she was once again invited to join her sons at Sandringham, and having agreed, then changed her mind (much to the relief of the Queen who was wearying of trying to keep the peace) and flew off to the West Indies with her secretary, Victoria Mendham. William and Harry joined their father in Norfolk.

*   *   *

In February, the divorce negotiations got serious. On the fifteenth, Diana had a meeting with the Queen at Buckingham Palace. It was attended by the Queen's deputy private secretary Robin Janvrin who took notes because, as the Queen had come to realize, 'bulimics rewrite history in twenty-four hours.'

One of the central questions that came under discussion was whether Diana would remain 'Her Royal Highness' after the divorce. In Diana's account, she was anxious to keep the HRH but told her friends that the Queen wanted her to surrender it. 'You don't say no to the Queen,' Diana declared.

On 28 February she had a 45-minute meeting, this time with Prince Charles at St James's Palace. The discussions were supposed to be private, but as soon as it was over the Princess issued a statement saying that she had agreed to the divorce, would continue to be involved in all decisions involving William and Harry—and that under pressure she would be giving up her HRH.

The woman clerk was still typing up the notes from the Queen's meeting with Diana. Astonished to see the details of what had supposedly been a totally private discussion broadcast on the news networks, the Queen immediately countered with an announcement of her own. In a strongly worded statement her press secretary, Charles Anson, insisted: 'The decision to drop the title is the Princess's and the Princess's alone. It is wrong that the Queen or the Prince asked her. I can state categorically that is not true.' Just in case

Diana chose to reinterpret what her 'enemies' were saying, Anson added: 'The Palace does not say something specific on a point like this unless we are absolutely sure of the facts.'

The Queen was furious at what she saw as Diana's attempt to reinterpret the truth as she saw fit. A member of the household confirmed: 'The Queen never mentioned her losing her title and neither did Prince Charles. It was a figment of her own imagination or manipulation to say this.'

The clerk had been worried that she would be blamed for leaking the details of the meetings. To put her mind at rest the Queen sent her a message telling her that under no circumstances was she to blame herself, saying, 'We know who it is.'

The following month, Diana telephoned Windsor Castle and asked if she could bring William and Harry round for tea. A few minutes later, in a carefully arranged double strategy, the Duchess of York rang and asked if she could bring Beatrice and Eugenie. It was the day after the Queen had visited Dunblane, the quiet Scottish town where sixteen children and their teacher had been shot dead at their school by a crazed gunman who then took his own life. Diana had been 'desperate' to get up to Dunblane. She was stopped by Sir Robert Fellowes who informed her that this was not her job. He was acting on the Queen's instructions.

The Queen had been deeply moved by the Dunblane tragedy. In a private meeting with the bereaved parents she had wept openly as she talked of 'grief and profound sympathy'. She had performed an essential role of the Sovereign by providing a focus for the nation's feelings. She was in no mood afterwards to deal with her daughters-in-law.

Up until then the Queen had been clear in her instructions as to how Diana should be received. She had told her staff on innumerable occasions: 'Treat the Princess of-Wales with kid gloves. Remember, she is the mother of the future king and her influence will go into shaping the Monarchy of the future.' Her attitude had changed in the weeks since *Panorama*, however. Told of Diana and Fergie's request upon returning from her morning ride, she said: 'Call back the Princess of Wales and tell her the boys can come, but she cannot. I can't face Diana. I don't know what she is going to do or to say. I just can't take it any more.'

Asked about the Duchess, she said: 'I can face her. At least she behaves herself when she is with me.'

Prince Philip who was there declared that he could not face either of them and would take tea in his study. Prince Edward, who was also at the castle, said that he could not face them either and would have tea with his father. The Queen was left in the Oak

Drawing Room on her own to entertain Fergie and her daughters and William and Harry who arrived shortly afterwards without their mother.

In April, the Queen had yet another reason for irritation. She had planned to celebrate her seventieth birthday party with a dinner at the Waterside Inn, a restaurant not far from Windsor. The story was leaked to the press, prompting the Queen to say: 'Thank you, Diana, for ruining another day for me.' The party had to be moved to Frogmore, a house on the Windsor estate.

The ground was now set for what proved to be a long-drawn out, and at times extremely fraught, squabble over the divorce terms. Captain Mark Phillips, whose own divorce settlement had been less than generous, visited Diana at Kensington Palace and advised the Princess that on no account should she agree to the start of proceedings until a final package had been agreed. Diana told me that the Earl of Snowdon gave her similar advice.

The Princess was impressed by their arguments. She told me: 'They both told me to get the money first. They were both treated very badly. That's why I held out. I was determined that was not going to happen to me.' She told her lawyers they should first work out the details of the finances, her future home, her future role and her title before she would agree to a divorce. She warned that she could delay matters by up to five years.

The Queen, who was anxious that the Princess should receive a generous and amicable settlement, was annoyed by the prevarication. There was method in the delay, however. Fergie was going through her own divorce at the same time and Diana's lawyer, Anthony Julius, was using that case as his guide. He went so far as to refer to Sarah as 'the yellow canary', a reference to the birds miners used to take underground with them to give warning of any poisonous gases.

To add to the Palace's feeling that they were being led up the garden path, Diana's team then demanded that Charles sign a confidentiality agreement. This the Prince refused to do on the grounds that his word was his bond and that to suggest otherwise would cast doubt on his honour.

When the negotiations did finally get started, the Princess opened the bargaining with a wholly unacceptable demand for £46 million. This was finally whittled down to a one-off payment of some £17 million. That still left the matter of the title, however.

Fergie had been stripped of hers. The Palace had looked at the Duchess's behaviour and drawn their own disparaging conclusions; the words the courtiers and Prince Philip used to describe her were unflattering in the extreme. There was no way they were going to allow her to fly the world, using her HRH as an international calling card, and in her divorce from Prince Andrew that April she was reduced to the ranks.

Diana was a different case altogether. She was the mother of the future king and many senior ministers and constitutional experts believed that she should carry the status befitting that position. Diana had overplayed her hand, however. She was no longer the virginal bride of yesteryear, but a mature and experienced woman approaching her middle thirties. She was the one who had brought the issue of the HRH to the negotiating table when she unilaterally announced that she was giving it up because that was what the Queen wished.

The Queen had said no such thing. She continued to harbour serious misgivings about taking it away and right up to the last moment had sought a way out of the impasse Diana had created. In the end Diana found it for herself. When she refused to give a commitment to work in cooperation with the Palace and insisted that she had the absolute right to set her own agenda, the Queen's hand was forced.

Diana made one last desperate telephone call to the Queen at Buckingham Palace and pleaded to be allowed to remain Her Royal Highness. The Queen replied that the matter was 'very difficult'. It was her way of saying no. As the Queen later remarked: 'She wanted to give up the title—so give it up she will.'

On 28 August 1996, Charles and Diana were divorced. The fairytale which had turned into a Gothic nightmare was almost at its end. Diana, Princess of Wales, had one year and three days left to live.

CHAPTER TWELVE

BUCKINGHAM PALACE

Buckingham Palace still stands in its pale magnificence in the heart of London, the enduring symbol of royal authority. Windsor Castle, the family seat of royalty since the reign of William the Conqueror a millennium ago, has been restored to its ancient splendour. Flowers are still laid by the railings at Kensington Palace but the crowds are long gone and a familiar calm has returned to British life.

But if the passions of those extraordinary days in September 1997 have been spent, the aftershocks continue to ripple. They mark, not the new beginning which many in the multitude that converged on the capital were demanding, and which for one tumultuous, clamorous week threatened to overwhelm the House of Windsor, but the end of a system which was put to the test and found wanting.

A Union Flag now flies over Buckingham Palace when the Sovereign is not in residence. It is a small concession to the demands of the people on the public side of the stately gates, but one which symbolizes the greater changes taking place within.

For the first time in its history the Palace is open to the public and it was the Queen, and not the taxpayer as was originally mooted, who paid for the refurbishment of Windsor Castle after the fire. The royal yacht *Britannia* has been turned into a tourist attraction and the Sovereign now flies by commercial airline and stays in hotels. The cost of the Monarchy has been slashed—from £53 million from the year before Diana's death, to £38 million two years after it—and the pomp and ceremony which was once deemed so appealing but increasingly came to be viewed as grandiose pretension has been streamlined.

Much of this downsizing was inevitable. Britain is a modern democratic nation ruled by a government determined to close the book on a past and its imperial pageants which it finds both embarrassing and irrelevant. But the legacy of Diana undoubtedly gave impetus and direction to the process.

Even royal weddings, once the sovereign hallmark of monarchy, have been moderated. When the Queen's youngest son, Prince Edward—or plain Edward Windsor, as he prefers to be known in business—married the commoner Sophie Rhys-Jones in 1999, there were no grand processions down the Mall, just a simple carriage drive through Windsor after a quiet family ceremony. And the bride and groom did not kiss afterwards. The rationale for such displays died in the tragedy of a Paris underpass.

The Queen does not like many of the changes that have been forced upon her. She is constitutionally required to remain above politics, but it is no secret that she is apprehensive about much of what is being done by a Labour government which still, in theory, acts in her name.

She disapproved of the abolition of the seven-hundred-year-old right of hereditary peers to sit in the House of Lords, seeing it as a move against the hereditary principle in general which would eventually lead to the Palace gates.

She regarded the suggestion that the homeless should be housed in flats above Admiralty Arch while she resided in Buckingham Palace at the other end of the Mall as cheap gesture politics of a cheap but dangerous kind.

She is irritated at the way Prime Minister Tony Blair has been late for their weekly meetings and, on occasion, even cancelled them, seeing it as a slight to her constitutional position.

She was also nonplussed at the way Blair

sidestepped the constitutional niceties and invited Diana to Sunday lunch at Chequers. She arrived with Prince William in tow and declared that she would like to be a peacemaker amongst fighting countries. That is not the role of a constitutional monarch and she felt it wrong that the Prime Minister should have given what she saw as encouragement to a princess who had renounced her official position.

On a more personal level, she detested a new, jazzed-up version of the National Anthem—'my song,' as she once quipped to Prince Philip.

In her final Christmas address of the last millennium, the Queen stressed the 'importance of history' when she said: 'The sheer rate of change seems to be sweeping away so much that is familiar and comforting . . . We can make sense of the future if we understand the lessons of the past. Winston Churchill said that "the further backwards you look, the further forward you can see".'

Sir Winston Churchill was one of her favourite Prime Ministers. Tony Blair is not.

There was no direct mention of Diana, Princess of Wales, in the Queen's Christmas speech. That is one piece of the past which the royal family would like to distance themselves from. The Monarchy survived the Abdication crisis of 1936 by retreating into itself and becoming worthy and dull. Diana gave it back its glamour—with dire result.

She captured the imagination of millions and in her brief, spectacular reign she swept away the preconceptions and expectations of what the royal family was like and how they really conducted themselves. By putting her marital unhappiness on to the national agenda, she called into question the relationship between the established Church of England and the Crown. By challenging the probity of the Palace courtiers, the civil service which serves the Head of State, she cast doubt on the integrity of the Monarchy itself.

In her demands for love and sympathy, she gave self-fulfilment precedence over duty. Princess Anne discharges nearly seven hundred engagements a year while the Queen, now an old-age pensioner, continues with her gruelling schedule of state visits on behalf of Britain and the Commonwealth, but it is the image of an embattled, badly treated young woman 'struggling to survive' which dominates the memory.

The recriminations continued in death. The Prince of Wales founded and runs Britain's largest charitable network dedicated to helping young people, but it is his relationship with Diana's replacement, Camilla Parker Bowles, which commands people's attention.

And such is the climate of suspicion generated by her life and death, that many saw a conspiracy behind that fatal car crash. The

Royal and Diplomatic Protection Department of the Metropolitan Police made their own study of the circumstances leading up to the accident, concluded that there was absolutely no evidence of foul play and now use it as a 'how not to' training exercise. Yet television and radio programmes gave Mohamed al Fayed the air time to make sweeping accusations which culminated in his allegation that Prince Philip was behind a plot to murder his own daughter-in-law.

In the confusion and hysteria which followed her death there was room, it seemed, to accommodate every crank and Diana's name has been used in a way which would have shocked her.

POSTSCRIPT

Prince Charles was Diana's first love. She was not his. She told me how, not long before their marriage, she had asked him about his previous girlfriends and were they 'better' than her. An unusual word, but I knew what she meant.

It is a question many young women ask. It is one any worldly man avoids answering.

Instead of side-stepping the subject, the Prince made the mistake of telling her about his other relationships. One name stuck in her mind. It was that of Camilla Parker Bowles. Diana could not shake it from her memory. It came to cloud her judgement and colour her actions. She convinced herself that whenever Charles was absent from their home, he was seeing Camilla.

It became her obsession. And in the end it became the reality.

Not until she was almost at the end of her life did Diana at last admit that there were other reasons for what happened to her marriage, and that Mrs Parker Bowles was not wholly responsible.

'He loved me when we got married and I loved him,' she said. She continued: 'We still love each other now, in a different way. At least, I love him. He is a good person. It is very sad about our marriage.'

By then, of course, it was too late. It is impossible to backtrack on a relationship or to press the rewind button and start again. But the thought occurs—and many who knew her well, especially in the early days, believe this to be true—that if Diana had never asked or, more pertinently, if Charles had not answered, the bitterness which tore them apart might have been avoided.

But Diana could not weather the marital storms, as her mother-in-law had done. She had neither the Queen's strength of character nor her ability to compartmentalize her life and put duty before all else.

The Queen did what she could to hold their union together. She wanted Diana to be happy, and gave her sympathy and support. But she also wants her son to be happy, too. She has come to accept how important Camilla is to her son. She has grown tired of their game of what she called 'cat and mouse' and believes that at some point in the future— though 'when' is one of those questions she is too astute to be drawn on—the two will marry.

If they do, the tragic irony is that the fear Diana willed on herself will indeed have come true.

BIBLIOGRAPHY

Barry, Stephen, *Royal Secrets* (Villard Books, 1985)

Royal Service (Macmillan Publishers Ltd, 1993)

Bedell Smith, Sally, *Diana In Search of Herself* (Times Books, 1999)

Benson, Ross, *Charles: The Untold Story* (Victor Gollancz Ltd, 1993)

Berry, Wendy, *The Housekeeper's Diary* (Barricade Books, 1995)

Blundell, Nigel, and Blackhall, Susan, *The Fall of the House of Windsor* (Blake Publishing Ltd, 1992)

Boothroyd, Basil, *Philip* (Longman, 1971)

Botham, Noel, *Margaret: The Untold Story* (Blake Publishing Ltd, 1995)

Bradford, Sarah, *George VI* (Weidenfeld & Nicolson, 1989)

Elizabeth (William Heinemann, 1996)

Crawford, Marion, *The Little Princesses* (Cassell & Co., 1950)

Dempster, Nigel, *Behind Palace Doors* (Orion, 1993)

Dimbleby, Jonathan, *The Prince of Wales* (Little, Brown, 1994)

Ferguson, Sarah, Duchess of York, with Coplin, Jeff, *My Story* (Simon & Schuster, 1996)

Friedman, Dennis, *Inheritance* (Sidgwick & Jackson, 1993)

Harris, Kenneth, *The Queen* (Weidenfeld & Nicolson, 1994)

Heald, Tim, *The Duke: A Portrait of Prince Philip* (Hodder & Stoughton, 1992)

Hewitt, James, *Love and War* (Blake Publishing Ltd, 1999)

Hoey, Brian, *Anne—The Princess Royal* (Grafton Books, 1989)
Mountbatten (Sidgwick & Jackson, 1994)

Junor, Penny, *Charles: Victim or Villain?* (HarperCollins, 1998)

Kortesis, Vasso, *The Duchess of York: Uncensored* (Blake Publishing Ltd, 1996)

Menkes, Suzy, *Queen and Country* (Grafton Books, 1992)

Morton, Andrew, *Diana: Her True Story—In Her Own Words* (Michael O'Mara Books Ltd, 1997)

Pimlott, Ben, *The Queen* (HarperCollins, 1996)

Rose, Kenneth, *King George V* (Macmillan Publishers Ltd, 1983)

Seward, Ingrid, *Diana: Portrait of a Princess* (Weidenfeld & Nicolson, 1987)
By Royal Invitation (Sidgwick & Jackson, 1988)
Royalty Revealed (Sidgwick & Jackson, 1989)
Sarah: HRH the Duchess of York (HarperCollins, 1991)

Royal Children of the Twentieth Century
(HarperCollins, 1993)
Prince Edward: A Biography (Century, 1995)
*The Last Great Edwardian Lady: The Life
and Style of Elizabeth, the Queen Mother*
(Century, 1999)
Simmons, Simone, *Diana: The Secret Years*
(Michael O'Mara Books Ltd, 1998)
Spencer, Charles, *Althorp* (Viking, 1998)
Wheeler, Bennett, *King George VI*
(Macmillan)
Whitaker, James, *Diana v. Charles* (Signet, 1993)
Winn, Godfrey, *The Young Queen*
(Hutchinson, 1952)